Richard Hooker Wilmer, Alonzo Hill

John Smith's Funny Adventures on a Crutch

The Remarkable Peregrinations of a One-Legged Soldier after the War

Richard Hooker Wilmer, Alonzo Hill

John Smith's Funny Adventures on a Crutch
The Remarkable Peregrinations of a One-Legged Soldier after the War

ISBN/EAN: 9783337307349

Printed in Europe, USA, Canada, Australia, Japan

Cover: Foto ©Thomas Meinert / pixelio.de

More available books at **www.hansebooks.com**

Richard Hooker Wilmer, Alonzo Hill

John Smith's Funny Adventures on a Crutch
The Remarkable Peregrinations of a One-Legged Soldier after the War

ISBN/EAN: 9783337307349

Printed in Europe, USA, Canada, Australia, Japan

Cover: Foto ©Thomas Meinert / pixelio.de

More available books at **www.hansebooks.com**

John Smith's

Funny

Adventures On A Crutch,

or the

Remarkable Peregrinations of a One-Legged Soldier after the War.

by

A. F. HILL,

AUTHOR OF "OUR BOYS, OR ADVENTURES IN THE ARMY,"
"THE WHITE ROCKS, OR THE ROBBERS OF
THE MONONGAHELA," ETC., ETC.

WITH ILLUSTRATIONS.

PHILADELPHIA:
JOHN E. POTTER AND COMPANY,
No. 617 SANSOM STREET.

TO THE

MEMORY

OF

ARTEMUS WARD,

WHOM THE WORLD OWES FOR A THOUSAND
HAPPY SMILES,

THIS WORK IS FRATERNALLY

DEDICATED

BY

THE AUTHOR.

PREFACE.

It is verily more difficult to write a good preface for a book than to write the book itself. We don't mind telling the reader, very confidentially, that this is not, by any means, our first effort at a preface for this work: and we earnestly hope that the public will not pronounce this *ninth* one so stupid as we deemed the eight preceding ones that we tore up.

It will be perceived that our hero bears the historic name of JOHN SMITH. Original old JOHN SMITH, the Virginia settler, met with many adventures—some of them funny and others *not* so funny—among the latter was the affair with Miss Pocahontas and her stern old parent: and we claim, for our own JOHN SMITH, as many adventures as his illustrious namesake—some of them quite as funny and others funnier.

(7)

Nothing in this narrative of real incidents is at all calculated to reflect on the excellent character of Mr. Smith : and this is because we esteem him very highly and not from any dread of the law; for John Smith is so multitudinous, that one *could* handle the name with impunity, and not incur any risk of prosecution for libel. What would a court say to an action against a writer for libeling JOHN SMITH, yeoman!—especially when the writer should plead that he never meant *that* JOHN SMITH, but quite another, unknown to the court.

There are those who will shrewdly guess that the hero of the narrative represents the author himself, the chief grounds for such inference being a striking similarity in the number of nether limbs. That, however, should scarcely be taken as conclusive; for, since "this cruel war is over," there are nearly as many one-legged men in the country as there are JOHN SMITHS!

PHILADELPHIA, *January,* 1869.

CONTENTS.

John Smith's

Funny

Adventures On A Crutch!

CHAPTER I.

The Way It Happened.

CRACK! went a rifle at the battle of Antietam.
Not that it was the only one fired, for they
were rattling away at the rate of a thousand
per second just then; but there was one rifle in particular discharged, which, so far as I was concerned,
was clearly distinguishable from all the rest. I did
not see it, nor am I confident that, in the din of battle,
I heard its report; yet I was made painfully aware
of its existence and proximity, and shall no doubt
entertain a recollection of it while life lasts, and
reason retains her throne.

That rifle, evidently fired by some one whom I
would have shot first, if I had had a good chance—
and therefore I couldn't blame him much for shooting
me—threw a leaden ball of one ounce in weight, and

(13)

similar to an acorn in shape; and that missile, travel-
ling at the rate of five thousand miles an hour—though
they rarely travel a whole hour without resting—
struck and wounded me, John Smith. It passed
through the thigh, lacerating that muscle vulgarly
known as the *tensor vaginæ femoris*, and causing a
compound fracture of the *femur*, barely below the
trochanter major; that is to say, it broke the bone
about three inches below the hip.

The ball had come diagonally from the direction
of my right and front, passing through the outside
portion of the left thigh, and coming out only an
inch and a half from where it had entered; and I
could not help, when I had regained my composure,
making some little geometric calculations on the subject. I reckoned that if the man who had fired the
rifle—allowing him to have been one hundred yards
distant, and the barrel of the piece to have been four
feet long—had moved the muzzle the one-hundredth
part of an inch to the right, I should have been
missed; if he had elevated it about the same distance
I should have been *missing*. My next thought was
that whereas my antagonist had discharged his rifle, I
must request the government to discharge *me*.

Some of my comrades carried me from the field,
and, after a little diversion in the way of fainting,
got me loaded into a one-horse ambulance—a vehicle
that can beat a wild-cat jumping on moderately rough
ground—and away it went, plunging diagonally across
a corn-field, like a schooner hove to in a storm. A
shattered limb is one of the most painful things in the
world, especially when its owner is jostled about like

old rusty nails. For good, solid, substantial pain, I know of nothing worthy of being spoken of on the same day with it. The toothache, in its worst form, is bliss compared with it.

There was another wounded "hero" in the ambulance, lying beside me; his leg was shattered below the knee; and I reckon that the yelling he and I did, jointly, wasn't the sort to be excelled by any other two youths of medium abilities.

We were driven to a small log schoolhouse that was used as a surgical hospital, and there unloaded. I do not know what became of my companion in misery—that is, in the ambulance—for it was as much as I could do to keep myself in view for some days following.

Within the schoolhouse were several surgeons busily engaged in amputating limbs; while without, beneath some oak trees that stood near, lay a great many sufferers awaiting their turn. I must give the surgeons credit for considerable dispatch—and no doubt they *dispatched* many a poor fellow that day—for I observed that every few minutes, a whole man, (in a bad state of repair, to be sure,) was carried in, and soon after carried out, in from two to four pieces. They did their work up with rapidity, and by evening, the arms and legs that were piled up against the wall of the schoolhouse without, would have amounted to a full cord—limb measure.

Well, as I do not intend to dwell on this part of the narrative very long, I will simply say that the doctors finally reached my case. I was carried into the little building, where so many pangs had been suffered that day, and laid on an operating-table; and after a slight examination of my wound, and a consultation of eight or nine seconds, they lulled me to repose with chloroform, and scientifically relieved me of my left leg. When I returned from the state of profound oblivion into which the chloroform had thrown me, I was glad to find that they had not made a mistake, and cut off the wrong limb—as a doctor was once known to do. They *had* amputated the *right* leg, because the *left* one was the *right* one—it being the wounded one—and my *right* leg was now my *left* one, because it was the only one *left*. Yet, the other was always the left one, and it has remained so, because it has been ever since *left* on the battle ground. However, that is all *right*.

What I suffered during the ensuing three months in Smoketown Hospital, several miles from Sharpsburg, I will pass over with but a thought and a shudder, and hasten on to tell of the curious and amusing adventures I have since met with, "on a crutch."

I will never forget my first attempt to walk on crutches. I thought it looked easy, to see others walking about the hospital on crutches; just as an inexperienced person is apt to think rowing a boat an easy matter, because he sees others do it with apparent facility. So, one day, when my strength had so increased that I thought I could bear my weight on my only leg, I urged the nurse to lift me up and let me try a pair of crutches.

He did so. He raised me up, and I stood holding tremulously to the tent-post—for I and five other unfortunates occupied a hospital tent—while he carefully placed a crutch under each of my arms. It was the first time for several months that I had been in an erect position, and you can't well imagine how I felt—without studying a good while about it. The ground on which I stood seemed so far beneath that it made me quite dizzy to look down on it, and I trembled at the awful possibility of falling.

With the crutches under my arms, and the nurse's strong hand on my shoulder to keep me steady, I made two or three feeble, timid strides, and concluding that walking on crutches was not quite what it was "cracked up" to be, I faintly said:

"Nurse, put me down on the bed again: I fear I will never walk well on a crutch."

"Pshaw!" said he, as he assisted me to return to my couch of straw; "you do well, and you'll do twice as well next time you try it."

"Twice as well would be but poorly," I rejoined. "However, I will do my best."

"Certainly! Don't think of getting discouraged."

As I now look back on that dismal scene, and remember the sinking heart that throbbed so feebly within me, and the wasted trembling limbs with which I attempted to flee from my prison-like bed, I cannot help smiling;—now, when I can skate as fast as any one, on my solitary foot, swim as well as I ever could, climb like a squirrel, jump on a saddled horse and ride at any pace I please, place a hand on a fence as high as my head and spring over in a quarter of a second, or walk twenty-five or thirty miles a day—all this with one good leg, a crutch and a cane!

2

When the spring came, and I could walk about with some ease, I went from my country home to Philadelphia, to get one of Palmer's artificial legs, supposing that I could wear one advantageously. While on the subject, I will simply say that I got one, but never used it much, because there was too little of the thigh left to attach it to firmly. Not that I would be understood to detract from the reputation of Palmer's patent limb; for we all liked the Doctor, and were most favorably impressed with his handiwork; and my subsequent observations have left no doubt in my mind that his are the most nearly perfect of any artificial limbs manufactured.

Major King, Assistant Surgeon-General of Philadelphia, sent me to Haddington Hospital, to wait till the proposed new limb should be ready for me; and it was there that I, JOHN SMITH, fairly began my somewhat eventful career—"ON A CRUTCH."

The hospital, located near the beautiful suburban village of Haddington, was set apart for such "heroes," as had lost arms or legs, and desired to replace them with substantial wooden ones. It was not unusual at that time to see fifty or sixty one-legged men strolling about the grounds, in fine weather; or squads of fifteen or twenty, supplied with passes for the day, clambering upon a street car and going into the city for a bit of a spree.

A person once asked me if it was not a rather sad sight, and if the boys in this condition were not rather morose and gloomy. The very thought is amusing. I never, anywhere, or under any circumstances, saw a livelier crowd of fellows than maimed and crippled soldiers at Haddington Hospital! They were nearly all young men, from seventeen to twenty-two, and a happier, noisier, more frolicsome set of boys I never saw! It was no unusual thing for some of them, in a merry mood, to carry on till they got put into the guard-house, by the impatient surgeons—sometimes when they scarcely deserved it; but of that, I will say more hereafter.

CHAPTER II.

JOHN'S ADVENTURES ·WITH A CRAZY MAN.

HADDINGTON HOSPITAL had its "characters," as every place has. I formed ties and associations during the spring of my stay there, which can never be forgotten. Nearly all who were there at the time, I remember with pleasure. There was "Chris." Miller, whose leg was amputated below the knee, and who walked splendidly on his "Palmer leg," when he got it. If there was one of the boys there whom I liked better than any other, it was "Chris." He was a jovial fellow, humorous and witty, and the boys were never at a loss for a laugh when he was about. When he got his artificial leg on tight he got tight himself on the strength of it, and made so much noise that the Doctors came to the melancholy conclusion that it was necessary to put him into the guard-house—which was Room No. 41, fourth story. There he made more noise than ever, sat in the open window with his feet dangling out— one a wooden one, you know—and threatened to jump down upon the roof of the piazza, a distance of twenty-five or thirty feet; so, the Doctors got scared, lest he should do so, and thus sprain the ankle of his new leg, and they had him brought down and locked up in the cellar, where there was not such a broad field for exercise.

Nor shall I ever forget Young, a reckless boy of the New York Fire Zouaves, whose leg was amputated five times. One evening when I was just about to retire, he came home from the city, more than tight, fell, as he came blundering up the steps, and bursted his unfortunate "stump" open, so that half-an-inch more of the bone had to be sawed off. He begged the privilege of keeping this fragment of himself, and when he got into a convalescent state again, he worked whole days at it with a pocket knife, and carved it into a very handsome ring, which he ever afterwards wore on his middle finger, both at the table and elsewhere.

There, too, was Mr. Becker, (a citizen,) the clerk of the hospital. He was a handsome fellow, with black curling hair; and he made love, *pro tempore*, to one of the village girls.

And there was Bingham, whom I shall never forget, a religious fellow who sung psalms of an evening, and induced the boys to make up money enough for him to go home on—athough it was subsequently ascertained that he had plenty of money himself at the time. He was the only mean fellow I remember; but he had lost a leg in the service of his country, and I will spare him.

One evening, a few weeks after I had been admitted to the hospital, a man named Thomas, who had been absent for ten days, returned and occupied a bed by the side of mine. He was a soldier who had been slightly wounded, and was doing guard duty at the hospital. He had been absent without leave, had been drinking all that time, and now returned in a very nervous and shattered state of body, and an uneasy and gloomy frame of mind. To add to his trepidation, he was apprehensive that he had been marked as a deserter, during his absence; and he retired to bed in uncommonly low spirits.

I was just falling asleep, and every thing was quiet about the hospital, when Mr. Thomas suddenly startled me by springing up to a sitting posture in his bed, and crying out:

"No you don't! I'll die first! I won't be taken! You want to try me for a deserter and shoot me with twelve muskets! I tell you, I'll not be taken!"

"What's the matter, Thomas?" I asked in alarm.

"Matter? Why, don't you see? There's a whole company of soldiers surrounding the house, and they want to take me for a deserter! Look!" he exclaimed wildly, pointing through the window. "Don't you see them?"

"No, no," I replied, perceiving that he was afflicted with a mild attack of the *horrors*. "There are no soldiers there. Lie down!"

"Yes, there are!" he exclaimed, springing out upon the floor. "See! See! Twenty! Thirty! Forty! Fifty!—I'll cut their hearts out if they try to take me! I will!"—— ——Here he swore a profane oath.

I confess that I felt rather uneasy in the presence of this madman, but calming my fears, I said, coaxingly:

"Come, now, Thomas, there's no one after you. Don't act so foolishly! Do lie down and go to sleep!"

"But I see them! They are down there by that car, now. Do you see? O, I'm watching them! They'll be sharp if they take me alive!"

The terminus of the Market Street and West Philadelphia horse railway is at the building then used as a hospital, and a car arrived and departed every forty minutes till eleven o'clock. At this time, there was one standing some fifty yards from the building, awaiting its time to depart for the depot in West Philadelphia.

"Yes, I do see them now," I said, thinking it better to humor him; "but it is very plain they have concluded you are not here, for they are getting on that car to leave."

"O, I know their tricks!" he replied, quickly. "They only want to make me think they are gone, so that I will go to sleep, and they can come and take me easily. But they don't catch me that way! I should think not! Ha! Ha! Ha!"

"Really, Thomas," said I, persuasively, "I believe they intend to go. Go to bed, and I will watch for you. If they do not leave on that car when it goes, and offer to come this way, I will wake you and tell you. Depend on me."

"Will you?"

"Yes, indeed I will. Lie down."

"I will, then; but, mind, don't let 'em get near They're sly as foxes. Watch 'em."

"Don't fear," I replied. "Go to bed, and I will wake you in good time if I see them coming."

Thereupon Thomas, who was a large strong man of thirty years, returned somewhat reluctantly to his

bed, while some of the other boys of the "ward"
began to wake up, and swear moderately because
their slumbers had been disturbed. The murmur
soon subsided, however, Thomas seemed to sleep, all
grew quiet, and I lay down again.

I was just getting into a comfortable doze, when
Thomas started suddenly, sprung out upon the floor,
between his bed and mine, making the whole house
quiver, placed his hands upon my stomach, and leaped
clear over me and my bed at a bound. At first, I
thought my "time had come," for I fancied he was
about to "slash" me in two with a knife; but having
executed the gymnastic feat just described, he withdrew his hands, and stood in a kind of crouching
position, trembling like a leaf—especially like an
aspen leaf.

"What's the matter?" I asked, trembling about
as much as he.

"Hush!" he whispered, in an awful manner.
"They're at the window! They were pointing their
muskets in! One of them touched me on the head.
Look! See their bayonets at the window! Where's
my knife? Reach and get it for me from my pants'
pocket! Do!"

"Wait a moment," I replied, "till I go to the door
and look out. I want to see how many there are."
My object was to get out into the hall, go and wake
the Doctor, and inform him of this sad case.

"No, no, no, no, no, no!" he said, quickly, at the
same time jumping about four feet high, and coming
down on the floor like a thunderbolt; "don't open
the door! They would all rush in!"

"Only the hall-door," I persisted, beginning to rise. "They're not in the hall. Stay here, and I'll get you a musket to defend yourself with."

The muskets belonging to the guards off duty were kept on a kind of rack in the hall, immediately adjoining the room I was in. I did not wait to hear any further remonstrances on the part of Thomas, but leaving him standing there trembling, as only a man suffering from delirium tremens can tremble, I seized my two crutches—for I used two then— stalked to the door, went out into the hall, closed the door after me and hastened to the room in which the Doctor slept, which was on the same floor.

It was some little time before I succeeded in getting him awake, and when I did, he growled out in an ill humor, asked what in the deuce I wanted, imagined I was some one come to rob him, seized his revolver, cocked it, threatened to blow my unhappy brains out, called to me to "halt, or I was a dead man;" and, in fact, he was, altogether, quite playful.

"Don't shoot! Don't shoot!" I fairly yelled. "It is I, Doctor—I, John Smith!"

"What do you want—waking a fellow at this time of night?" he demanded. "Are you sick? Do you want medicine? Go to the cadet and tell him to give you:

  R. Sac., Satur. ʒi,
   Ext. Vr. Viride, Ɖii,
   Emetia, ʒi,
   Ol. Tiglii, gtt, xx.
   Acid. Tannicum, ℥iss,
   Fowler's Sol. Ars., ℥ss,
   Aqua distillata, ℥iiiss.
  Coch. mag. every ten minutes, till relieved;
   and if——"

"Stop! stop, for suffering humanity's sake!" I interrupted. "I am not sick, at all. On the contrary, am quite well—thank you. But—— "

" Well, what is the matter ?"

"I came to tell you that Mr. Thomas is raving mad. He imagines that a provost-guard is after him, and that he is to be shot as a deserter; and he is scampering about over the ward, like a rat in a hot stove. He talks strangely about cutting people's hearts out; and he may hurt some of the boys."

" O, is that it ?" said the Doctor, now wide awake. " Well, I'll attend to him !" And he hurriedly turned out and drew on his unmentionables.

Accompanied by the Doctor, a light, and a guard of two men armed with muskets, I soon returned to "Ward A," and found Thomas raving like a " wild man of the woods." He imagined himself already attacked by a company of soldiers, and he was hammering away at my empty bed with his big fists, and cursing and swearing like an officer of the Regular Army. All the boys of the " ward" were now wide awake, and more than scared. They were all cripples, and some of them still in a weak condition, and they really had much to fear in case of Thomas's becoming generally pugnacious.

" What do you mean, Thomas ?" demanded the Doctor, angrily. " Do you want to go into the guard-house right now? or will you lie down and take a night's rest ?"

" They've surrounded me !" vociferated Thomas, with a profane oath. " And I'll not be taken! I'll sell my life as dearly as possible! I will!"

"Confound you!" said the Doctor, vexatiously.
"You'll cheat the man that buys it, then!—seize him,
boys, and put him in the cellar. Put on your pantaloons, Thomas; you must sleep in the cellar to-night.
You shall not carry on in this way."

Much to my surprise, Thomas at once cooled down,
and became perfectly tractable. He offered no resistance, nor showed any signs of disobedience, but
straightway drew on his trousaloons, put on his
blouse, placed his cap on his head, with the visor
shoved down over his eyes, and quietly accompanied
the guard, and allowed himself to be locked up in a
strong room in the basement. So, our peace and
tranquillity were no more invaded till roll-call in the
morning.

When one of the guards went to give Thomas his
breakfast, he found him sitting with a grave air on a
low stool near the door of his prison, with a large
bloody pocket-knife in his hand. There was a pool
of gore on the floor at his feet, and his neck and
breast were terribly gashed.

"Why, Thomas!" exclaimed the horrified sentinel,
"What have you done?"

"Some fellow,".returned Thomas, in a calm, and
even dignified tone, "murdered my father last night
in the room above, and——" pointing to the blood
on the floor—"his blood ran down here. Some
of it fell on me, but how could I help that?"

"But what are you doing with that knife? You
have surely cut yourself."

"O," he retorted coolly, as he pointed to his lace-
rated breast, "I have been merely trying to get my

heart out. I had hold of it once, but it slipped out of my hand."

There was a wild look in his eye, and he presented a rather dangerous appearance with the gory knife in his hand, and his clothes stained with blood. The entinel paused a moment, then duty triumphing over fear, he advanced boldly, and said, in an authoritative tone:

"Give me that knife!"

Without a word, Thomas submissively handed him the bloody instrument, with which he had been attempting self-destruction. It was a large knife with eating-fork attached, such as was much used by soldiers during the war—the blade being about four inches long.

Having secured this weapon, the sentinel closed and locked the door, then hastened to inform the Doctor of what had occurred. Thereupon Thomas was conducted to an upper room, his wounds—twenty-two in number—were examined and dressed, and he was put to bed. There were two Doctors at the hospital at the time, and both expressed a like opinion on the case of poor Thomas. They said they wouldn't be surprised if he should die, but yet, that it was possible he might get well—if "kept quiet:" so, by this non-committal course, they did not endanger their reputation.

CHAPTER III.

Proposes to Leap From a Third-Story Window.

FOR some days, the recovery of Mr. Thomas was very doubtful. Some one had to stay with him continually, and especially at night, for at that dreary hour, "when churchyards yawn," and one experiences an inclination to sup on "hot blood," (*vide* Hamlet,) he was in the habit of raving a good deal, and of threatening to destroy himself, and the greater portion of the human race.

By and by, "sitting up" with him got to be a rather sleepy task, and as there were not very many whole men about, it was necessary for the cripples to take turns at it.

One night, a week or so after the attempted suicide, my turn came. I was told early in the evening that I was detailed to get up at twelve o'clock, and stay with the sufferer till three. At the appointed time I was awakened by one of the nurses, arose, dressed, and proceeded to the invalid's apartments. I entered the room with some misgivings, and relieved a one-armed "hero," who had been watching since nine o'clock. The latter retired at once, and left me alone with the patient. The latter was asleep at that time, and the single candle that was burning in the room shed a ghastly light over his ashen face, and the white bandage, slightly blood-stained, that was bound around his unhappy neck.

"He is asleep now," the one-armed soldier had said, before withdrawing, "and may not give you any trouble. If he should awake and try to hurt you, ring the bell."

The bell-wires, *et cetera*, used when the building was a hotel, were still in good working order, and all that lent me courage was the bell-pull that hung down close to my ear, when I had taken a seat on a chair near the door.

I was just getting into an uncomfortable doze, when the patient waked up, awoke me, and raising up quietly in bed, remarked:

"I believe I'll jump out of this window."

He said it as coolly as a man in good health would say: "I believe I'll take a walk."

It was a third-story room, and the bed stood immediately by the window. I thought of the disastrous consequences of such a proceeding on the part of Thomas, and earnestly advised him not to think seriously of embarking in such a colossal enterprise. The window was raised about two feet, it being a warm night, and he gazed wistfully out into the sombre darkness.

"Don't do it, Thomas," said I, with earnestness. "We are at least thirty feet from the ground, and in your present condition it would not be judicious. Wait till you get well, at least."

"*You* jump out," he suggested, turning and looking upon me with a wild stare.

He seemed to have just thought of it. What could be my excuse, for not taking a flying leap in the dark, I being in sound health—what there was of me?

I glanced furtively at the bell-pull, and replied:

"O no; not from that window. You see, that is a back window. The laundress has some clothes hung out to dry just below, and it might injure them. Besides, I am in the habit of doing my leaping from a fourth-story front window. You'll always find, Thomas, that a man of refinement prefers a leap from a window of the fourth floor."

He sat awhile, in a sort of thoughtful attitude, while I kept one eye on the bell-cord, and the other on him; then, to my relief, he deliberately lay down again, drew the covers close up to his chin, and glided off into a gentle slumber.

I had no more trouble with him. Thomas got well, in the course of a month, left off drinking, and got to be a pretty sensible sort of fellow. The last time I saw him was one day, some months after I had left the hospital, when I returned to the old place on a brief visit. He was engaged in a four-hand game of euchre, and I observed, just as I arrived, that he held in his hand both bowers, ace, king and queen: would you believe it?——he had the temerity to play it "alone," and the extraordinarily good luck to make "four times."

CHAPTER IV.

Locked Up.

THE inmates of the hospital were allowed passes, after roll-call in the morning, to go into the city, or whither they pleased; but it was imperative that they should return by half-past seven in the evening, positively, without fail. One morning, as usual, I got a pass to go into the city, and as the Doctor handed it to me, he said:

"Don't fail to be back at half-past seven."

"I won't," I replied, with the best intentions in the world.

As new patients arrived almost every day, some of whom might be ignorant of the rules and regulations, the Doctor had got into the habit of repeating this injunction every time he gave out a pass; and as he gave, on an average, about one hundred and fifty per day, Sundays excluded, he must, in the course of a year, have said, "Don't fail to return by half-past seven," forty-six thousand nine hundred and fifty times.

I had just stepped from the street-car in the heart of the city, when I ran squarely against one of the boys of my own regiment, whom I had not seen since the battle of Antietam.

"Hallo, Charlie!" I exclaimed, delighted to see the

familiar face of my comrade; "what are you doing here?"

"I have been in the Chestnut Hill Hospital," was his reply, as we shook hands. "I was wounded at Fredericksburg, and am just well enough now to return to the regiment: I go to Washington to-day. What are *you* doing here?"

"I am staying at Haddington Hospital," I returned, "waiting to have a Palmer leg fitted on me that is made of willow, and only weighs three ounces and a half."

"Come and go to Washington with me," he said, as the thought appeared to strike him. (It struck me rather forcibly about the same time, I confess.)

"I couldn't—I—I—"

"Why couldn't you?"

"Because I only have a pass till evening."

"Oh, that will make no difference. They will hardly be so strict with the cripples."

"When do you go?" I asked, thoughtfully.

"At eleven o'clock."

"Where is the regiment?"

"Lying at Upton's Hill. Come—you'll go with me!"

"I might get into trouble," I said, wavering. "I only have a pass till half-past seven, and if I should go away and stay whole days——"

"O, pshaw! They wouldn't care. You have no duty to perform there."

"No, but——"

"O, come," he urged—all I wanted was a little urging—"the boys would be so glad to see you!

3

You don't know how they felt about your losing a
leg at An ietam!"

This argument completely disarmed me. I had
not been with the regiment since I was carried away
from it in the smoke of battle, and, O, I knew that
he boys would be glad to see me! No one who has
not been a soldier knows how dear one's comrades
are to him! And especially his messmates—those
with whom he has slept many a time on the cold
ground, and under the same narrow tent; those with
whom he has drank from the same canteen, or eaten
from the same scanty dish! The attachment that grows
up among companions in arms is like no other. It is
not like paternal or fraternal love; it is not like the
love of lovers; but it is as fond, as deep, and as lasting!

I accompanied my comrade to Washington, thence
to Upton's Hill, and saw the "boys;" and I think I
never enjoyed so much true happiness, in the same
length of time, as I did during that pleasant visit. I
never thought of my being absent without leave, till
I neared Philadelphia again. Then I began to wonder
if "any thing would be done with me" on my return
to the hospital. I tried to persuade myself that there
was no danger of any thing of the sort, but something
would keep whispering to me that I was going to
"get into trouble."

I arrived at the hospital again just one week from
the day I had left. The roll was regularly called,
both in the morning and in the evening, and I could
not suppress an involuntary shudder, as I thought of
the fourteen roll-calls I had evidently missed, and of
the fourteen *black marks* that were surely placed, by

this time, opposite the honest, unassuming name of Smith, John.

However, I put on a bold face, walked up the hospital steps, paid no attention to the guard, who said, " Where the deuce have you been all this time?" walked in, and calmly reported myself to the surgeon.

"Doctor," said I, "it isn't half-past seven yet, is it?" (It was about two o'clock, *post meridian.*)

I had hoped he would enjoy this joke, and good-naturedly laugh the affair off, but I saw no such indications on his stern countenance.

"Where have you been, Smith?" he asked. Do I say *asked?* I should say, *demanded.* That is putting it mildly enough.

"I went to Upton's Hill to see my regiment," I replied.

"Exactly. Upton's Hill. Let me see—that is—"

"Upton's Hill," said I, " is about eight or nine miles from Alexandria, by the pike. From Washington, it is situated——"

In fact, I was going on to deliver a first class lecture on geography, when he interrupted me with :

"So you went there, eh? A pretty way to act! I gave you a pass a week ago to-day, as the records will show, telling you to return by half-past seven, and, until now, have not seen you or heard of you!"

"Well," said I, still hoping that the affair might be accepted as a joke, "I am back, you see, before half-past seven. The mere matter of a week——"

"Go to your ward," interrupted the Doctor, who did not seem to be in a joking mood.

"Glad to get off so easily," I muttered to myself, as I withdrew. "I really did begin to get a little scared; but it's all right now. I believe I'll go and write a letter or two."

Now, there was at the hospital, acting as sergeant of the guard, a contemptible little fellow named Kinsley, who had never been wounded, and probably had never seen any active service. I do not remember what regiment he belonged to. He was very fond of displaying his sergeant's stripes, paper collar, and delicate little mustache. I had not been in my ward long, when this pompous little fellow came in with a *key* in his hand, approached me and said:

"Come and go with me, Smith."

Observing the key, I at first supposed that new quarters had been assigned me—in truth, I was nearly right—and I arose and followed him. He led the way up one flight of stairs, then another, then another. We had not quite reached the fourth story when the horrible truth suddenly flashed upon me. *I was. to be put in the guard-house*—yes, the GUARD-HOUSE!

"Sergeant," said I, pausing on the stairs, "I half believe that you contemplate locking me up."

"So I am ordered," he replied.

"I've considered the matter," I continued, coolly, "and have come to the conclusion not to go."

"But you've got to go," said he. "There's no use in ——"

"No, I really don't think I'll go: not right away,

anyhow," I said, coolly ; and I turned about and began
to descend the stairs.

He quickly followed me, and roughly seized one of
my arms. Letting my crutches fall, I turned im-
petuously upon him, and with all the fire of assailed
dignity, seized the foppish little sergeant by both
arms, and hurled him down the stairs with all my
might. I tumbled down after him, however, for I
had not then such command of my equilibrium as I
have since acquired, and we landed at the foot of the
stairs all in a heap. I was up first, and snatching up
one of my crutches for a weapon, I stood with my
back to the wall, and proposed to "split his skull" if
he should dare to approach. He did not dare, however, but with a savage oath for so small a man, he
picked himself up and ran down the other two flights
of stairs. I deliberately followed. I was half-way
down the last flight, when the Doctor and two guards,
armed with musket and bayonet, appeared in the hall.

"Doctor," said I, "did you order me to be put in
the guard-house?"

"Yes," he replied, frankly.

"You have no right to do it," I said, with some
force. "I am a sergeant, and cannot, without a trial,
be confined in a guard-house."

"But you can," he retorted, "if there are men
enough here to carry you up. Go, boys, and put him
in No. 41."

The two guards came up to me, and one of them
said :

"Come, now, you see we are ordered to do it. We
don't like to, but——"

"I will go with *you*," said I, "for I know you are a soldier; but if that dandified little sergeant comes within reach of me, I will break his head!"

I again ascended the stairs, for I saw that resistance would be both useless and wrong; and one of the guards, inserting the key, opened the door, and I walked in. Just then, the cowardly little sergeant made his appearance, rushed to the door, drew it to, turned the key, and tauntingly said:

"Now I've got you, my fine fellow! You see a sergeant *can* be put in the guard-house!"

I could not help acknowledging the truth of this, but did not do so to him. I merely promised to lick him as soon as I should get out.

"You know nobody would hurt you, because you are a cripple," he replied, "or you wouldn't talk that way."

"And you," I retorted, "who never went into danger enough to lose a limb, can well afford to lounge about a hospital, and bully over the cripples!"

No reply was made: I heard them going down stairs, and I was alone in my prison!

Fortunately, during my youthful days I had not neglected one important branch of my education. I had read, with deep interest, minute and graphic accounts of the daring adventures and hair-breadth escapes of Claude Duval, Dick Turpin, and Sixteen-string Jack, contained in a series of twenty-four octavo volumes, of one hundred pages each, handsomely bound in orange-colored paper, and illustrated with numerous spirited lithographic engravings, done on brown stone.

There is no sort of learning that will not come in play at some time or other; and, with my extensive theoretic knowledge of prisons, it is not to be supposed that an ordinary hotel-room, with the lock on the *inside* of the door, would hold me very long. I looked about me for means of escape. The window was too high to think of taking a jump from it, as it will be remembered I had led Thomas to believe I was in the habit of doing, and as Chris. Miller had threatened to do; so I resolved to force the door open or die in the attempt.

There was a stove in the room, without fire, of course, and I opened the door and peered in. It contained about eighteen quarts of ashes and cinders, and ——a small iron shovel with an iron handle. I seized it with joy. I saw *liberty* beaming all over it. First I tried to insert the handle between the lock and the iron "catch," into which the bolt went, which was only secured by a couple of one-and-a-half-inch wood-screws. The crevice was too small, or the shovel-handle too big. I next tried a corner of the shovel itself: it entered the crevice, but it proved too pliable—it bent. Then, with some effort, I wrenched the handle from the shovel, and tried that end. It was smaller than the other end, and success stared me in the face. I inserted it in the crevice, and, with a reasonable expenditure of strength, pried the "catch" off, and it fell to the floor, in a somewhat bent and dented condition. The door swung open. I was free.

Thus liberated, I walked calmly down stairs, and went out on the piazza, where the Doctor and a

number of the boys were sitting, airing them
selves.

"Doctor," I said, coolly, as I boldly confronted
him, "I am not accustomed to sleeping in the fourth
story: couldn't you give me a room lower down?"

CHAPTER V.

ACCOMMODATED WITH A "ROOM LOWER DOWN."

I NEVER saw a man stare with such pure unalloyed astonishment as the Doctor did on this occasion. Not five minutes had elapsed since he had had me locked up in the guard-house, and yet, there I was—free. He stared at me for a moment as though I were an apparition from the dead, then stammered:

"Why—why—is—is—this—John Smith?"

"So I am called," I replied, coolly taking a seat on a bench.

He arose from his seat, stared for a moment, again, with contracted brows and a puzzled expression of countenance, then said:

"I—I—thought you—were put—in No. 41!"

"So I was," I calmly replied. And I deliberately took a newspaper from my pocket and cast my eye over the late items.

"How—how—in the name of sense—did you get out?"

"O, that was easy," I replied, carelessly, as I regarded the paper more attentively.

"Sergeant Kinsley," said the Doctor, calling to the insignificant little sergeant who was standing at the other end of the porch, "come here."

The sergeant approached.

"Didn't you put Smith in the guard-house?"

"Yes sir," returned Kinsley.

"Here he is," said the Doctor, pointing to me.
' How did he get out?"

Kinsley, who had not before observed my presence,
started back, turned pale, and said: "I—I—don't
know."

"Go and see," said the Doctor.

Glad to get out of my presence, Kinsley ran up
stairs, and in a minute or so returned, and reported
what had been done.

Now, if the Doctor had possessed the heart of a
human being he would have suspended his persecu-
cutions, after that—in a word, would have "let up"
on me—but he seemed entirely impervious to good
jokes, practical or otherwise, and was more than ever
determined to punish me.

"Sergeant," said he, no doubt thinking *he* was per-
petrating a joke—but *I* couldn't see it—"Smith
wants a room *lower down*, he says. I think we can
accommodate him. *Put him in the cellar!*"

There was, in the basement, a dark apartment with
an iron door—the same room in which crazy Thomas
had been confined—and that was the "room lower
down" assigned me on this melancholy occasion.

"Will you go?" said Kinsley, standing off at a
respectful distance: "Or will it be necessary to call
the guard?"

"It will be necessary to call the guard," I replied,
folding up my paper, arising and taking a hostile
attitude.

"You might as well go with him quietly, Smith"—
the Doctor began.

"No I won't," I interrupted. "Should I do so, it
is not positively certain that he would get back in a
sound condition, and you might lose a valuable ser-
vant, who is not scrupulous about turning his hand to
any sort of work."

"Call the guard," said the Doctor.

The guard was called.

I was put in the cellar.

Only a few dim rays of light found their way into
my dismal prison, and they came struggling through
a small crevice in the double partition of thick pine
boards that divided the "cell" from the knapsack-
room. On this formidable partition I at once went
to work, with extraordinary *nonchalance*, with a small
six-bladed knife I had in my pocket. I think this
course was much more laudable than that pursued by
Mr. Thomas, when confined in the same apartment,
with a knife for a companion.

I worked diligently, cutting off one thin shaving
after another, till night came; by which time I had
actually cut a hole in the thick partition through
which I could easily thrust my arm.

Next morning, after a miserable fragment of repose
on an old mattress, I arose early, and resumed my
work. I had not been long at it when Sergeant
Kinsley came down with some provisions for me,
consisting of *bread and water*. I took the large tin
cup of water from his hand, dashed it in his face,
slammed the iron door to, braced it with one of my
crutches, and went at my work again; while he,

strangling, sputtering and swearing in wild rage, locked the door, and rushed up stairs.

Cutting, splintering and shaving, I worked away, and by noon, I had made an aperture in the wall through which one might have thrown a hat—that wasn't too wide in the brim.

By and by, I heard some one coming down the steps, and a light from the door above shone down through the bars of the iron door. Some one unlocked it and entered. It was one of the guards—one who had been wounded in the service.

"I have brought you your dinner," said he. "They only gave me some bread and water for you, but I stole a nice piece of boiled beef from the cookhouse. Here it is."

"Thank you," I said, gladly accepting the repast. "What did Kinsley say?"

"O, he's as mad as a hornet! He said you threw the water in his face."

"So I did."

"Served him right," said the guard, laughing. "He's an overbearing young puppy, who never heard a bullet whistle in his life. I knocked him down one day, and he has been civil towards me ever since. Not very comfortable down here, is it?"

"Not very."

"Well, you'll soon be out. I heard the Doctor say he would let you out this evening. He told me not to tell you, and I said I wouldn't. I meant, I wouldn't till I'd see you."

I eat my dinner with a relish, and, after he had gone, I worked away at my new window—merely for

pastime. I did not make it much larger that afternoon, but I trimmed it up around the edges, and got
it into some shape, thinking it might do to put a pane
of glass into, some day.

That evening I was released, and informed by the
Doctor that my name should go on the "Black List,"
for the space of one week. The "black list" was a
list of the names of those who, for misdemeanor,
were denied passes for a certain time. And on this
roll was the noble name of JOHN SMITH, to be placed
for seven days! I thought the Doctor would relent
by Monday morning, so I called on him at his office,
and said :

"Doctor, I should be most happy to visit the city
to-day, and if you will have the kindness to favor me
with——"

"No, no, Smith," he interrupted, in a decided tone;
"You can have no pass to-day."

"But——"

"No use talking: you can have no pass to-day."

I saw that he "meant it;" so I turned away for
the time, and called again the next morning.

"Doctor," said I, with a beaming smile, "there is
a friend of mine in the city, whom I would like to
see, and if——"

"You can have no pass to-day, Smith," he interrupted: "nor till your week is up. We have discovered how you cut the partition-wall when you were
in the cellar. What did you do that for?"

"To get out," I replied.

"If I had known it," said he, with some severity,
"I would have kept you in three days longer!"

"Then I am glad you didn't know it," said I.

"At least," he rejoined, "you can have no pass till your week is up. That will be on Saturday."

I gave it up for that morning, but promptly returned and renewed my importunities on Wednesday morning. I was refused, as before, and peremptorily ordered not to solicit a pass again till Saturday. In accordance (?) with this order, I promptly returned on Thursday morning, and most earnestly request d the favor of a pass, stating that it was indispensable that I should visit the city that day. The Doctor refused again, and threatened to put me in the cellar again for three days, and place my name on the "Black List" for two weeks, if I should "bore" him for a pass again, sooner than Saturday.

Therefore, I concluded to go to the city anyhow. So I slipped out the back way, threw my crutches over the fence, climbed over after them, and, without being observed by the guard, made my way to the street-car that stood awaiting its starting-time, and got aboard of it: thus I clandestinely went into the city.

There, the first thing I did was to call on Doctor Levis, at his residence. He was controlling surgeon of Haddington Hospital, and I determined to make a "point." I informed him that I had not been very well treated at the hospital, talked nice to him, used the best language of which I was master, introduced foreign words and phrases, made vague allusions to law and history, touched on chemistry, gave him to understand that the assistant surgeons at the hospital were the most tyrannical fiends in existence, and that *I* was the very paragon of all human excellence; and, finally, requested him to do me the slight favor of giving me a standing pass—that is, an order addressed to the assistant-surgeons at the hospital, commanding them to allow the bearer, John Smith, "who had friends in the city, with whom he might desire to stay a night now and then,"—to pass in and out of the hospital, day or night, for all time to come. This, Doctor Levis,—who, I must say, is a perfect gentleman, and was beloved by all the wounded soldiers under his charge—wrote, signed, and gave to me, without a word of objection; while I poured out the overflowings of my grateful heart in the most profuse thanks, and earnestly begged him, in case he should ever visit Western Pennsylvania, where I then resided, to call on me by all means, assuring him that he would be as welcome as a brother. The Doctor smiled, and, with renewed thanks, I put on my cap, picked up my crutches, saluted him *a la militaire*, bade him a cheerful " good morning," and withdrew.

CHAPTER VI.

THE WAY SMITH GETS BORED.—AN EPISODE.

HAVING taken a stroll of six or seven hours about the city, I proceeded to Market street, and got into the first car going westward. Soon after, a dignified gentleman, whom I liked the appearance of,—and I modestly think he liked the looks of me,—got into the car, and occupied a vacant seat directly opposite. He glanced at my crutches, then at the vacant space where my left leg should have been, if I had possessed one, and said:

"How do you do, sir? You lost your leg in the army, I suppose?"

Just here, reader, before I tell you who this excellent gentleman was, pardon a slight digression. Did it ever occur to you that one who has lost a limb in the service of his country, finds it necessary to answer "a question or two" now and then—to put it mildly—for some time after his return? He is looked upon as public property, and is almost bored to death with questions, by the many curious strangers he meets. No one who has not experienced it, can imagine what a nuisance this quizzing is. I can never have a moment's rest in any public place. I no sooner take a seat in a car, restaurant, or lecture-

room, than my right-hand or left-hand lady or gentleman commences. I give below an impartial list of
the questions they ask, and which I, at first, answered
with pride and pleasure; but which, however, after I
had answered them a few hundred thousand times,
grew rather stale. Here they are: they have been
asked me so often, as to become stereotyped upon
my heart and brain:

Did you lose your limb in battle?

What battle?

Did a cannon ball take it off?

A rifle ball, eh?

Did it knock it clear off?

Did it sever an artery?

Did it hit the bone?

Did it break it?

Did you afterward find the ball?

Was it crushed out of shape?

Did you fall when hit?

Did you walk off the field?

Who carried you off?

Did you feel much pain?

How long after you were wounded till it was amputated?

Who performed the operation?

Did you take chloroform?

Did it put you to sleep?

And didn't you feel the operation?

Not even the sawing of the bone?

Could not your limb have been saved?

Was it taken off right where the wound was?

Can you wear an artificial leg?

4

Would the Government furnish it if you could?

Do you draw a pension?

How much?

How old are you?

What is your name?

What did you do before the war?

Don't you often wish you hadn't lost your leg?

How does a person feel with a leg off?

Does it ache when the weather changes?

Would you rather lose a leg than an arm?

I have heard persons say that an amputated limb still feels as if it were on—is that so?

How do you account for that?

All these questions, dear public, I have answered thousands of times, and may have to answer thousands of times yet, if my miserable existence is lengthened out for many years. Imagine how it must torment me! The same old questions, to me long since devoid of interest, I must meekly answer, over and again, day by day, week by week, year by year! How would you like to commence and repeat the A B C's five thousand times every day, as long as you live?—Be pleasant, wouldn't it?

But this is not all. After the affable stranger has asked all the ridiculous questions he can think of, he commences, without being solicited for a narrative, and entertains (?) me with a glowing (?) account of the army experience of one of *his* relatives—his son, nephew, cousin, or wife's uncle's brother's cousin, and I must patiently listen. He, poor fellow, goes the story, was wounded, too: arm or leg nearly torn off, barely hanging by a bit of the hide. Doctors wanted to carve it off. He wouldn't let 'em. But they said he'd die unless his limb was amputated Said he'd die all in one piece, then, and save the trouble of digging two graves: wasn't going to die a piece at a time. Doctors said they knew best and limb *must* come off. "Hero" declared they didn't, and that it shouldn't be cut off, and, moreover, he'd shoot 'em if they tried it. Hence, limb left on. Patient got well, although Doctors said wouldn't live a day, "and to-day," continues the narrator, "the limb is sounder and stronger than before it was wounded." I have heard ten thousand such stories told of persons I never knew, never saw, and never heard of, and never wished to hear of. Yet I had to sit and listen. How interesting! ! !

Nor is this all. I occasionally meet with one who, in addition to all this, asks a few questions and makes a few remarks too ridiculous to be believed. Once, a gentleman who had been quizzing me for half-an-hour in a street-car, gravely asked:

"Don't you think there are a great many *unneces-sary* legs taken off, by army surgeons?"

He meant, I suppose, "legs taken off unnecessa-rily," and I thought so; but he had been boring me till I felt pale and looked like fainting, and I replied:

"Yes. I think that, strictly speaking, all that are taken off are unnecessary, for those who lose them manage to live without them."

He didn't bother me any more.

On a similar occasion, a gentleman asked:

"Do you ever go away and forget your crutch?"

When too late, he perceived how ridiculous the question was; but I gravely replied:

"Yes, I once went away and left it standing in the corner of a restaurant. I went several hundred yards before I missed it; and I then had a deuce of a time getting back to it."

Another once thoughtfully asked:

"Now, suppose you had lost your left arm instead of your left leg, where would you have placed your crutch?" He never considered that in such a case it would not have been necessary for me to use a crutch at all.

"Then," I replied, "I would have used the crutch under the right shoulder, and a cane in my left hand."

Another idiot, one day, after having asked the usual questions and entertained me with the usual incidents, consolingly remarked:

"Well, you don't have to pay so much for shoes."

"I never pay any thing for shoes," I replied.

"For boots then," he suggested, with a complacent smile.

"No, nor for boots either," I replied.

"Why so?" he asked, with some curiosity.

"I buy neither boots nor shoes."

"How then?"

"I buy *only one.*"

Thus, dear public, am I, John Smith, tormented for having sacrificed a leg for my country. How often have I felt that I would be far happier if I were still a mark for the bullets at Malvern Hill, Bull Run, or Antietam! This accursed *quizzical* disposition on the part of the public has made me feel, at times, that life was actually a burden to me!

One day I met an elderly lady in Philadelphia who stopped me on the street, asked a profusion of questions, and wound up by giving me an accurate history of her son. She said he had gone into the army, had been missing ever since a certain battle, and she feared he was no more. Ever after that, whenever we met—and it happened frequently—she would hail me, commence with, "I've never heard from my son yet!" and talk at me till I felt weak in the knee. At last, I met her one day, and pretending I did not see her, I was passing by, when I felt her grasp on my elbow, and was obliged to stop.

"My son's dead," she said. "I've heard from his officers, and they say he was killed."

O, how I envied him! Sleeping peacefully in a quiet grave, somewhere, with nothing to trouble him, and no one to torment him with questions, he must have been happy compared with the wretched John Smith! The old lady began again to give me his full history, as she had related it to me many times before, while the cold perspiration started from my frame, and I felt as though death was not two doors from me.

Thus am I bored without mercy. No one spares me, except such as have been in the army themselves. Men, women, children, foreigners, fools and even negroes, subject me to this systematic torture.

One day I was walking in front of the Naval Asylum, when two little girls passed me, on their way to school.   When they had passed, I heard one of them say :

"O, look at that man with one leg !"

"Hush !" said the other.   "How would you like it if *your* pa had but one leg and a little girl would call out that way."

"*He* aint anybody's pa," retorted the first.

"How do you know ?" rejoined the other.

CHAPTER VII.

JOHN SMITH'S FRIEND.

NOW let me proceed. The gentleman in the Market-street car spared me. The questions he asked were few and to the point. He was an exception. When I replied in the affirmative to his first question, he said

" Where do you live ?"

" In Western Pennsylvania," I replied.

" Where are you staying now ?"

" In Haddington Hospital."

" I suppose you will soon be discharged ?"

" Yes, I shall soon take my discharge."

" Have you any employment in view ?"

" No, sir; none."

" If you would like to remain in Philadelphia awhile, when discharged from the service, I will get you a situation."

This rather took me by surprise, but I had the presence of mind to say,——

" Thank you : I think I would like it."

" Then," said he, " call at my office near Fifth and Chestnut and I will do as I promise. My name is M* * * * * * *: I am United States Marshal."

" I am truly obliged," I said.

"Not at all," he returned. "When I do any thing for a soldier I am only paying an honest debt."

I returned to Haddington in triumph, and exhibited my pass to the assistant-surgeon who had put me in the guard-house.

"Didn't you know," said I, with dignity, "that Doctor Levis and I were particular friends?"

"No," said he, turning slightly pale. "Are—are you acquainted?"

"Acquainted!" said I. "I should think so! We've known each other for—for—I don't know how long."

I didn't know exactly how long, but knew it was something short of twenty-four hours.

"Ah? You should have told me. I am sorry. Well, go in and out of the hospital whenever you please."

"I will," said I.

From that time forth I had perfect liberty, during my stay at the hospital.

In June I got my artificial leg, which I have never worn much—finding a crutch and cane far superior as a means of locomotion—and having received my discharge, I called one fine morning at the United States Marshal's office. It was early, and he had not come in yet. To pass the time, I walked to the corner of Fifth and Chestnut streets, and stood for a moment gazing at the good old clock in the State-house steeple. Streams of people were passing up and down the street; and I had not stood long before a man came up and held out his hand as though, I thought, to shake hands. Supposing him to be some old acquaintance, whose visage had faded from my memory in the course of the sanguinary scenes through which I had lately passed, I was about to seize his hand, and request him to remind me where and when we had last met, when I observed that there was a ten-cent note in the extended hand, and he seemed to be offering *that* to me, and not the hand. I stared in astonishment.

"Take it," said he: "you're welcome to it."

I was dumb with amazement. Was the man an escaped lunatic? Might he be dangerous, like Thomas of the hospital? I felt like "getting."

"Take it," he repeated, still presenting the trifling bit of fractional currency: "I owe it to you."

I was still lost in wonder. Could it be possible that it was some country gentleman to whom I had lent the sum of ten cents before the war, and that he was so honest and upright as to return it on the first opportunity? No, he must be mistaken. I had never seen him before, certainly.

"My dear sir," I said, "you are mistaken. I never lent you——"

"O, not that," he interrupted. "You've served your country; you've fought my battles for me, while I stayed at home; you've got crippled, and now——"

"Really, sir," I interrupted, smothering my indignation, "I am not in need of pecuniary assistance. On the contrary, my income is ten thousand dollars a year." (That was a big one.) "If you wish to do good to the amount of ten cents, pray give it to some one who needs it. I thank you." I spoke the latter words with dignity, and turned away disgusted.

Since that day, I have ever feared to stop a moment at a street corner, no matter how tired I might be, lest some other unpardonable fool should chance to be near, and bring a burning flush of crimson to my face. The idea of being suspected of soliciting pecuniary assistance, simply because I stood resting at a corner with a crutch in my hand! It is so revolting to me that I can not look back on that little—extremely little—incident without a shudder. Another reward for serving my country. O, John Smith! John Smith!

I saw Mr. M * * * * * * *, who, remembering me at once, gave me a letter to Colonel C * * * * * *, a blunt, but good-hearted old soldier, who at once procured me a situation in the United States Arsenal. I remained in my situation eight months, during which I saw a great many queer things, and got a pretty fair idea of the purity, (?) probity (?) and integrity (?) that prevail among the men who have charge of such public institutions.

CHAPTER VIII.

JOHN THOUGHT HE WOULD LIKE TO TRAVEL.

J HAD always been of a literary turn; so, while employed in the Arsenal, I concluded to write a book, and give to the world, therein, an account of soldier life, as I had experienced it; and I had very little doubt that eighty or ninety thousand dollars might be made out of it. I carried out my determination, writing in the evenings, after my daily labors; and when I left the Arsenal, I had completed the manuscript of my work, which, when published, a few months after, constituted a duodecimo volume of over four hundred pages.*

I did not make "eighty or ninety thousand" out of the work, as my sanguine nature had led me to anticipate; but I made a "few thousand," and I concluded to travel a little and see some of that porti n of the world lying within the boundaries of the United States: and it was while thus traveling,

---

* OUR BOYS. Comprising the personal experiences of the author while in the army, and embracing some of the richest and raciest scenes of army and camp life ever published. By A. F. Hill, of the Eighth Pa. Reserves. With portrait of the author on steel, and several characteristic illustrations on wood. 12mo. Cloth, price $1.75.

(John E. Potter & Co., Publishers, Philadelphia.)

chiefly in our own country, that I met with a great
many funny adventures which I shall relate in this
book.

The first time I visited New York, I went to remain a few weeks as correspondent of a Pennsylvania
newspaper. I think any stranger's first impression
of Gotham is, that it is a busy sort of a place; and
the longer he stays there the more he " keeps on
thinking so." The bustle of Broadway has been so
frequently dilated upon, that I will not attempt to
enter upon a regular description of it. It must be
seen to be appreciated; and I concluded to see it the
first thing. So I hailed an omnibus that came
thundering along, and somewhat astonished the
driver by climbing nimbly to the *top* of it, instead of
taking a seat within.

"You get up quicker than a two-legged man," was
his brief comment.

"Havn't so much weight to pull up," I replied;
and paid my fare.

From my lofty perch I had a good view up and
down Broadway, as well as on each side. Number-
less pedestrians thronged the sidewalks, while vehicles, of all kinds, shapes and sizes, crowded together,
rolled along and swayed to and fro in the street like a
mighty torrent.

We had not proceeded far up Broadway, when
cluck! went one of the front wheels of our "bus"
against another one that was coming down—they got
tangled and a "jam-up" ensued. Although I could
not see that it was the fault of either driver, they
cursed each other in round terms. One driver swore

at the other, and the other swore at him; then they swore at each other, in concert, for a quarter of a minute, in the course of which they were very earnest and emphatic in advising each other to emigrate to a certain fabled climate where the mercury in the thermometer seldom falls to the freezing point. The way these drivers curse each other is frightful. If all the men told to go to that hot climate in the course of a year by Broadway drivers, should go, the place would be crowded to suffocation. The expression I refer to seems to be a favorite one among the drivers of vehicles on Broadway; and I presume, that on that thoroughfare there are more men urged to visit Erebus in one day, then there are warned against it in all the rest of the land in a whole year.

For about two miles up Broadway, the rattle of omnibuses, express-wagons, drays, furniture-cars, buggies, barouches, cabriolets, etc., was really bewildering. As I looked upon the busy streams of men that hurried along the sidewalks—their faces all strange to me, yet no two alike—and saw the rumbling carriages, all crowding forward as though life depended on their speed, I could not help thinking of this stanza in Byron's Childe Harold:

> "But 'midst the crowd, the hum, the shock of men,
>   To hear, to see, to feel and to possess,
> And roam along the world's tired denizen,
>   With none who bless us, none whom we can bless;
> Minions of splendor, shrinking from distress!
>   None that with kindred consciousness endued,
> If we were not, would seem to smile the less,
>   Of all that flattered, followed, sought or sued,
> This is to be alone ; this, this is solitude!"

Every one who has had any experience in the matter, must have observed that a person is more lonely in a crowded city, where he is unacquainted, than in the depths of the forest where no human being is seen.

As I had no money to throw away, I stayed at a modest hotel in Park Row, where one could live on less than twenty five dollars a day. I shall never forget a brief acquaintance I made there. The first evening I stayed in New York, I was seated in the hotel trying to make up my mind whether to go to the theater or not, when I observed, sitting near me, a sedate gentleman of prepossessing exterior, fifty or sixty years old, and dressed in plain clothes and a broad-brimmed silk hat, of a grave and dignified appearance. I could not help fancying that he was at least an ex-governor, or something of the sort; and I felt somewhat flattered when he moved his chair closer to mine, with the obvious intention of addressing me. He opened his mouth to speak, and I nerved myself to reply with respectful dignity, when he said, in a low tone:

" Would you lend me fifteen cents?"

The man was a "dead beat." I resolved never to place much reliance on appearances again.

Having made up my mind to go to the theater and see John E. Owens play "Solon Shingle," I walked out. At the door I met a solitary boot-black, who greeted me with, "black 'em?"

"You may black *it*," I replied, "for you see I have only one to black."

"All right," said he; whereupon I seated myself

on a low railing that guarded a cellar-way, and placed my foot on his box.

He had soon "shined" it sufficiently, but was still brushing away at it, when I said:

"There, that will do; what do you charge?"

The dirty, ragged little fellow looked thoughtfully and earnestly up into my face, and replied:

"O, I won't charge *you* any thing; you're only got one."

I compelled him to accept a ten-cent note, of course, assuring him that I had "bushels of 'em;" but the intention was no less kind in him; and such a noble thought, though the poor little heart from which it sprung be clothed in rags and filth, will shine in heaven when the rust has long covered and hidden the millions of gold which men of wealth have contributed to "charitable institutions!"

Before leaving New York, (which is ironically styled Gotham, from an old English town noted for the stupidity of its citizens,) let me say one word about its early history. New York, the great commercial metropolis of this country, is built on an island fourteen miles long, and from one fourth of a mile to two miles and a half wide, called, originally, Manhattan Island. This island was purchased from the Indians many years ago for twenty-four silver dollars. No wonder that race of people have had such bad luck during the last century; for any people who would extort such a sum of money from simple, inoffensive Europeans, don't deserve any providential favors. Poor, impoverished New York has been struggling ever since to get out of debt, but in vain;

this colossal sum, which the heartless savages demanded in ready hard cash, completely "strapped"
the mayor and city council, and they have never
been able to struggle up to an independent pecuniary
position since.

Shortly before leaving the city, I was taking my
usual stroll, when, turning the corner of Broadway
and Fulton street rather abruptly, I accidentally
planted my crutch fairly upon the unfortunate toes
of an elderly gentleman.   He proved to be one of the
irascible sort—and no doubt it *did* hurt like the
deuce—and he turned angrily toward me, brandished
a cane, and vociferated:

"****'* fire and ***nation! If you were not a
one-legged man I'd knock your head off!"

Thus, you see, that having lost a leg saved my
head.

I felt a little riled at first, but seeing that he was
an old man, I curbed my fiery passion and calmly
replied:

"If I were not a one-legged man, sir, I would not be
using a crutch; and hence it wouldn't have happened."
And we went our ways.

Without getting robbed, or garroted, or murdered
in cold blood—in fact without getting "done" in any
shape, I spent several weeks in New York, visiting
many places of interest in the vicinity, such as Central
Park, High Bridge, and the various islands in the
bay and harbor; and finally returned to Philadelphia,
my adopted city, with the impression that New York
wasn't such a bad place after all.

CHAPTER IX.

Sea-Sick.—Ugh!

IN January, 1865, I concluded to visit the New England—otherwise called the "Yankee" or "Eastern"—States; and thought I would at once strike for Boston, Massachusetts, which is called the "Hub of the Universe," and make that city my head-quarters during my stay in the "land of steady habits:" that means the six New England States: Maine, New Hampshire, Vermont, Massachusetts, Rhode Island, and Connecticut. The habits of the people of all the rest of the United States are very *unsteady.*

I fancied that a "sea voyage" must be a delightful thing, according to all that poets and novelists had said about the "deep blue sea," the "ocean wave," the "rolling deep," and the like; so, I determined to go by sea. I took passage aboard a large propeller one squally day, and away we went, amid the ice and snow, down the Delaware river, down the bay, and out upon the bosom of the "mighty deep." Yes, and it is "mighty deep," as Davie Crockett would have said—a "mighty sight" deeper than is really necessary, merely for the encouragement of navigation and the cultivation of whales and sharks!

5

I had heard of such a thing as "sea-sickness," but I believed it was half imagination, and that any brave heart could bear up against it. In a word, I resolved not to get "sea-sick" myself. The mate of the vessel told me that it was "more than likely" I *would* feel a little "squeamish" when we should get out where it was "rough"—that was, if I had never been to sea before. I didn't believe it, though.

We started on Saturday morning, and it took us all day to get "outside." During that time I eat three hearty meals on board the propeller, for traveling on the water lent me an appetite. It was only *lent*, for I returned it.

Well, about dark that evening, we got out where it was "rough." The vessel began to roll, pitch, and plunge, and I heard the sea roaring, the waves splashing over the deck, a few loose articles on board rattling and tumbling about; and I began to wonder if everything about the vessel was secure. I sat on a sofa in the cabin, and presently, I began to feel—well, I felt, in a word, that a "voyage" was, like all other enjoyments, not quite what one anticipates; but still, well enough. Then, immediately, I felt a little—just a little—"worse." I didn't like the way the cabin was throwing itself around: it made my head feel queer. I thought that if the vessel would just stop rolling for half-a-minute, I would feel all right again. It didn't stop, though, and I rapidly began to feel all wrong. In a word, I grew dizzy.

Dizzy? O, no! That's no fair expression. I rather felt as though I was a large cask filled a little too full of mixed white lead, putty, or something heavy that way, and that the head was forced down upon it with considerable pressure—especially about the stomach, where I fancied one of the hoops of the imaginary cask might be located, and about the "brow," where the upper hoop might be, did I experience this indescribable heaviness. I imagined the heavy cask (myself, John Smith,) to be rolling and tumbling about loose, and the white lead or putty straining to get out. I couldn't stand that thought. The mate came into the cabin, asked me if I wasn't sick, remarked that I looked "deathly pale," and advised me to "turn in" as quickly as "the law would allow me."

"Where?" I asked, as I rapidly grew sicker. "O, dear! Where'll I sleep?"

"Here!" he said, hastily opening a stateroom door very near me. "Get in there. I'll help you. Take the lower bunk. You will be the only passenger in this room." In fact, there were but few passengers aboard.

As I attempted to rise, the ship gave a playful lurch, laid over on her side, then quickly tossed herself upon the other side, and if the mate had not caught me, I should have plunged clear across the cabin and tumbled back again, far more quickly than a man could have walked it. My crutch and cane escaped me, however, striking an opposite stateroom door in less than a second, and throwing themselves savagely about over the cabin floor.

"Never mind them just now," said the mate. "I'll help you in." And he helped me in.

" There's a bucket hanging to the side of the berth,"
said he. " If you should feel a little sick——"

Ugh! Human nature couldn't stand it any longer.
I tumbled recklessly into the berth, and—O, wasn't I
sick! Even now, after the lapse of several years, I
shudder to think of it! Supper, dinner, breakfast—
all eaten in vain! Bauh-gosh-gslish-shesh! O, lordy!
The ship was tossing about like a man intoxicated,
and I, worse still, was tossing about like a man sick
drunk; I heard the wind howling, for it was blowing
hard, the waves dashing overhead, the ship creaking
and groaning; and I groaned, and prayed for land or
death! Then I regretted that I had ever been born.
I also reproached the fates for having sent me to sea
in such stormy weather, and solemnly vowed—and I
kept that vow for nearly a year—that, in case I ever
reached land, (which I now thought rather unlikely),
I would never, never, never venture out upon the
broad ocean again! O, O, O, O, Ugh! Gushshshsh!

O, how I wished the ship would stop rolling for
just a moment! But it wouldn't stop at all. It rolled,
and plunged, and tossed, and tumbled, and pitched;
and I got sicker, and sicker, and sicker, till I imagined
myself at " death's door," with my hand on the bell-
handle.

To gain a slight conception as to how I felt, fancy
how a boy would feel, if, when sick on his first cigar,
he were not allowed to throw it away, but forced to
retain it in his mouth and smoke away! Thus it is
with one who is sea-sick. The motion of the vessel
causes it, and when a fellow grows dizzy, and feels
wretched about the bottom of the vest, he can't throw

that motion away, like a cigar. It has made him sick, it makes him sicker, and don't even stop when he gets "deathly sick." To treat a patient scientifically, physicians remove the *cause* of his illness; but in this case, the cause—that is, the motion of the vessel—cannot be removed, and there is nothing left for the unhappy patient but to get "used to it."

The only thing I remember of that fearful night, except pure, unbroken, unalloyed misery, is that I asked the captain, as he passed through the cabin, if it was actually storming. He carelessly replied:

"O, it's only blowing a fresh little nor'-wester;" and passed on.

A fresh little nor'-wester! I groaned in agony, and rolled about in my berth, thinking that if that was only a fresh little nor'-wester, what a fearful thing a *stale big* nor'-wester would be!

Next morning at daylight the steward came to my berth and asked me if I could "eat something?" Eat! Whew? Ugh! The very thought came near bringing on a relapse. "No, no, no!" I shuddered; and buried my face in my bunk.

About ten o'clock he passed through the cabin, and I asked him if we were "out of sight o' land?"

"Out o' sight?" he returned. "Yes, and have been for ten hours!"

I felt somewhat better—in fact, a good deal better than during the terrible night just passed—and I determined to make my way to the deck to view a scene that had never before blessed my eyes. The wind had abated, but the waves ran high, and the vessel was still rolling considerably. Feeling light-

headed and queer, I got out of my berth, grasping
something all the time to keep from being spilled out
into the cabin, got my crutch, left my state-room, and
began to move toward the companion-way. By hug-
ging the wall, grasping state-room door-knobs, and
the like, I reached the foot of the staircase without
falling, and looking up—the hatch being open—I saw
the blue sky staggering about overhead. Holding
firmly to a polished brass railing, I ascended to the
deck and took a seat on the companion-hatch.

Before me and all around me was the long wished-
for sight. Our ship, the dark-green sea, the sun, the
clear blue sky and a few wild sea-birds flitting about,
were all that the eye could find to rest on. The sea
and sky met on all sides, forming a grand and mighty
circle around us. I remember remarking to myself,
in my enthusiasm, that to see such a sight as this,
was " worth risking a fellow's life !"

To do " old ocean " justice, I must say that there is
nothing in the world more delightful than to be at
sea a little while in mild weather ; but when a gale is
blowing, as I have since seen it, the ship going to
pieces every hour, and the waves foaming, and snarl-
ing, and gnashing their teeth, as it were, in their impatience to get you and strangle you; then you naturally wish there wasn't such a thing as a sea in the
world; or that your lot had been cast in the " new
world," where " there was no more sea." (Revelations xxi. 1.)

On Monday we came in sight of Cape Cod, and I
thought we should never get round it. Those who
have noticed Cape Cod on the map have no doubt

observed that it is shaped like a human foot; and we went gliding along near its sole, traveling from heel to toe. For hours, I was every moment expecting to go "round the point," which I imagined I could see all the time a little way ahead: but it kept receding all the while, like an *ignis fatuus*, till I began to fancy that the foot belonged to some great giant, who was bending his knee, and drawing it back stealthily, in order to straighten it out again and give us a kick.

CHAPTER X.

THE "HUB."

WE arrived in Boston Harbor Monday afternoon about four o'clock, and entered a very dense fog about the same time. The fog was so thick for several minutes that objects could not be seen from one end of the vessel to the other. The engine was quickly stopped, and we narrowly escaped a collision with a steamer. But in the course of ten minutes, the heavy mist swept down the harbor in a body, and left all clear around us; when we were somewhat surprised to find ourselves within one hundred yards of the shore. We floated up to the pier at the foot of State street; the propeller was soon made fast, and I immediately went ashore, in the midst of a soaking rain that seemed to be sent just then for my express benefit. I got into a carriage— one that had sleigh-runners substituted for wheels— and rode to a good comfortable hotel which the Captain had recommended.

It rained till after dark; and, in fact, I retired to my room, went asleep and left it raining. I remember that I heard some one remark, just before I retired, that if it kept on raining,—he didn't say how long—it would spoil the sleighing, and wheels would come into requisition again : for in the New England States, especially Massachusetts, and those lying north of it, a vehicle with wheels is seldom seen in the depth of winter. The sleighing usually continues good till spring, and the wheels are removed for a time from all vehicles, and runners are adjusted in their stead. Not even the street-cars or omnibuses are any exceptions: they, too, cease to rattle, roll and rumble over the streets, and go gliding about with so little noise that one gets the queer idea into his head that they are barefooted.

Next morning I discovered that it had cleared off, and that the thermometer had gracefully descended to zero. [Well, that was *nothing*.] In fact, during the ensuing six weeks which I spent in the New England States, the sleighing continued excellent, and the thermometer ranged pretty generally from about five degrees above zero to five below. To be sure, we had a cool night or two, now and then, when it went down to ten or fifteen below; but no one thought much of that. Such is the character of the winter in New England—the good old-fashioned kind that a fellow likes to see.

I glanced over toward Charlestown early on the morning after my arrival, beheld Bunker Hill Monument towering far above the smoke-stacks and steeples in the perspective; and I determined to visit it at once. I accordingly climbed to the top of an omnibus, cold as it was—for I wanted to see all I could—and rode over.

It is not universally known that the battle of Bunker Hill is so called because it was fought on

Breed's Hill. The latter is near Bunker's Hill, and it is on Breed's Hill that the monument now stands—and always has stood since it was built, (for they never moved it.) The reason the battle was called the battle of Bunker Hill, and, consequently, that the monument is styled the "Bunker Hill Monument," is, that the engagement *should have been* fought there. Colonel Prescott was sent with a thousand men to throw up earthworks on Mr. Bunker's Hill, which overlooked Charlestown Neck; but either mistaking his instructions, or not being acquainted with the vicinity, he took possession of Breed's Hill instead, and threw up an earthwork there in rather unpleasant proximity to the British fleet in the harbor.

The monument is built of granite, is about twenty-five feet square at the base, and about twelve or fifteen at the top; which top is accessible by means of an interior winding stone stairway, dimly lighted with rather small jets of gas that are too few and too far between. At intervals of about twenty feet there are narrow apertures to let in air; and that cold morning they let in too much. During the previous night, too, the rain had blown in and frozen on the stone steps, so that fully one half of them were perfectly enameled with ice.

To ascend these with a crutch under such circumstances was no less than a dangerous undertaking. The superintendent advised me not to try it, but I could not act upon his advice, from the fact that I had "made up my mind" to go up. (It's a wonder I didn't "go up," in another way.) If there had not been a small iron railing to cling to, I could never have reached the head of that almost interminable staircase. As it was, I came near falling backward, and only saved myself by clutching this railing.

Should one start to fall down these steps, nothing would save him. They wind around and around, with here and there only a narrow landing, not more than twice the width of a stair, and too narrow to arrest the progress of a descending form. One might as well leap down from the top, either outside or within the circular shaft around which the stairs wind, as to go tumbling around and around, down, down, down, the solid spiral stairway, thumped and beaten by the edges of two or three hundred stone steps; for in either case I suppose that brandy and water wouldn't save him.

I reached the top pretty tired, after having ascended two hundred and ninety-five icy steps; and from this height of two hundred feet, had a good view of Boston, Charlestown, Roxbury, and the harbor.

Finding it rather cold up there—for there were several good sized windows open for the wind to blow in at, and visitors to look out of—I soon made up my mind to descend; in fact the cold was so severe that it had a rather benumbing effect on me; and as my thigh and the calf of my leg fairly ached from my recent exertions, I fully realized the danger of descending, and fancied I would have made a considerable pecuniary sacrifice to be safely at the base of the tall structure. There was no way to get there, however, but to *walk* down, if it might be so called, and I began the perilous descent. I was not half way down when my crutch and cane both slipped

from an icy step, and I fell. O, what a fall there
would have been, my countrymen, if I hadn't caught
the iron railing! I gripped the cold iron with my
right hand, and arrested my crutch with my left; but
my cane escaped me, and away it went, tumbling knocking, cracking rattling and clattering, till it reached the
bottom. I fancied it took it something like a minute
to make the descent, but the probability is that the
time it occupied in the journey was not more than
ten seconds. It's last echo had just died away, when
I heard the voice of the superintendent calling to me
from below; and his voice had a kind of twisty
sound by the time it wound its way up to me.

"Did you fall?" he asked.

"No," I replied, telling a white one, "I merely
threw my cane down because I can get down better
without it."

I did, however, get along better without it, for I
could now grasp the railing all the time with one
hand while the other held the crutch.

Well, it is not my intention to write an ordinary
book of travels. That has been done too often. All
the places I have visited have been described time
and again; and I will only entertain the reader with
my (John Smith's) odd adventures therein.

While in Boston I had the pleasure of an introduction to Mrs. Partington. That amiable old lady is a
jovial, round-faced old *gentleman* of fifty-five or sixty.
His name is B. P. Shillaber, and he is connected with
the Boston *Gazette*. He is a noble-hearted, excellent
gentleman; and the people of this country owe him

their thanks for the many happy smiles his eccentric and inimitable pen has called out upon their faces. Long life and many happy years to Mrs. Partington!

I remained in New England during the rest of the winter, and had a pleasant time and many sleigh-rides. I visited Lexington, Lowell, Lawrence and most of the large towns of Massachusetts; Manchester, Concord and Portsmouth, New Hampshire; Bellows Falls, Rutland and Burlington, Vermont; and Portland and some smaller towns and cities in Maine.

In the city of Portland I hired a horse and sleigh one morning, and resolved to drive a few miles into the country. It was snowing vigorously, but was not very cold; I had a spirited horse before me; a good light sleigh under me; and away I went, bounding over the road, neither knowing nor caring whither I went. By and by, when I had traveled five or six miles, and distanced a number of other travelers, in similar vehicles, on the way, I saw a town just ahead of me. The snow was still falling so briskly that I was almost in the town before I saw it. As I drove along, I asked a boy what place it was, and he said, " Westbrook." I entered the village, and found it to be one of considerable extent. In fact, I drove half-a-mile, and still there was no end of houses. On the contrary, they became thicker and thicker; and I began to conclude that " Westbrook" must be quite a city. By and by I found myself on a street that reminded me forcibly of one I had seen in Portland; and, what made it more remarkable, I observed that it rejoiced in the same name. What a coincidence! But I marveled more still, as I followed this street a little way and passed an hotel that was the very image of the one I stayed at in Portland—and lo! there stood at the door a porter who was dark-skinned and cross-eyed, exactly like the porter of my hotel in that city! Was I dreaming? No, not exactly; but I must have been during my drive, for I had wandered around among the country roads in the snow-storm, lost my reckoning, and actually entered Portland again. I had come in through a little suburban village, north of the city, called " Westbrook ;" and hence my delusion.

In Rutland, a beautiful little city nestling in a kind of basin high up among the Green Mountains of Vermont, I arrived one night at a late hour. I went to a good comfortable hotel—for they have such there—and asked for a " single room." The host regretted that he had no single rooms unoccupied. Passengers from the earlier trains had taken them all. He could put me in a double-bedded room where another guest had just retired—one who appeared to be a " perfect gentleman :" that was the best he could do. It was the best *I* could do, too; so, I was shown to the room.

I had a few hundred dollars in my pocket, and, not being perfectly sure that the man in the other bed was a perfect angel, I thought there would be no harm in placing it in the watch-fob of my unimpeachables, and placing the same rolled up in a ball, under my neck. I did so. When morning came, the " other fellow " got up first, and I felt somewhat amused when I chanced to observe—for I was awake, and dreading to " turn out " on account of the sharp morning air—

that he had done so too. We had both taken each other for rogues.

Well, that is the right way to view every stranger when you are traveling. Look on every man you meet, and especially if he speaks to you, as a deep-dyed villain, till you have had the most incontrovertible proof that he is not.

I made Boston my head-quarters, while visiting different portions of Maine, New Hampshire, Vermont and Massachusetts; and about the last of February, I departed for Philadelphia. I didn't try the "dark-blue sea" again; but took the "Shore Line" railroad, stopping a short time in Providence, New Haven and New York.

I arrived in New York one March evening, and, allowing my baggage to go on to Philadelphia, resolved to remain in the city that night and go to the "Quaker City" next day. I wanted to go *via* the Camden and Amboy Railroad, and was told that the boat—for passengers on this road take the boat from New York to South Amboy, a distance of twenty-eight miles—would leave at six in the morning. That evening, while in the sitting-room of my old hotel, I observed two suspicious-looking fellows eyeing me rather sharply, and I felt that they were entitled to a little watching from me. So, I watched them. When I retired, I locked and bolted my door and even braced it with my crutch. [A handy thing to have in a house, sometimes.] I slept soundly till five o'clock, at which time the porter, according to instructions, knocked at my door and awoke me.

There was no one in the hotel below, when I went

down but a sleepy porter, and I was wondering wh-re my suspicious-looking friends (?) were, and where they stayed, and congratulating myself that I was escaping them nicely by going away at that early hour in the morning, when the street-door opened and the two identical gentlemen stepped in, and took a seat by the stove. Pretending not to notice them, *I* stepped *out*.

It was still far from daylight, and the snow was flying merrily. The wind was howling, and each blaze of gas in the street-lamps was fluttering and struggling as though it might go out at any moment. I wanted to go to Pier No. 1, North River, from which the boat was to start, and I walked as fast as I could—and that was not slow—toward Broadway, glancing back over my shoulder at intervals of two seconds, to see if my villains were coming. It was the quietest hour I ever saw in New York. Not a stage, carriage, cart or car was astir in that part of the city ; and neither policeman nor "any other man" was to be seen. The snow and wind combined were fairly blinding, and it was very far from being a "fine morning."

I had nearly reached Broadway, when I looked back and saw the two dears coming, a square distant. They were passing a lamp-post, and the glimpse I caught of their figures convinced me of their identity. Without exhibiting any haste or trepidation, I walked on to the corner of Broadway and Park Row and turned to the left ; but instead of walking down Broadway, suddenly stepped aside and stood in the door-way of Barnum's old Museum—which was still standing at that time, but over whose ashes Bennett's majestic marble palace now stands—leaned my cane up in a corner, drew my revolver, cocked it, and awaited the attack.

I had just completed my preparations for a defence of my position, when the happy pair came. The light of a street-lamp at the corner shone full upon them, and I must have been blind indeed if I had not recognized them. Their hats were drawn down over their eyes, to shield those organs from the driving snow, and as I was in the shade, they failed to see me, and rushed by. They were running, their footsteps soon died away, and their "forms" faded down Broadway, which was then as quiet as a country lane. I was very well satisfied to escape an encounter with them, because I preferred not to shoot them, as I would certainly have found it necessary to do had they seen me.

I knew they would soon discover that I had dodged them, and return; so, replacing my revolver, taking my cane, and keeping an eye down Broadway, I glided across the silent thoroughfare, went down Vesey Street to North River, and thence down West Street to Pier No. 1, which was not really much out of my way.

I reached the boat in good time, and arrived in Philadelphia that day by twelve o'clock.

6

CHAPTER XI.

NARROW ESCAPE IN A ROW AT BALTIMORE.

ABOUT the middle of March I concluded to take a tour to Baltimore, Harper's Ferry, Antietam Battle-field, Hagerstown and Harrisburg: at all of which places—and especially ANTIETAM—I had been before. I intended to occupy three or four weeks, and made arrangements to act meantime as correspondent for a paper.

Nothing unusual happened to me on the way to Baltimore, except that on looking from a car window at Havre de Grace, a small particle of cinder from the engine flew into my eye; which kept it red and inflamed, and furnished me with first-class pain, at intervals, for the ensuing two weeks.

A bit of cinder from a locomotive, with all its "fine points," is, I think, the severest thing that can work its way into a man's optic organ. Had railroads been in vogue in the days of King John, what a point young Arthur might have made, when remonstrating with Hubert who had been authorized to burn his eyes out with a red-hot poker, and eloquently descanting on the sensitiveness of the eye, by reminding him how it felt even when a cinder from a locomotive got into it. For example, how would the passage read in this shape?——

> "O, heaven! that there were but a mote in yours,
> A grain, a dust, a gnat, a wand'ring hair,
> *Or the ten-thousandth part of a dead spark*
> *From the smoke-stack of a lo-com'-o-tive;*
> Any annoyance in that precious sense!
> Then, feeling what small things are boisterous there,
> Your vile intent must needs seem horrible!"

It will be perceived that the two lines in italics are my (John Smith's) own production: the rest is Shakspeare's. I will not venture to predict what critics will say of the relative merits of the two authors in this case.

As the trains from Philadelphia enter Baltimore, they cross a wide, clean, quiet street, called "Broadway." It bears no resemblance to the Broadway of New York, as it is occupied chiefly by private dwellings. The trains always stop there a minute or two to allow those who wish to get off. This street runs north and south and of course crosses Baltimore street, the principal business thoroughfare, which runs east and west. The Baltimore-street railway extends down Broadway, and as several cars are always in waiting when trains arrive, many passengers get off the train here, take a street-car, and ride into the heart of the city. I always do so when I visit the "Monumental city." I did so on this occasion, having first instructed the baggage-express agent to send my trunk to my hotel.

As I jumped from the train, (before it had quite stopped,) and walked toward the street-car that stood waiting on Broadway, a soldier approached me, and tapping me familiarly on the shoulder, said:

"Why, Locke! how are you?"

I saw at a glance that he had mistaken me for some one else, and soberly replied:

"I believe this isn't I."

"O, so it isn't! Excuse me," he said, perceiving his mistake and laughing at my joke.

I got into a crowded car and rode to my hotel on West Baltimore street; for the principal street is divided into East and West Baltimore streets by a canal, which it crosses near the center of the city.

Having a week or two before me, with very little to do, I determined to see all the places of interest in the vicinity, for I had, theretofore, neglected to visit them, although I had frequently been in Baltimore. I had never even visited the Washington Monument there.

Here let me commend Baltimore for being the only city that has ever erected a monument to the memory of that pure-hearted patriot to whom we are indebted for our liberties and free institutions— GEORGE WASHINGTON!

Baltimore has another monument which was erected in honor of the Maryland soldiers who fell in the war of 1812; and is hence styled the "Monumental City."

The Washington Monument is indeed quite a fine structure. It is built of marble to the height of about two hundred feet, and its top is adorned with a large statue of the "Father of His Country." Within, is a spiral stairway of stone, like that in the Bunker

Hill Monument; but it is not lighted with gas, nor has it any embrasures for the admission of air and daylight. The superintendent, or some one employed for the purpose, accompanies each visitor, who wishes to ascend, carrying a lantern. He may well be termed a man who has a great many "ups and downs" in the world. From the top of this monument, the view of the city is excellent; almost every house in it can be seen.

Of course, I visited this monument, but as nothing extraordinary occurred, and especially nothing funny, I will not entertain the reader with a full description of my visit, nor of the monument itself.

I was always fond of rowing, and as the weather was mild and pleasant next day, I concluded to go down to the harbor, hire a boat and take a row. I was told that I could get one at the foot of a little street running obliquely toward the piers from the junction of Broadway and Pratt streets, the latter being the street on which the Philadelphia trains run into the city—and I took a street-car and went down.

When I asked the man for the boat, he looked at my crutch and said:

" Can you row ?"

I told him that reminded me of a lady friend of mine, who shortly after my return from the "field of glory," asked me if I didn't find my corporeal defect very inconvenient about eating. " Why shouldn't I row ?" said I. " A man don't hold the oars with his toes, any more than he holds his knife and fork in them when eating at the table—which would look rather odd, and render it necessary for him instead of sitting in the usual manner to take a somewhat novel position."

No further doubts were expressed as to my ability to row, and I got into a fifty-cents-an-hour boat, and rowed out into the harbor.

"Be careful," was the owner's admonition as I pulled away, "that you don't get caught in a squall and be driven away. The weather is uncertain in March."

"No danger," I replied, and my boat glided out to where there was a stiff breeze blowing, and was soon dancing on the waves.

I moved toward the southeast a mile or so, rested awhile near a ship that was lying at anchor, and had a chat with one of the mates. I was beginning to pull away from the ship, when I heard an excited voice toward my right sing out:

"Look out there! Where the deuce are you going?"

Immediately followed a confusion of voices, the ringing of bells, and the shriek of a steam whistle. I turned in the direction, and was somewhat alarmed to discover that I was about to cross the bow of a propeller, that came dashing along. Had I pulled the oars but once more, nothing would have saved me from being run down. My boat would have been shivered to pieces, I would have been stunned and my chances of being saved from a watery grave would have been as one against a hundred. With all the presence of mind I could command, I "backed oars," and checked my boat, which of its own accord turned side-wise; and the propeller rushed by, at such a trifling distance from me as to strike the blade of my right-hand oar.

"Whew! my young man," said the mate with whom I had been talking—for he still stood by the bulwark—"you came near going down."

I fully realized this, and quite satisfied with my row, put back for shore. The wind had increased, and I now noticed, for the first time, that some dark clouds were coming from the west. I had a good mile to row against the wind, which, as well as the waves, was every moment increasing in violence. I was yet a quarter of a mile from the dock in which the boat belonged, when a regular squall came on. Then I had a time of it. Throwing off my coat and hat, and placing them in the bottom of the boat, I grasped my oars and pulled away with all the strength and energy I possessed. I made rather slow time, and when within one hundred yards of port, perceived that I was just making out to lie still against the wind. I was nearly exhausted, and felt like throwing down my oars in despair; but seeing what a short distance was yet to be accomplished, I nerved myself for a final effort; and such a battle as I had with the wind and waves no one need want to engage in. After ten minutes of the most strenuous exertion, I arrived in the dock, trembling from exhaustion, perspiring from exercise, and wet all over with spray.

I concluded, taking my narrow escape into consideration, that rowing in the harbor was no delightful recreation, and solemnly vowed never again to venture out there in a row-boat. I kept my word faithfully till next afternoon; when the weather being very delightful, I broke it, went out again, and had a very pleasant row in the same boat.

At four o'clock one evening I left Baltimore for Harper's Ferry, *via* the Baltimore and Ohio Railroad, having first sent my trunk back to Philadelphia by express. I arrived at Harper's Ferry by nine o'clock. A great many soldiers were there—for it will be recollected that the war was not yet ended—and I found it difficult to secure a comfortable lodging. Every private house was acting the part of an hotel, furnishing supper to many soldiers and a few sorry-looking travelers; while those desiring a night's lodging were packed into rooms at the rate of from seven to twenty-seven in each.

By paying a few dollars extra, talking politely, and pretending that I was not in the best of health—although I eat an astonishing supper for an invalid—I succeeded in securing a small room to myself, to which I retired immediately after supper; and having carefully fastened the door, I lay down on a clean bed and slept comfortably till the morning.

CHAPTER XII.

HOW SMITH TRAVELED A-FOOT—AND MORE.

WHEN morning came, I tried for an hour to get a conveyance to Sharpsburg, near Antietam Creek, twelve miles distant; but in vain. Not a horse or carriage of any kind was to be had for love or money; and I made up my mind to walk it, although I had never yet walked any such distance on one leg. When a man makes up his mind to do a thing, however, he will do it, if he has firmness, no matter whether he has any limbs or not.

At eight o'clock, I went to the office of the provost-marshal to get a pass over the bridge—for it will be recollected that the village of Harper's Ferry is on the Virginia side—but he had not come in yet. Wishing to start as soon as possible, I thought I would try to face my way over. So, I went to the bridge, bade the sentinel a cheerful good-morning, and was moving on, when he said:

"Have you a pass?"

"No," I replied, stopping. "I am not in the service. Is a pass necessary?"

"No," said he, after a slight pause. "Your crutch is pass enough. I suppose you got that in the Army?"

"Yes," I replied, "at Antietam. I am going up there to-aay to see the old ground."

" How are you going ?"

"I'm going to walk."

" Walk !   Why, can you do it ?"

" I think I can, although I have never yet walked so far on a crutch."

" You'll have a good walk of it.   It is fully twelve miles."

" Yes, so I have been told; but I could get no conveyance, and must try it."

" I hope you'll get along well."

" Thank you."

I passed on.   When I reached the middle of the bridge, I could not refrain from stopping to admire the scenery, which had never before appeared so grand to me.   Harper's Ferry presents a romantic picture indeed.   All around are tall majestic wood-covered hills that gaze down upon the village and bridge with quiet and awful dignity; and the beautiful river, wandering silently about among them, looks as if it would never find its way out.   It was the twenty-fifth of March, the morning was pleasant, the sun was smiling on the heights and glancing down on the little village and the pure river.   I thought I had never before seen such a beautiful sight.

I passed over the bridge, turned to my left and walked up the tow-path of the canal.   The first two or three miles I got over in an hour or so, very smoothly; but after that I felt weary at times, and **found it an advantage to rest every mile or two.**

By a quarter to twelve o'clock I had reached the mouth of Antietam Creek, ten miles from Harper's Ferry, and had now to leave the river and strike over the hills for Sharpsburg, two miles distant. Nothing had happened to me during my walk, save that a stray bullet from beyond the river had now and then whistled about my ears. They were no doubt fired at random by some of our pickets there who did not see me.

I had now to cross the canal, in order to direct my course toward Sharpsburg. This was no easy matter. There was no bridge or lock near, and no ordinary jumper could clear it at a bound. I did fancy that I might make it in two jumps, but did not try. It was not full of water, and, seeing no plan but to wade through it, I removed my shoe, and other apparel liable to get saturated in the course of such an enterprise, and stalked in. I did not find it deeper than twenty inches, but its temperature felt very little above thirty-two degrees, Fahrenheit, and it made my foot and the calf of my leg ache clear through by the time I got across.

Having passed this obstruction and replaced my shoe, etc., I went to a house not far off, where I inquired the way to Sharpsburg, and was directed to follow a country road that took its way over the hill; and did so. I reached Sharpsburg by one o'clock having walked a little more than twelve miles in five hours. There was an hotel there and having taken dinner, I started for Smoketown, three miles distant, where I had lain in the hospital. I visited the village—a village consisting of two dwelling-houses and a corn-crib—then returned to the battle-field and spent an hour or two traveling about in search of the spot on which I had received my wound.

I failed to find the interesting place, although I had felt confident of being able to walk directly to it n a straight line. It is remarkable what a change takes place in a year or two in the appearance of the ground on which a battle has been fought. Thirty months had now elapsed since the battle of Antietam, and a casual observer would not have noticed any trace of the conflict.

I saw a Mr. Miller plowing in a field opposite the little Tunker Church by the pike—a building that had been nearly knocked to pieces in the fight, but had since been repaired—and he showed me a full set of "bones" lying in a fence-corner, which he had just "plowed up." He said they had been scarcely under the surface of the earth; but that he would bury them deeper. This was the famous cornfield in which the struggle between Hooker's and Longstreet's corps was so terrible, and where so many of the Pennsylvania Reserves were killed. I found in this field several oullets, a fragment of shell, and a few canteens, straps, etc., lying about.

As evening approached and I had walked from eighteen to twenty miles since morning, I started for Keedysville, several miles distant, with the intention of staying there all night.

After the amputation of my leg at Antietam, as mentioned in the first chapter, I had lain in a barn near the creek, a week or two; and this evening, after crossing the creek and walking a little way toward

Keedysville, I recognized this same barn, although I had never known its precise location: and O, what recollections of misery it brought back to me! My sufferings in that barn were so terrible, so far exceeding any thing that might merely be termed pain, that, as I look back now, the time spent there seems more like a horrible dream than a reality!

The sun was sinking as I stood in the road gazing thoughtfully at the barn; and I thought of the evenings I had lain within, almost dead, and seen the sun's last red rays struggling into that somber apartment of misery, through the crevices. While I thus stood, a lady, who had come out of an adjacent house, approached me. Her footsteps as she drew near aroused me from my train of thought.

"Good evening, ma'am," said I.

"How do you do? Will you walk into the house?" was the response.

"No, I thank you," I rejoined. "I am on my way to Keedysville, and was just looking at this barn, which I recognize as one in which I lay for some days after the battle here."

"Ah," said she; "were you one of the wounded ones who occupied the barn?"

"Yes, ma'am. Who is the owner?"

"Mr. Pry—my husband."

"I have been on the battle-ground," I observed, "trying to find the place I was when wounded."

"And did you find it?"

"I am sorry to say that I failed," said I.

"A pity. Where did you come from to-day?"

"Harper's Ferry."

"How did you get up?"

"Walked."

"Walked! You surely did not walk it on one leg?"

"Yes, ma'am, and this crutch and cane. I reached Sharpsburg by dinner-time, and have spent the afternoon in rambling over the battle-field and visiting Smoketown."

"You surprise me. I did not suppose a person on crutches could do all that."

"Nor did I till I tried it."

"Well, you must go no further to-night. You were our guest before, and must be again, now that we are better prepared to accommodate you."

"Why, really, I——"

"You musn't think of going any further. Why, you've walked twenty miles to-day—and on a crutch! No, indeed, you must not pass my house. Come in. Mr. Pry is just coming in to supper. Come, no excuses."

I did not further decline the proffered hospitality of this excellent lady. I was ushered into the house, and was made no less welcome by Mr. Pry, his sons and a beautiful and amiable daughter.

An excellent supper, a pleasant evening chat, a tidy bed, a comfortable chamber, and, O, such a delicious, dreamless slumber, after my day's exertion, made me forget all my weariness; and I awoke next morning—the beautiful Sunday morning of March twenty-sixth—with all the vigor of youth. Never let me forget the Pry family for their cordial welcome and hospitable entertainment!

CHAPTER XIII.

ROMANCE IN JOHN SMITH'S "REAL LIFE."

THAT Sunday morning I determined to visit the battle-ground again, and try to find that part of the field on which I had had the honor to be shot; then walk to Hagerstown, a distance of twelve miles. Having discovered, the previous day, that I was something of a walker, I now thought nothing of going that distance on foot. My excellent friends urged me to stay till Monday morning, but I declined.

I have now to record a little incident such as we sometimes read of but seldom gain cognizance of through our own auricular and optic organs. It may well be termed a "Romance in real life."

Once, while in the army, I had picked up a small white pebble on the battle-ground of Bull Run, intending to keep it as a relic of that famed field. I had put it in a port-monnaie, and carried it with me through all my battles. While lying in the barn alluded to, I had lost my port-monnaie, which only contained, besides the pebble, a small bit of white paper on which I had made some notes of marches and their dates; and since then I had scarcely given it a thought. In fact, it had gone quite out of my mind.

Well, on Sunday morning, March twenty-sixth, 1865, before I left Mr. Pry's house, Mrs. Pry showed me a small fancy basket of curiosities, such as little shells, bullets, and the like, and as she handed it to me to examine, she said:

"You will find among those shells a little white pebble, to which there is probably some story attached."

"Ah?" I replied, moving the shells about. "How so?"

"Why, I think," said she, "that it must have been the property of some soldier who, no doubt, carried it as a relic. Our boys were fishing one day, not long ago, and one of them drew up on his hook a port-monnaie—and what a fish he thought he had!—when _____"

"A port-monnaie!" I exclaimed, as the recollection of my pebble suddenly flashed upon my mind for the first time since my leaving the army.

"Yes," she went on; "and in it was the pebble _____"

"And this is it!" I interrupted, as I found it at that moment among the shells and instantly recognized it by its peculiar shape and a little dark streak running through it.

"Yes, that is it."

"And do you guess whose it is?"

"Is it yours?"

"Yes, ma'am. I recollect it distinctly now. I picked it up on the battle-field of Bull Run, when visiting the ground one day, before I had ever been in a fight, and carried it with me through all my campaigns, till wounded; and I lost it from my blouse pocket while lying in the barn. Was there not a piece of paper in the port-monnaie?"

"Yes, so the boys said."

"With some marches and their dates noted down ——"

"Exactly."

"Well, is it not rather romantic!"

"It is, indeed. The pebble is yours now. Take it."

"Thank you. I am indeed glad to see it again; but if you prefer to keep it, as you have established an undoubted right to it as property, by rescuing it from the depths of the waters, I will cheerfully leave it with you."

"No, no," said the good lady. "It is a pleasure to me to be able to restore it to you, after the lapse of more than two years. I am so glad I happened to mention it. If I had read of such an incident I could scarcely have believed it."

"Nor any one. I thank you a thousand times! To think that, after thirty months, I should recover a little thing like that!—and that after it had been associating with the fish at the bottom of Antietam Creek! To think that it should so happen that I should stop at this house all night and that you should happen to mention it to me just before departing! It is indeed romantic!"

"It is, truly. Be assured that I am as happy to restore it to you as you are to recover it."

I took the pebble, and have it yet in my possession. Any one calling on John Smith at his residence,

7

(wherever that is,) will have an opportunity of seeing it, and of thus satisfying himself that this story is true.

Accompanied by Mr. Pry's two sons, I departed for the battle-ground, in the midst of the most earnest solicitations to remain till Monday morning, and made another tour of the battle-field. At last, we succeeded in finding the identical spot of ground on which I had stood when shot, which I recognized by unmistakable landmarks. Especially did I remember a little ledge of rocks in the midst of a small grove of trees, over which we had climbed in advancing, and where two men had fallen back, shot dead—one at my right hand and the other at my left. I also found and recognized the identical tree against which I had leaned my rifle on finding myself to be too badly wounded to continue firing. There were some graves in the quiet little grove, and on a small head-board I found the name of one of my old regiment. Among some of the sunken graves, were also visible whitened bones that had barely been covered with earth, and were now, after the rains and storms of more than two years, entirely unearthed and exposed to view.

Between ten and eleven o'clock, I started for Hagerstown. The boys wanted me either to go back to the house or wait there till they should get a team ready to convey me to my destination, but I declined, assuring them that I could walk easily, and would really prefer to do so, as the weather was fine.

I made my way to the Hagerstown pike, and had not traveled far, when I fell in with a farmer who was returning from a Sunday-school he had been attending at the little church, and he urged me to go nome with him and take dinner. Not wishing to stop so soon, I declined, with thanks. I met with several similar invitations on the pike. I must say, that the hospitality and kind-heartedness of the people of Maryland cannot be too highly spoken of. They had no fair opportunity to show these good qualities while whole armies were passing through their land, although even then they did all they reasonably could do for us; but let a person travel through the country districts, especially if he be crippled or laboring under any physical disadvantage, and he will meet with kind smiles of welcome from all, regardless of political sentiments.

Having traveled four or five miles, I was passing a house where dinner was just ready, when a good-natured old gentleman came out to the gate and said:

"How do you do, sir? Stop a moment. Which way are you traveling?"

"I am going to Hagerstown," I replied, pausing.

"Well, you have not had your dinner yet," he said with a tone and manner that distinctly added, "So, of course, you simply walk in at this gate and up into the house and get your dinner, to be sure."

"No," I could not help admitting; "but——"

"But What?——in the name of sense."

"I am not decidedly hungry, and would like to walk a mile or two further before I stop."

"O, nonsense! Come in!" And he opened the gate with such an air that I could not have remained

in the road without insulting him. "Did you say
you intended to walk to Hagerstown?"

"Yes, sir; such is my intention."

"Well, you mustn't think of it. Come in, take
dinner and rest awhile, and I will hitch up to my
spring wagon and take you to Hagerstown in less
time than it would take you to walk a mile! Come."

I could no longer resist, and allowed myself to be
smiled and welcomed into the house. The good people therein—an elderly lady and her daughter—were
somewhat astonished when I told them of my walk
of the previous day.

"Is it possible you couldn't get a wagon?" said the
old gentleman.

"I could not."

"If I had known it," said he, while his noble heart
shone out all over his face, "I would have hitched
up and come down for you! Surely, there ought to
have been some one there—However, people get
pretty hard-hearted where soldiers are quartered so
long."

"Very natural," I observed.

After a good dinner, which I had the appetite to
enjoy, this hospitable gentleman, despite my protesta-
tions, hitched up his horse and wagon, and took me
to Hagerstown. I offered to pay him, but he regarded
that idea as one of the best jokes he had heard lately.
No, indeed; I mustn't give a thought to such a
thing!

"The idea of taking pay from you!" he said; and
laughed till we both forgot about it.

I stayed at Hagerstown that night and next morning took an early train for Harrisburg, arriving there about noon.   I only spent a couple of hours in Harrisburg, then took a train for Philadelphia, where I arrived that evening, and found my trunk awaiting me.

CHAPTER XIV.

THE HUDSON.

I SPENT the remainder of the spring and the first two months of the summer in New York, but as the extreme "caloric" of the "heated term" began to make the giant walls and solid streets of the metropolis next to intolerable, I determined to take a little tour up the Hudson, and out by the lakes into Ohio : and did.

But my grateful heart will not allow me to pass quietly by New York again without briefly acknowledging the sincere thanks I owe, for distinguished favors, to the following excellent gentlemen: Manton Marble, Editor of the WORLD; Drexel, Winthrop & Co., Bankers, Wall street; Willy Wallach, Stationer, John street; Paschal S. Hughes, Merchant, Broadway; Henry S. Camblos, Broker, New street; and E. S. Jaffray, Merchant, Broadway. I can say no more.

Having made arrangements to correspond with a certain well-known journal, I started, about the first of August, on my projected tour, taking passage on the handsome steamer DANIEL DREW for Albany.

They have on the Hudson river some of the finest boats in the world—low-pressure boats of immense size, that never think of bragging on speed that falls below twenty miles an hour. Some of them, by straining a muscle or two, have made twenty-five miles an hour, and felt none the worse for it next morning.

We started at eight o'clock one August morning; and what a change of atmosphere we experienced as we left the hot streets of the city far behind us, and glided up the Hudson—that most picturesque and romantic of rivers! The sky was bright and clear; and, however hot and close may have been the narrow and crowded streets of New York, the air with us was charming.

Most of the passengers sat on the cabin deck, which was protected from the sun by an awning, that hovered over us like the ghost of some broad sail that Old Ocean might have swallowed. We had not gone far, when a band of musicians from the land of Horace, Virgil, Cicero, Titus, Vespasian and the Cesars, treated us with some melodious strains on the violin, harp, and some other instruments. Although we would have regarded them as a nuisance in front of our doors in the city, we now really appreciated their talent; and when they had played half-an-hour, and one of them came round with an empty hat in his hand, there were but few, if any, who did not acknowledge their approbation by contributions of ten cent notes, or the like.

They had just disappeared, and I was beginning to regard the delightful scenery that began to unfold itself to us along the shores, when a very black African made his appearance on deck, and leaning over a kind

of sky-light, called out to some one below in a loud
tone :

"Hillo, Bill, down dah!"

"Well, what does you want?" was the response
from below. It was evident that William was also
a gentleman from the land where snakes, crocodiles,
and savage beasts grow to their full size.

"Are you gwine up to Albany?" asked the darkey
on deck.

"Yes, reckon I'se gwine up dah," came from
below.

"How'd you leabe all de folks?"

"O, well enough—but don't ask so darned many
questions," said Bill, testily.

"Gettin' rudder techy, ain't you?"

"O, don't bodder me! I didn't git no sleep last
night—I didn't."

By this time the attention of the passengers in the
vicinity was attracted, and all eyes were turned upon
the darkey. As for myself, I felt somewhat annoyed,
and wondered why the black cuss didn't go below and
carry on his animated chat with his friend, instead of
standing up there, yelling down, and disturbing the
tranquillity of the passengers.

"Well, why didn't you sleep? It was your own
fault."

"O, let me 'lone, Sam," came from below. "I don't
want no foolin'!"

"I won't let you 'lone. You ain't gwine to get no
sleep dis day, you isn't," said Sam, thrusting a cane
he had in his hand down through the open sky-
light.

Some one appeared to seize it from below, and at the same time the voice of Bill said:

"Now, look yere, I say, I'll break dis 'ole cane fur you, if you don't look out!"

"Yes, you bettah try dat," said Sam, thrusting the cane down several times, as though he were stirring a 'possum out of a hollow log.

"Now you be keerful!" vociferated the voice below, angrily; and the stick was seized again and an effort made to wrench it from Sam's hand.

"Let go o' dat now, I say," said Sam, at the same time freeing it with a savage jerk.

"Den you let me 'lone," said Bill, in a kind of compromising tone.

The passengers were looking on in astonishment. It was rather singular that this black *employé* of the boat, as he evidently was, was allowed to come up among the passengers, and go to raising such an altercation through the sky-light with some one below. One passenger, who had been reading, seemed very much annoyed, and at last testily said:

"O, let the fellow alone—whoever he is!"

"I'll let *you* 'lone if I come up dar!" retorted the voice below, evidently addressing the irritated passenger.

"Look out, Bill," exclaimed Sam; "dat's a white gemman you's talkin' to! d'ye know dat?"

"Don't car for dat. He's no wuss dan a black gemman," retorted Bill. "De white cuss!"

"Confound him!" exclaimed the angry passenger, rising and going to the sky-light. "Where is he? I'll punch his head!"

"Don't you wish you'd ketch me! Ha, ha, ha, ha, ha, ha!" laughed the voice, in taunting exultation; and now, to the astonishment of all, it sounded distinctly as though it were on the awning above our heads.

All looked up as though expecting to see the shadow of some one there, but only the broad beams of the sun covered the canvas from side to side.

"Ha, ha, ha! What's de mattah?" yelled the same voice. "Ha, ha, ha!"

First it appeared on the canvas, then under the deck, next toward the cabin-door, next toward the bow of the boat, and, after apparently making a rapid circle around us, finally subsided in our midst—in fact, in the very mouth of the darkey who stood on deck. He was a ventriloquist—a skillful one, too—and had been thus beautifully "doing" us all this time. As for "Bill," the darkey below, he was of course a fictitious personage. A loud laugh came from the passengers, as they realized this, and the irascible man, who had threatened to punch Bill's head, returned to his seat, trying to look unconcerned. Sam passed around his cap for tokens of our appreciation of his powers, and each one—including the irascible passenger—contributed from five to twenty-five cents. That was the last "tax" we paid that day.

I might give a long, and even interesting, account of my journey up the Hudson; but such is not my intention. There are already numerous books of travel extant, which describe the Hudson as well as it can be described in words. My object is to amuse;

and if I relate all the funny things that happened to me, I shall succeed. I might describe the view of the Catskill Mountains, the towns of Hudson, Peekskill, Newburg, West Point, etc., but will leave that to tourists, as already hinted.

But I must not pass by without mentioning one or two points on the Hudson. The Catskill Mountains, viewed from the river, present so lovely a picture that neither pen nor brush can convey any adequate idea of them. No one should live and die without viewing such scenery as this.

A few miles above West Point, and on the same shore of the river—the western—rises a mountain peak called the Crow Nest. Joseph Rodman Drake, an American poet who died in 1820, at the age of twenty-five, thus exquisitely depicts this delightful region, in his poem entitled, "THE CULPRIT FAY:"

"'Tis the middle watch of a summer's night—
The earth is dark, but the heavens are bright;
Nought is seen in the vault on high,
But the moon, and the stars, and the cloudless sky,
And the flood which rolls its milky hue,
A river of light on the welkin blue.
The moon looks down on old Crow Nest,
She mellows the shades on his shaggy breast,
And seems his huge gray form to throw
In a silver cone on the wave below;
His sides are broken by spots of shade,
By the walnut bough and the cedar made,
And through their clustering branches dark,
Glimmers and dies the fire-fly's spark—
Like starry twinkles that momently break
Through the rifts of the gathering tempest's rack.

"The stars are on the moving stream,
  And fling, as its ripples gently flow,
A burnished length of wavy beam
  In an eel-like spiral line below:
The winds are whist, and the owl is still,
  The bat in the shelvy rock is hid,
And nought is heard on the lonely hill
But the cricket's chirp, and the answer shrill
  Of the gauze-winged katy-did;
And the plaint of the wailing whip-poor-will,
  Who moans unseen and ceaseless sings,
Ever a note of wail and woe,
  Till morning spreads her rosy wings,
And earth and sky in her glances glow.

"'Tis the hour of fairy ban and spell;
The wood-tick has kept the minutes well;
He has counted them all with click and stroke,
Deep in the heart of the mountain oak,
And he has awakened the sentry elve,
  Who sleeps with him in the haunted tree,
To bid him to ring the hour of twelve,
  And call the fays to their revelry."

CHAPTER XV.

John at Saratoga

WE reached Albany at five o'clock, and I stepped ashore and walked carelessly up the street, trying to look as though I had been there before. I don't think I succeeded. It is the most difficult thing in the world to step off a boat or train in a strange city, and not fancy that at least half the assembled spectators are looking at you and saying:

"There's a fellow who never was here before: that's clear."

I went up to an hotel, gave my check to the porter and told him to bring my baggage from the boat. I have hitherto forborne to give the names of hotels, because it might look like surreptitious advertising; and John Smith is above that sort of thing. But, it might be urged, why not mention the names of the good hotels, that travelers who read this work may know where to stay when they visit such cities as I mention? One reason is, this is no traveler's guide; and another is, that an hotel that was comfortable and well-conducted two or three years ago, may have changed proprietors, and become quite the reverse by this time. I have seen this demonstrated myself, as I may have occasion to mention in the course of this work.

I remained at Albany a week, during which time I visited the penitentiary—*only* as a visitor, remember—and other places of interest. I also visited Troy, six miles above, on the east side of the river, and some of its manufactories. At a nail and horse-shoe factory there I saw the largest wheel in this country. It is a monstrous water-wheel, which runs the machinery of the whole establishment. I was told that its diameter was seventy-four feet. It was in operation while I was there; it revolved rather slowly, and looked like the world turning around on a cloudy day. At Troy I also saw a Trojan horse; though not the one Homer tells about.

Before going westward, I paid a visit to Saratoga Springs, the great fashionable summer resort, which is about thirty miles from Albany. Do not infer that I went there to spend the fashionable "season." I am above such a place as that. So is any one that hasn't too much money. It is there that glittering wealth and giddy fashion congregate during the hot weather, and that merchants from New York and other cities go to gamble away in a week—sometimes in a single night—all they have made in a year.

"Faro" prevails there to an alarming extent. So do poker, roulette, billiards, nine-pins and horse-racing. I stood by a faro-table for an hour, and the amount of cash I saw change hands in that time was something frightful. Thousands seemed but a trifle at that board. I saw one gentleman looking on with idle interest, while others were betting, losing and winning, and I said to myself, "That fellow is going to try his luck: I can tell by the way he looks."

And he did try it.

"I'll put that V on the ace," said he, laying down a five-dollar greenback.

It lost.

"Pshaw!" said he; to which nobody paid any attention.

The betting went on. Presently my man tried it again.

"Here's an X on the ace."

And he put an X on the ace.

It lost.

"Confound it!" he exclaimed, vexatiously. "Here's twenty-five for the deuce."

He put two Xs and a V on the deuce.

The ace won this time, and the deuce lost. And *he* lost. He was now forty dollars "out."

"Give me some checks," he said, handing a hundred-dollar bill to the banker. He was evidently going into it more extensively.

The banker quietly took his hundred dollars, and counted him out some ivory checks used to represent cash in the game.

The betting went on. He laid down five dollars' worth of checks on the ace and won. He laid down another five and lost. He laid twenty on and lost. He laid twenty more on and lost.

"Confound that unlucky ace!" said he, "I will not ry it again."

So, he tried betting on two others at once. He laid five on the seven, and thirty on the eight. The seven won and the eight lost. He won five dollars and lost thirty.

"Blast the luck!" said he. "Here are the rest of the checks on the ace. I'll try my luck on it again." And he placed the remainder of his hundred dollars' worth of checks on the ace.

And lost.

He then abruptly mentioned the vulgar name of a place that is also called Hades and Erebus, and wished ugly wishes on himself if he'd bet any more. But he soon thought he would like to try it again—just once. He resolved to risk one bet of a hundred dollars, and if that should lose, he wouldn't try it again.

"Let me see," said he, "I'll put it on the ace. No, I won't. The ace is unlucky for me. I'll put it on the seven; that won for me once."

He put it on the seven and lost. If he had put it on the ace that time he would have won.

He then used profane language, and spoke very disrespectfully of the cards in general, and of the seven-spot in particular. Then he left the room.

Presently he returned with a roll of bills in his hand—a thousand-dollar one being placed conspicuously on the outside, as a kind of index, to show what was within. He handed a thousand-dollar bill to the banker, and said:

"Change that."

The banker changed it.

He then laid down five hundred dollars on the ace, and lost. He laid five hundred more on it and lost. He took another thousand-dollar bill from the roll, laid it down, and lost. He laid down another, and won.

"Good luck, at last," said he. "I believe that ace

will win again. It will be sure to: it has won so
little of late." So he put three thousand dollars on
it. Others followed his example, and two thousand
dollars more were laid on the ace. All who sat at the
table now, or stood by, looked for the issue with
much interest.

It lost.

This most unfortunate of the gamblers made a
slight movement of the hand, as though to place his
remaining cash in his pocket and quit; but he hesitated a moment, then placed the whole "pile" on the
ace.

"There," said he, "are seven thousand dollars."

Yes, seven thousand.

The ace lost that time.

The unfortunate man, who had now lost about ten
thousand dollars, articulated a number of bad words,
and, turning away, left the room with as sad-looking
a face as I ever saw under a hat. No one paid any
attention to him. The game went on, and he was soon
forgotten.

Of course, others were betting, winning and losing
all this time, for there were a score around the table,
and it would be no exaggeration to say that at least
a hundred thousand dollars changed hands while I
was standing there. I have merely mentioned this
one gentleman in particular, because his case was,
perhaps, the saddest of any that came under my notice, and made the greatest impression on my mind.
Whether he returned with any more cash, or whether
he could raise any more, I do not know, as I soon
after left the room and returned to Albany; but, if

8

he was able to raise any more "spondoolix," there is little doubt that he tried it again that evening, for the more bitter lessons of this kind a man learns, the more they don't do him any good. "I will try it again till I at least win back what I have lost," is his plea. If he has been fortunate, and won, he will say: "I seem to be pretty lucky; it's worth trying again." He does and often finds it *is* worth trying again— to the banker. Win or lose, a gambler will be a gambler.

CHAPTER XVI.

THE SAIL BOAT.

NEXT day I left Albany for Rochester, *via* the New York Central Railroad. Those who have done much traveling by railroad must have been annoyed and tormented from time to time by the flying dust, and the smoke and cinders from the locomotive. Every dying spark that flies from the chimney seems to go right for the eyes of any unhappy visage that dares to thrust itself from a car window for a breath of fresh air or a glance at the scenery ahead. And O, how it does hurt! The sting of a bumblebee is joy compared with it.

On this occasion I determined to adopt a plan that would enable me to thrust my head out all the time if I chose, and stare at the locomotive with impunity. Before leaving Albany, I purchased a pair of fifty-cent goggles—window-glass focus—which I wore during my journey from Albany to Rochester (a distance of over two hundred miles). Hence, my eyes being secure, I paid no attention to the smoke and dust I was continually *breathing;* and the result was, that next morning my throat and lungs were so sore as to interfere materially with my articulation, and for some weeks I was afflicted with a regular "graveyard cough," that I had reason to fear would merge into some permanent pulmonary affection. I got over it, though, and I also got over wearing goggles on an express train.

To this day, I can not help shuddering as I contemplate what a frightful appearance I must have presented with those goggles on. A good-looking young man like myself, on a crutch, with such an immense round patch on either side of his nose, must have been a marvel to look at. I regret that I did not procure a mirror, and take a look at myself while wearing them, for I have never had the courage to put them on since.

My memory records that several passengers, with subdued smiles on their countenances, manifested the most intense interest in my welfare, and asked me what was the matter with my eyes? In reply to this impertinent question, I gave them to understand that it was an hereditary weakness of the "windows of the soul;" and intimated that the Smith family had, from time immemorial, been amateur astronomers, and had done a good deal of gazing at the moon and stars.

The New York Central Railroad takes its way through the beautiful Mohawk valley. That valley is famed in history, and we read of a great many bloody scenes enacted there by the savage Mohawk tribe; but I think that now, with its green meadows, its fields of grain, its grazing sheep and cattle, its farmhouses and dairies, with PEACE smiling over all, it is far more beautiful and interesting than it was in its wildness, when the red-skinned son of nature made it his home, and followed killing bears, deer, and the pale-faces for a living.

There is one grand picture in the Mohawk valley which I can not forbear to mention. It is an enchanting cascade. The amount of water is not great, but it comes streaming down from a height of two hundred feet, sparkling in the sunbeams, and bounding from rock to rock like a thing of life. For calm, quiet enjoyment, I would rather sit among the trees that hover about this romantic cascade and listen to its murmurs, than on the banks of the Niagara, and hear the roars of that grand old cataract.

It was after night-fall when we reached Rochester, and as I wanted to stay there a few days, I went into an hotel that was in the same building with the depot *itself*, and registered my name. Next morning I walked out and looked about me. Rochester is a very pleasant city of about sixty thousand inhabitants, and is situated at the Falls of the Genesee river, seven miles from Lake Ontario. I say *at* the Falls, for the city is built on all sides of the cataract, except one. It occupies either shore, and one of its principal streets, with its solid rows of buildings, actually *crosses* the river on an arched bridge or viaduct about two hundred yards above the Falls.

It will be remembered that it was at these Falls that Samuel Patch, Esquire, made his last leap; and here I am compelled to dispel a very popular delusion that prevails in regard to the matter. I do not wish to detach a particle from the glory and honor of Mr. Patch, for he was an American, like myself—not exactly like myself, either, for he is said to have had two legs—and I feel a kind of national pride in holding him up before the world as the paragon of jumpers. But what I wish to say, is this: Patch did not stand in the water below, as is generally supposed, and jump *up* over the falls. On the contrary, he stood above on a platform erected at the brink of the precipice, where there was not much water pouring over at the time, and jumped *down;* and who couldn't do that? I saw persons in Rochester who saw him make his last leap, and they told me all about it, confidentially.

Another thing: It is generally known that Patch leaped over the Falls of Genesee twice, but it is not generally known on which of these occasions he killed himself; some suppose it was the first: but I can assure them, on the best authority, that it was his second leap at Rochester, and not his first, that proved fatal.

On one occasion Daniel Webster was called upon to speak at a public dinner given at Rochester. "Gentlemen," said he, "Athens had her Acropolis, and Rome her Coliseum, but, gentlemen, they could boast of no such falls as those of Rochester!" Here, being slightly under the influence of the wine which he had been drinking, he paused, and hesitating, was about to sit down, when some one whispered to him "The national debt!" Rising to his full height the great orator exclaimed: "And then, gentlemen, there is the National Debt! It should be paid, gentlemen. It must be paid, gentlemen." And then, in louder tones, "I'll be d——d if it *shan't* be paid. *I'll pay it myself!"* pulling out his pocket-book. "How much is it?"

Two miles below Rochester there is a wharf where steamboats and other lake craft land, and where a man keeps boats to let. The street-cars run to within three quarters of a mile of the place, and I got on one and rode down. On leaving the car at the terminus of the city railway, I walked to the river bank, and found a graded wagon-road leading down to the landing, the bank being about two hundred feet high; and very steep.

When I reached the landing I concluded to hire a sail boat and have a little ride on the river.

" Can you manage one?" asked the owner.

"O, yes," I replied. "That is, pretty well." The truth was, I had never tried it, and therefore didn't know whether I could manage one or not.

"Well, take that one," said he, pointing to a small sail boat of about three quarters of a ton burthen. "There are oars in it, and if you can not manage it you can row it back."

It was well enough, for without those oars I could never have brought it back. I got in, the sail being set, and he pushed me from shore. A stiff breeze was sweeping down the river, and I did not like to run before it, lest it should blow me out upon the lake and clear over to Canada. So, I thought I would try tacking, and run up the river a little way, in order to have easy sailing back. With the helm in one hand and a line attached to the boom in the other, I went flying across the river, which was only about four hundred feet wide, and presently brought up against the other shore. I looked quickly around to see if the owner was observing me, found he wasn't, pushed my boat off with an oar, got the sail set right for the other tack, and went sailing for the western shore again. This time, I "tacked" in time, turned the boat pretty skillfully, and the boom sweeping around before the wind hit me a deuce of a "belt" on the head and knocked my hat off into the water. I then lowered the sail and shipped the oars. Recovering my hat, I then unshipped the oars, and hoisted my sail again.

I had seen persons "tack" before, and make pretty good time against a head-wind. It looked simple and easy; but with me it went rather awkwardly. I couldn't make any "time" up stream at all, but found after each "tack" that I had drifted further and further down. I had better have cast anchor and waited for a port or starboard wind, so far as making "time" was concerned.

At last, much disgusted with a sail boat, I lowered my sail and took her in with the oars, vowing never to try a sail boat again: another vow I kept for nearly a year.

I then hired a light row boat and went up to the "Lower Falls"—that is, a cataract of some seventy or eighty feet, about a mile and a half below the principal Falls of Genesee. I had some stiff rowing to get up, too, for the current was very swift near the Falls. But didn't I come back, though, when I started to return! I only used my oars to keep the boat straight, and the current carried me down as the wind bears a feather before it.

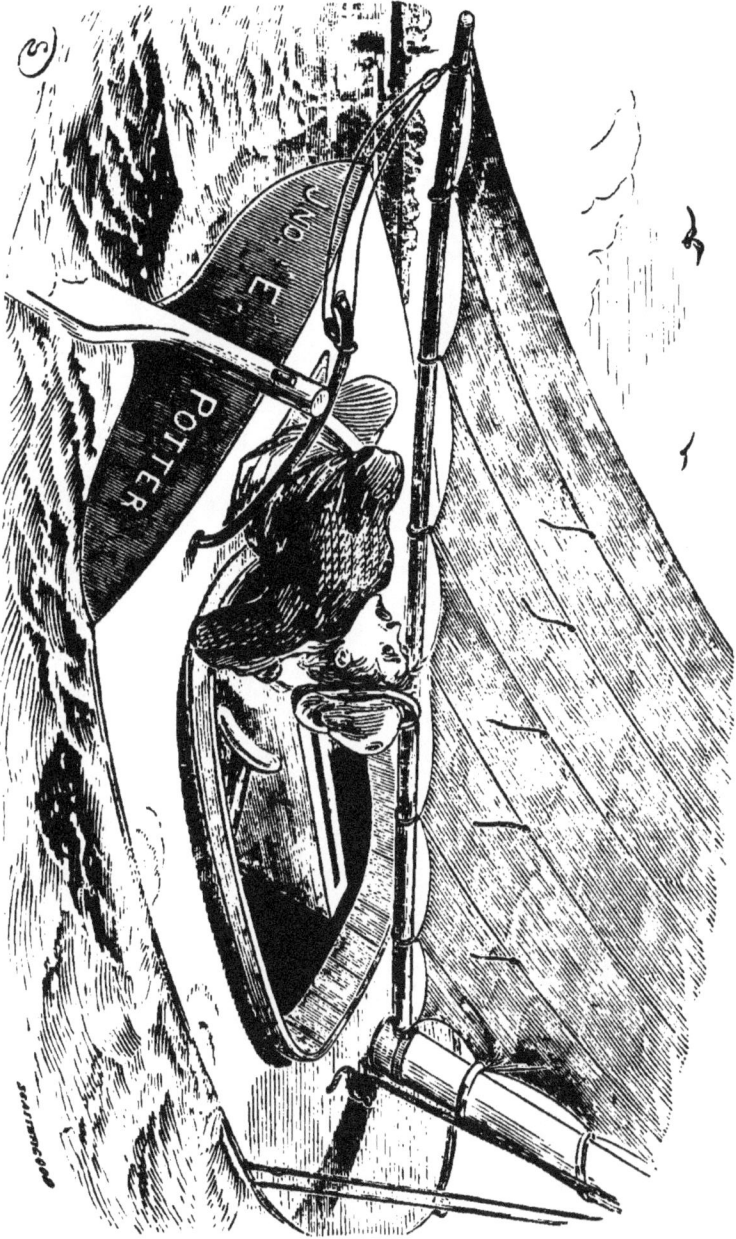

"The boom sweeping around before the wind, hit me a deuce of a 'belt' on the head and knocked my hat off into the water."—*Smith on the Genesee.* *Page 120.*

The next day was Sunday, and learning that a small steam pleasure boat was to make a trip that afternoon from the landing, to a little harbor on the lake shore, some eight or ten miles from the mouth of the river, I went down and embarked for the voyage.

The boat started early in the afternoon, crowded with pleasure-seekers. It was the slowest boat and about the lightest draft steamboat I ever had the honor to travel on. We were three or four hours reaching our destination : and on entering the harbor, she plowed through the shallowest water I ever saw navigated. The water in the lake was low at that time, and we passed over some places where the rushes grew up so thick that at a little distance the water could not be seen at all. It looked a little more like navigating a meadow than any thing I ever saw. At intervals, when we could see the water ahead of us, it did not appear to be a foot deep. And, O, the way our boat stirred the mud up! I pity the fish that lost their way in our wake : they must have been a long time finding it again.

The voyage was a little tedious, in consequence of the slow " time " we made, but not unpleasant. It was nine o'clock that evening when we returned to the landing in the Genesee river, and a two-horse spring wagon waited there for all who preferred a ten-cent ride up the long hill to a free walk. I pre-ferred the ride and got in. But I wished myself out again before we reached the upper end of the perilous road, for I never enjoyed the luxury of a more dangerous ride. It was extremely dark—so dark that you couldn't have seen a candle, if it had not been lighted —and the wagon was crowded. As we moved up the road there was a high perpendicular bank on our right hand, and on our left was the brink of a steep precipice, whose height became greater and greater as we advanced; and I could not help contemplating the fearful consequences of a possible accident, such as the balking of the horses, the break-ing of the traces, or the giving way of the earth at the brink of the declivity beneath the weight of the wheels. It was, in truth, a perilous ride, and before we reached the top of the tall shore half the passen-gers had got scared and jumped off: but I had paid for my ride, and was determined to have it at the risk of my neck. So I stayed in.

We reached the head of the narrow road without accident, and half-an-hour later I was in my bed, re-posing after the pleasures and perils of the day.

CHAPTER XVII.

NIAGARA FALLS.

ON the following Wednesday morning I took the accommodation train for Niagara Falls. When I say "accommodation train," do not fancy that we went jogging along at the rate of six or eight miles an hour. That is not the style of the New York Central. The accommodation trains make twenty miles an hour, including numerous stoppages, which is better time than is made by the express trains of some roads I have traveled on.

So, I arrived at Niagara, eighty miles from Rochester, by nine o'clock; where I left my trunk at an hotel and walked out to see the sights.

It would be presumptuous in any man to attempt a regular description of Niagara Falls, with the expectation of doing the subject justice—much more so in the unpretending John Smith. No one can form a fair idea of the mighty cataract without having seen it. Nor will one mere glance be sufficient. You may spend whole days there before you arrive at a just appreciation of it. The mind cannot grasp it at once.

A friend had told me that I should, on first visiting Niagara, experience a sense of disappointment—that

the Falls would not appear quite equal to their reputation and my consequent anticipations; but that, by
and by, as I should come to contemplate them more
maturely, I should be led to regard them as infinitely
grander and more majestic, than my loftiest anticipations had painted them. I found it true. As the
train approached, I heard the roar of the cataract,
and saw the green waters tumbling down with their
white robes of spray; but I somehow thought they
did not come up to my expectations, or rather experienced a vague, indescribable impression that I had
seen the like before. But when I walked down to
the bank, stood in the midst of the mighty thunder,
felt the earth tremble beneath the giant leap of the
great river, saw the dashing spray, arising like clouds
of smoke and dust from the sudden ruin of some great
city; when I remembered that for ages and ages, from
time lost in dim obscurity, day and night, winter and
summer, never ceasing, never tiring, the mighty waters
had been tumbling and plunging down from the dizzy
height, as now; and when I thought of the future,
when I mused of the unknown ages to come, fancied
generation after generation to have passed away; when
I imagined this great round sphere to have made
thousands of annual revolutions around the sun, and
pictured the grand old cataract, with none of its
vigor lost in the maze of centuries, still thundering
away, with the same old strength, young, mighty,
glorious, majestic as ever : then did I begin to realize
the magnitude of the lofty cataract, the work of the
Almighty Maker of heaven and earth, and feel the
littleness, the nothingness, of man!

The following lines written in the immediate presence of the great cataract, by David Paul Brown, Jr.,
Esquire, of the Philadelphia Bar, are highly worthy
of perusal:

"Niagara! O, Niagara! long thy memory will remain
A source of mingled wonder, of happiness and pain.
When burst thine awful grandeur on my raptured, ravished
    sight,
My senses broke from Reason's chain, in frenzied, wild delight;
But as the God-like attribute resumed its sovereign sway,
A calmer feeling soothed my breast—its tumult passed away,
The spirit bowed, and then a tear—my Nature was subdued,
A thrill of awe swept through my frame, I worshiped as I viewed;
A moment more I silent gazed, then humbly bent the knee,
As, in Niagara's mightiness, I felt God's majesty!
I saw His glory shining round where tremblingly I stood,
I cast a glance to His bright realm then on the foaming flood:
And is there strength, I humbly asked, in the Almighty will
To calm this boisterous element, and bid its rage be still?—
To sweep it e'en from Nature's face, with but a single breath,
Resistlessly as human life is swept away by death?
And can Niagara not rebel, with all its force and power,
When crumbling Nature shall give way at the appointed hour?
Must its fierce torrent tamely hush—its giant rocks then fall?
The still voice of my soul replied, 'Yes, yes, frail mortal, all!'
Then let me meekly bow the head before such Power Divine—
The only Power that never ends—NIAGARA'S GOD AND MINE!"

I am sure you will not quarrel with me, reader,
for introducing these graphic and eloquent lines, and
for growing sentimental over my remembrance of
Niagara Falls. They are too grand to be passed over
lightly. Thus far, since my arrival at Niagara, you
have not found much of the John Smithian tone in
my narrative.

I had heard a good deal about the "Cave of the Winds," and thought I would like to visit it. So, after standing for a full hour, wrapped up in the glories of the thundering cataract, I inquired of a respectable-looking gentleman where the "Cave of the Winds" was?

"You must go over on Goat Island to see that," he said; "but I hope you don't think of going down?"

"O, yes," I replied.

"What——on one leg?"

"Yes, I shall certainly take it with me."

"But it is dangerous. You will have to go down a steep flight of wooden steps, and pass behind the sheet of water where you cannot stand up. The spray will blind you, and the wind will take your breath and lift you off your feet——"

"*Foot*," I interrupted.

"Yes, will lift you off your *foot;* and one mis-step is certain death. Many strong men with two legs are afraid to try it."

"They have two feet, and are therefore just twice as apt to slip or make a mis-step."

"Well," said he, "go and see it, and I don't believe you will venture down. A look down into it will satisfy you. It will remind you of all the accounts you have heard of Hades——"

"Where I thought *water* was not so plenty," I interrupted.

"You are ahead of me again," said he, laughing. "Well, follow the bank of the river till you reach a bridge: that will take you over to Goat Island."

"Thank you."

I walked up the shore of the river a little way and came to the bridge—a suspension bridge of four or five spans—and went over to Goat Island. This island divides the turbulent river, just before it takes its fearful plunge, into two cataracts. That on this side is termed the "American Fall;" that between Goat Island and Canada being termed the "Horseshoe Fall," because of its shape. The American Fall is nine hundred feet wide and one hundred and sixty-four feet high; while the Horse-shoe Fall is two thousand feet wide and one hundred and fifty-eight feet high. By far the larger portion of the water tumbles over on the Canada side of the island, no doubt because the rocky bed of the river is six feet lower on that side; the cataract on either side, however, is stupendous enough for all practical purposes.

In this connection I am reminded of an anecdote, with which I will conclude this chapter. Two Yankees, one of a sentimental and the other of a practical turn of mind, were standing side by side, gazing on this prodigy of Nature.

"How sublime!" exclaimed the former. "To think that it falls one hundred and sixty-four feet at a single leap!"

"What's to hinder it?" responded the other.

CHAPTER XVIII.

CAVE OF THE WINDS.

IN order to reach the " Cave of the Winds "—I don't see why it should be so styled, for the winds never *caved* there yet—I had to descend a winding stairway within a wooden tower at the north-western margin of the island.   On arriving at the base of the tower, I found myself on a shelf about forty feet above the water-line below the Falls, with the American Fall on my right hand and the Horse-shoe Fall on my left. The " Cave of the Winds " is simply a vacant space between the great perpendicular wall of rock over which the torrent leaps, on the American side, and the broad sheet of descending water itself. A flight of wooden steps takes the visitor down nearly to the water level, behind the foaming, dashing folds of this fearful curtain ; and from the foot of the stairs a narrow plank walk extends some distance, to a point where the sheet of water is again parted by a project-ing rock at the brink far above.   The visitor, after reaching this welcome recess in the furious torrent, can pass out and take a seat on a great heap of rocks at the foot of the mighty cataract, where he hears nothing but the eternal thunder of waters and a cloud of mist hides the whole world from his view !

Pardon me for coming down from the sublime to the common-place, and for stating that a suit of water-proof clothes is provided for the visitor.

At a little house near the entrance to the "Cave of the Winds" I met a man whom I asked where the guide was.

"I am one of the guides," said he: "but *you* don't want to go down into the Cave of the Winds?"

"Yes, I had rather thought of going down," I replied.

"O, dear me!" he said, decidedly. "You can't go down!"

"Why?" I asked.

"I wouldn't let you go down for a thousand dollars! you would be drowned, certain. Just step this way and take a look down.—Did you lose your leg in the army?"

"Yes," I replied, as we walked to the head of the wooden stairway, "at the battle of Antietam, in Meade's Division, Hooker's Corps—got struck with a rifle-ball, and the leg was amputated the same day about six hours after; I draw a pension of eight dollars a month, but can't wear an artificial leg on account of the shortness of the stump; I am never troubled by change of weather—am twenty-two years old and my name is John Smith.—That place down there is the Cave of the Winds, is it?—Well, it's a much milder-looking place than I had expected to find it."

It will be perceived that I gave all this voluntary information to save time, by sparing the guide the trouble of asking the usual questions; for every hour

9

a man stays at Niagara costs him from two to five
dollars, if he is economical.

"What do you think of it?" he asked, in a loud
voice, so as to be heard above the roar of the cataract.

"A fine place," I coolly shouted.

"Wouldn't think of going down, now, I hope?"

"I'll go down now, by all means," I calmly yelled.

"O, no; it would be recklessness," he shouted.
"We've never lost any one here yet, and we don't
want to."

He didn't want me "lost."

"No danger," I shrieked.

"I can't give my consent," he yelled, decidedly.

"If you don't," I screamed, "I'll jump down
without it. I've traveled eighteen hundred miles for
the sole purpose of going down in the Cave of the
Winds, and I'll not return to my free home in the
Rocky Mountains without it! Give me a water-
proof suit!"

That began to tell on him. A man who lived in
a free home among the Rocky Mountains might be
dangerous. So he yelled, in a softer tone:

"Well, if you will only go to the foot of the stairs,
and will not try to follow the walk to that heap of
stones out there, I'll give you the water-proof clothes,
and you may go down."

"John Smith never rejected any thing like a reasonable compromise," I replied; "so I will promise
to go no further than the foot of the steps. Get me
the water-proofs."

He gave me the oil-cloths, and I donned them and
carefully descended into the famous Cave of the

Winds, and stood on the frail plank walk, between the thundering torrent and the black, rocky wall over which it tumbled. As I began to descend, I felt as though I was leaving the face of the earth for ever; but who can describe my emotions as I stood at the very heels of the raving and raging cataract? Who shall describe that awful place? It exceeded all the wild storms I had ever dreamed of. The spray dashed into my face, and fairly blinded me; while the fierce, unceasing wind rushed violently upon me from all sides, took the very breath from me, and seemed about to snatch me up from the frail plank on which I stood, and hurl me under the mighty torrent! It was wildly, fearfully bewildering. The wind and spray and the roar of the cataract fairly took away from me the senses of sight and hearing; I was conscious that the water had thrust its way beneath my water-proof clothes, and that I was wet all over, but could not feel the dampness; I coul l scarcely command my mind so as to think or reason. I scarcely knew whether I felt, thought, or was conscious at all, so absorbed were all my faculties in that eternal storm. I fancy that, if one were to remain there long, he would lose all consciousness, sink prostrate, tumble from the walk, plunge under the wild torrent, and be no more.

On returning to the face of the earth again, and removing my water-proof clothes, I realized how wet I was. I fancied it would not help my cough very much, but although I got wringing wet four different times during the few days of my sojourn at Niagara, it never injured me: which is a strong point in favor of the water-cure system ; *i. e.*, if it don't cure, it, at least, is not quite certain to kill.

" What is your charge ?" I asked of the proprietor.

" Nothing at all," was the reply. " We charge visitors two dollars each when we attend them through the whole walk; but, under the circumstances, we won't charge you any thing."

" I am willing to pay, if——"

" No, no ; not a cent. If any one ought to pay, I ought to pay you ten dollars for the privilege of seeing you go down there. You are the first and only one-legged man that ever ventured into the Cave of the Winds."

I returned to my hotel, took a lemonade, changed my clothes, imbibed another lemonade, took dinner, then another lemonade, and was about to start for the river again, when the host said :

" Are you going to see Leslie walk the rope ?"

" Walk the rope ? Where ?" I queried.

" Just below the railroad bridge—the large suspension bridge, two miles below."

" At what time ?"

" Four o'clock. You will have an hour or two yet to get there."

" I will go, by all means," I said, much delighted at this opportunity. "I thank you for mentioning it."

I went out, and walked leisurely down to the Suspension Bridge. I found a great many people collected on the bridge, and on either shore, and observed that there was a rope stretched across from bank to bank, not far from the bridge.

This bridge is one of the grandest of structures. It is an iron bridge with a single span of eight hundred feet, and is suspended two hundred and fifty feet above the water. The trains run over on top of it, while on a level with the bank are a carriage-way and a walk for pedestrians.

I paid twenty-five cents to be admitted upon the bridge, in order to view the feats of Mr. Leslie. It was crowded with spectators, but I succeeded in getting a good position, from which I could see the rope.

Not long after, Mr. Leslie, arrayed in the garb of a circus actor, and carrying a long pole in his hands, as a man is apt to carry a fence-rail when constructing a worm fence, made his appearance on the American shore, stepped boldly out upon the rope, over the fearful abyss, and walked leisurely toward Canada. He moved nimbly till he had traveled more than half the length of the rope, when he seemed to lose his confidence for awhile, stopped, and tottered from side to side. At this point, the ladies all became pale, a great many of them said, "O, Lord!" fervently, and turned away; while we stronger-hearted men gazed on with the most absorbing interest and anxiety. Leslie soon regained his composure and equilibrium, and resumed his perilous walk.

On reaching the Canada side, he was saluted with thunders of applause from both shores and the bridge; and, after resting awhile, and taking a glass of lemon-ade (probably), he again stepped upon the rope, balancing-pole in hand, and a coffee-sack over his head. He thus again accomplished the fearful walk, and was again greeted with cheers. Then he went out upon the rope, with only the balancing-pole, stopped about the middle, and performed some gymnastic feats.   He laid his pole carefully down—one end resting on the main rope, and the other on one of the guys—hung there by his hands a moment, two hundred and fifty feet above the foaming waters, that were still angry from their recent leap, then hung suspended by one hand, then by his chin, then by his feet, and finally by one foot.   To use the very mildest expression, it looked dangerous.

His hanging suspended by one foot was his last *feat* for that day; the crowd soon after dispersed, and I got into an omnibus and returned to Niagara.

CHAPTER XIX.

CANADA.

EARLY next morning I started for Canada. Just below the Falls a flight of three hundred steps, protected by a weather-boarded frame-work and roof, descends the steep bank to the water's edge, and beside the flight of steps is a track for small cars, that are drawn up and let down by means of a windlass run by water-power. I got on one of the cars and rode down to the water; but before taking the boat for Canada, visited the foot of the Falls near by, and got completely wet with spray again. Here the wind created by the vast masses of water continually tumbling down is very strong, and the flying spray is equal to a violent rain; so that this place reminded me of the "Cave of the Winds." I had to climb over a huge heap of slippery rocks that had at one time fallen from above, and I got my shin scraped and bruised, and my knee cut in the operation. O, what difficulties a mortal will overcome for the sake of novelty. Charles Dickens thus speaks of this place in his "American Notes:"

"Climbing over some broken rocks, deafened by the noise, half-blinded by the spray, and wet to the skin, we were at the foot of the American Fall. I

could see an immense torrent of water tearing head·
long down from some great height, but had no idea
of shape or situation, or any thing but vague im·
mensity."

After getting as wet as I wanted, I (John Smith,)
returned to the foot of the stairway and got aboard
the ferry-boat. This is only a kind of yawl that will
accommodate twenty or twenty-five passengers, and
is rowed across the turbulent stream by *one* strong
man. It was crowded with visitors, of both sexes
and all ages; and when we reached the middle of the
stream, where the waves were rolling, and the boat
rocked handsomely, a lady grew dizzy and pale,
dropped her parasol in the water, fainted, and fell
back in the boat, into the arms of a friend. I seized
the parasol before it could float away, sprinkled a
little of the sparkling water upon her face, and she
revived. We soon after reached the Canada shore
and she was all right again.

When we landed, the passengers all arose from
their seats in the crowded boat, and made a rush to
see who should be first ashore, just as though the
first would see the most. The result was that one
fell overboard, and another, in making a leap from
the gunwale of the boat, miscalculated the distance,
and alighted in water of such a depth that it just ran
into his watch-pocket to see what time it was. Both
were rescued, completely saturated, and terribly
scared. I quietly retained my seat in the boat till the
rush was over. As I stepped ashore, last of all, the
boatman, whom I shall always remember gratefully
for his kindness, slyly said to me:

"You are going over here for the first time, I suppose; be careful that you don't get beat. Do not buy any thing or hire a carriage without first making your bargain, or you will be charged six prices."

I thanked him, and treasured up his advice.

On the Canada side, a carriage-road winds its way in a serpentine course up the steep, high shore; and, on stepping from the boat I was immediately assailed by half-a-dozen drivers of carriages, who expressed a curiosity to know whether I desired to ride up or not. But I replied that I lived "just over the hill," and would walk up. One of them winked at the other, and I passed on.

On gaining the top of the high shore, I visited Table Rock, from which prominent point I had an excellent view of the whole cataract. I was again assailed by cabmen.

"Do you want to go to Lundy's Lane?" "Do you want to go to the Burning Springs?" "Do you want to go to the Suspension Bridge?" "Do you want to go to Brock's Monument?" I was asked in a second.

"Yes, but I'm going to walk," I replied.

"Walk! You can't! It's four miles to Lundy's Lane." [It's only a little over a mile, reader. J. Smith.] "It's five miles to the Burning Springs." [It's only one and a half. J. Smith.] "It's ten miles to Brock's Monument." [It's only five or six. J. Smith.] "It's three and a half to the Bridge." [It's only two. J. Smith.]

"Is that all? Then I'll walk, certainly."

They left me—having probably come to the conclusion that I was a heathen.

I was told that there was a place on the Canada side similar to the "Cave of the Winds," where one could go behind the sheet of water. Desiring to see all that was to be seen, I went into an adjacent building, in which was a museum, got a water-proof suit, and, with others, explored this dangerous place.

It is a fact worthy of remark, that the Canadian in charge of the place, did not offer a single objection to my venturing upon the perilous walk; nor did he offer a single objection to accepting the fee of two dollars. Why? 'Cause I was a "Yankee."

We walked fifty feet behind the sheet of water, on a narrow and slippery path. The wind and spray here, as in the "Cave of the Winds," formed a perfect tempest. It is really surprising that so few accidents happen at this place. Many ladies visit it. I believe only one person ever fell from the path, and that was a gentleman. He lost his footing, rolled down a steep and slippery declivity, fell under the resistless torrent, and, of course, never breathed again.

Having returned to the building and removed my water-proof clothes, I went into the museum awhile, where I saw a mummy, a native of Egypt, that had reached the remarkable age of three thousand years, and there wasn't a gray hair in his head. He had a healthy and vigorous appearance, and looked as though by being careful about his diet, and avoiding damp weather, he might live a thousand years yet. I also saw the skeleton of a mammoth that had been discovered at the bottom of an oil-well. It was chiefly made of the best seasoned oak timber, and constructed with an eye to strength and beauty combined.

On leaving the building, I saw a very black seventeen-year old negro sitting lazily in a buggy, and I approached him and asked:

" What will you charge to drive to Lundy's Lane?'

" Why," he replied after regarding me attentively for a moment, "dey charges six dol——"

' O, never mind," I interrupted. " I'll walk it!" And I turned away.

" No, no ; wait a minute," he said, quickly ; and I stopped to learn what he might have the honor to represent.

" Dey charges six dollahs," said he, " but you git in an' I'll take you dar an' to de Burnin' Springs bofe, fur dat. Did you want to go any oder whar?"

" Don't know," said I. " But come, I'll tell you what I'll do. I may want to visit several places, or may only go to Lundy's Lane. Now, I'll give you a dollar an hour for the time we're gone."

" O, dat's too——"

" Very well," I interrupted, walking away.

"Hold on! Wait!" he called, excitedly. " Let's see. Well, don' car. May be I kin afford it. Git in.—Or, I'll help you."

He was going to get out to help me in, but I placed one hand on the buggy and the other on the top of my crutch, and sprung up upon the seat with ease.

" Golly!" he exclaimed. " You kin git up better'n anoder man!"

" Certainly, old coon," I replied. " You awkward two-legged fellows can't get about in the world.—

Drive on: don't waste my time. Let me see——" I
looked at my watch—"it is just ten o'clock."

"Whar'll I go de fustest?"

"To Lundy's Lane. Move it, now."

My ebony companion touched up his horse, and we
got over the ground pretty fast. He might have
jogged along slowly, to extend the time, as he was
paid by the hour; but he saw I was up to all that,
and it wouldn't do.

On the old battle ground of Lundy's Lane, there is
a wooden tower fifty or sixty feet high, from the top
of which one can see not only all the ground on
which the battle was fought, but also a vast expanse
of country on both sides of the river, including the
vicinity of the Falls, and also many miles of the
river, its mouth and a portion of Lake Ontario.

The tower is ascended by means of a winding stairway; and a surly old cove, who pretends that he was
in the battle of Lundy's Lane—but I'll bet my hat
he wasn't—stays there and acts as guide. He accompanied me to the top of the tower, and showed me a
telescope supported on a pivot. With this I proceeded to sweep the wide, wide landscape before me,
and I began to ask the old "soldier" a few questions.
He was very reticent, and his answers were not only
very brief, but also very vague, ambiguous, and un-
satisfactory. I soon discovered why. His tongue
had to be greased with a trifle of change—for he was
only employed by the owner of the tower, who kept a
drinking saloon at the bottom—that is, the *base-m'ant.*

"Is that Brock's Monument?" I queried, perceiving

a tall column of masonry in the direction of Lake Ontario.

"A-hem," he replied, reluctantly, and with an apparent difficulty of articulation—"I—I—it bothers my head to talk much, ever since I got my wound in this battle. That is Brock's—A-hem—I—Visitors usually gives me—a—a—they generally—a little—a —a—ahem——"

"O, to be sure," said I. "It's perfectly right they should not forget your services."

I gave him a quarter, and found his speech much improved. Still, it was not so fluent as I could have desired, and I further touched it up in this way :

"Do you ever drink any thing?"

"Yes, sometimes," he replied, distinctly, brightening up.

"The gentleman below keeps something, does he not?"

"Yes, I believe he—Yes, he keeps a little on hand."

"Then," said I, "we will take a little of a good article when we go down. It always does me good to take a little something strengthening that way with an old soldier—especially one who, like yourself, has that graceful military air that can leave no doubt of his having served his country with distinction."

This was certainly piling it on pretty strong, but not too much so, it seemed, for he took it all with as good a grace as a toper would take his "bitters" in the morning. He grew extremely affable, and gave me all the information I wanted; and more, too, for I am satisfied he made up about thirty-nine or forty lies and told me—among which was this one: That he was captured at Lundy's Lane and taken before General (then Colonel) Winfield Scott—whom he pronounced the noblest soldier that ever lived—and that the latter gave him a drink of most excellent rum, and said to him: "You have an air of greatness about you—you have. Are you not a British general in disguise?"

The veteran guide also told me that Buffalo was clearly visible through the telescope, and tried to point it out to me. I will not deny the fact that it was visible from the tower, but I couldn't "see it."

When we went below, I treated him, as I had promised, tasting something myself; then I asked the proprietor what was to pay for drinks and visiting the tower?

He let me off for a dollar.

Returning to my sable friend in the buggy, I got in again and told him to drive to the Burning Springs, "as fast as the law would allow him;" and in less than half-an-hour we were there.

The water of these springs is characterized by an accompaniment of inflammable gas—sulphuretted hydrogen, I think—and when a lighted match is applied to it a blue flame springs up over the surface, like the flames of burning spirits.

I returned to the Falls and found that we had been gone a little over two hours and a half. I then gave the darkey three dollars, and told him to drive me down to the river; which he cheerfully did.

The ferry-boat was just leaving, as I jumped from

the vehicle, but the boatman saw me, and began to push back. To reach the boat, I had to step over some stationary rocks that protruded from the water, and in attempting to step from one of them to the boat, I slipped, lost my footing, and down I went into the river, striking my chin on the sharp edge of the rock, as I descended, and cutting it to the bone. I went in up to my neck, and would have gone lower still had I not clung to the rock. I scrambled up into the boat, with some assistance, and the boatman recovered my crutch and cane that were floating on the water.

The gash on my chin healed up in a few weeks, but it left a scar that will be unpleasant ground for my barber to get over as long as I live.

A couple of days later, having visited all the points of interest in the vicinity of Niagara, I departed for Buffalo, a city at the head of the Niagara river, twenty-two miles from the Falls. I did not leave however, without regret: I fancied I could never grow tired of Niagara Falls. The great cataract, whose youth, and vigor, and might are the same they were a thousand years ago, could never grow old to me!

CHAPTER XX.

Colonel John Smith at an Hotel.

I LOCATED in a delightful place called "Cold Spring," in the suburbs of Buffalo, and there remained two weeks; during which time I recovered from my cough, and the gash on my chin healed up. I made some pleasing acquaintances at Cold Spring, and became as much attached to the beautiful locality as though I had lived there for years.

From Buffalo I went to Erie, Pennsylvania; thence, to Cleveland, Ohio, a beautiful city of about forty-five thousand inhabitants, situated on the shore of Lake Erie.

As I desired to remain at Cleveland a week or so, I took lodgings at an hotel about two or three miles from the city, near the terminus of the City Railway, where the air was clear and pure and the green fields lay spread out around me; and yet where I could jump on a street-car and ride into the heart of the city in twenty-five or thirty minutes.

While at this hotel, a little incident happened to me, which some might term "funny"—but I did not think it so at the time, because it was rather calculated to wound my pride and dignity—and which further illustrates the mortification to which an unhappy one-legged fellow is sometimes subjected, through the pardonable ignorance or want of judgment of others. I was sitting on the piazza of the hotel one delightful evening in September enjoying the mild balmy air and admiring the glowing sunset, when two charming young ladies, in a buggy, drove up to the pump in front of the hotel obviously with the intention of quenching their delicate thirst by quaffing the pure, sparkling water. One was about to jump out for the purpose of getting the water for herself and her companion. No one else was near. Could I sit there and see the beautiful creature climb out for a draught of the water, when it was in my power to help them both to it where they sat, and thus save them the trouble? Not while my name was John Smith—and thus far the Legislature of my State had not been petitioned to change it.

"Do not get out, miss," I said, rising, taking up my crutch, and walking to the pump. "Do not get out: I will hand you a drink.—Fine evening."

"Yes, very.—But, I am afraid it's too much tr—"

"O, not at all," said I, taking the pump-handle in one hand, and with the other holding the tin cup that was at the pump under the spout. "Pray remain where you are."

"You are so kind——"

"O, not at all," I interrupted, as the sparkling water gushed from the spout and overflowed the cup.

I handed the cup to the nearest fair one, and she handed it to her companion.

"*You* drink," said her companion.

"O, no; *you*," said the fair one nearest me.

10

"No *you* drink first," said the other."

"I won't: *you must* drink first." So, the one farthest from me took the cup and drank.

I describe this little episode in the incident, because I suppose it to be a scene entirely new, and one that no person ever saw any thing like before (?).

When the lovely one on the other side had drank, the lovely one on my side took the cup, which was yet half full, drank it off and handed me the vessel, with a sweet,

" Thank you."

" Will you have some more ?"

"No, thank you."

"Perhaps, the other lady——"   It will be seen that I was getting extremely gallant.

"No, thank you; no more," interrupted the other lady.

They had been driving in the country—driving at a lively pace, probably—and I noticed that the horse was perspiring and looked tired and thirsty; so, my humanity being fully equal to my gallantry, I said:

"Here is a bucket at the pump—perhaps your horse would—"

"O, *you* couldn't——"

"Yes, I can easily give the animal a bucket of water."   And I set the bucket under the spout.

"If I thought you could, easily——"

"I can, I assure you."

I pumped the bucket full in three seconds and a fraction, picked it up and held it to the mouth of the "noble steed."   He drank it, seemed satisfied, and **looked volumes of thanks at me with his big eyes.**

Considering my mission at an end, I set the bucket down, and stood by the pump in a position favorable to touching my cap gracefully to the ladies as they should thank me and drive off, which I supposed they would now do. But here comes the mortifying part. One of the ladies held out her hand. Was she going to shake hands with me and bid me an affectionate farewell? No. My brain reeled, as I looked closer at the hand.

"Here, please take it," said she.

Take——not the hand, but a ten-cent note which she held out and desired me to "take" in return for my distinguished services. I felt the hot blood rush to my cheeks, but mastering my emotion, I said :

"O, no, miss, I thank you, indeed. I am not the porter here now. I used to be, but my Uncle Charles Exeter Johnson Smith died two days before last Christmas a year ago, and left me a large fortune; since which time, I have only been a boarder here. I thank you. Good evening." And I turned and walked away, while they drove slowly toward the city.

I can only impute the young lady's conduct to the grossest ignorance. I was not miserably clad, or any thing of that sort, and her reason for offering me the little contribution could only have been that I had lost a leg, and she no doubt thought it naturally followed that I was "needy." A great mistake. The wealthiest man in the world would have lost his leg had he been standing where I was when I was shot.

Having spent a week at Cleveland, I departed for the smoky city of Pittsburg; where I arrived one evening at five o'clock. Before returning to Philadel phia, I desired to visit the celebrated " White Rocks," near Uniontown, about seventy miles south of Pittsburg; and as no train was to leave for Uniontown till next morning, I was obliged to remain in Pittsburg all night—a thing I never do if I can help it, because I never spent a comfortable night in the smoky old place: nor do I believe any other civilized person ever did.

Before the train reached Pittsburg, I had given orders to a baggage-expressman to send my trunk to the St. Charles hotel, which had once been a first-class house, but which, without my knowledge, had of late degenerated to some extent. At the depot I got into a " bus" and rode to the St. Charles; when I saw at a glance that it had changed proprietors and was not conducted as of yore. It was in the hands of two or three brothers who were lineal descendants of the patriarch Abraham. One of them was acting as clerk. He was blustering about the office, like a rat that had got into a hot brick-kiln and couldn't find its way out, giving orders to the porter, talking to several guests at once, and getting very little accomplished.

" Can I get a single room, to-night?" I asked.

" I ton't knows," he said, in the odious dialect of a Teutonic Jacobite, "I sees apout it pretty soons direcklies leetle whiles;" and he kept on talking with some body about nothing.

I stood by the counter for some minutes, entirely unnoticed by the contemptible fellow; and beginning to think that "pretty soons direcklies leetle whiles" had about expired, I said:

"My friend, my trunk will be here presently, and I would like to know if you can accommodate me with a room."

"In vun meenutes," he said. "We's some fulls now, don't knows."

Had I not already ordered my trunk to this hotel, I would not have trifled there many seconds, but would have gone at once to another house. Wondering why he seemed so inattentive to me, I glanced at my apparel and was thereby reminded that I was not well dressed. I seldom wear good clothes during a journey of several hundred miles in a railroad car, for the smoke and dust will ruin a good suit of clothes in half that distance. I had on, for one thing, a military coat which I had worn considerably, and it immediately suggested an idea to me. I opened the register, with a commanding and dignified air, put on expressly for the occasion, took up a pen, examined it, found it very good, but dashed it impatiently down, as though not quite good enough for me, then took up another, found it good enough, dipped it savagely into the ink, and wrote:

"JOHN SMITH, COLONEL U. S. A., NEW YORK."

"There is my name," said I, turning the book around, and pointing to what I had written. "Try to hunt up a single room for me, and put my trunk in it when it comes. My name is on it. There is my check for it. I am going out awhile." And I gave him the check of the baggage-express agent.

The disgusting groveler glanced at my name, and fairly jumped from the floor: he was all obsequious-ness in a moment.

"Certainly, Colonels," he exclaimed, and I fancied he would have embraced me if the counter had not been between us, "I tends to it right aways." And he immediately wrote the number of a room opposite my name. "Porters, see eef Colonels Schmidt's drunks comes yet aready now. Ven it ish comes put it in Numbers Finf. We sees to it, Colonels. You says you goes out? Vell, you have suppers any times vat you vants it."

All eyes were turned on me. Those present must have thought me a rather young-looking colonel. I have no doubt that a great many went to the register and examined my signature, after my back was turned. They were no doubt proud of the honor; too.

I walked out, and had just descended the steps of the hotel, when I ran against a young man who had a cane in his hand and walked a little lame.

"Excuse me," I said.

"No harm done—" he began, then opened his eyes wide with surprise and interrupted himself with, "Why, John Smith! this you?"

It was "Chris" Miller, whom I had known at Haddington Hospital, and he was walking on his artificial leg.

"Hollo! Miller, my boy! How do you do?" I exclaimed, as we shook hands.

"Fine," he said.

"**Do you live here?**"

"Yes—or rather, in Alleghany City."

"I am glad we have met. I stay at the St. Charles to-night. I hope you are not engaged."

"No."

"Then you must take supper with me. Come up a moment; then we will take a walk."

I re-entered the hotel, accompanied by Miller, and opening the register again with the air of the owner, I wrote immediately under my name:

"MAJOR C. MILLER, Pittsburg Arsenal."

"Major Miller," said I, addressing the clerk, "will take supper with me."

"All right, Colonels," was the obsequious reply; "any times you blease."

Miller and I walked out for a stroll, and I explained to him, somewhat to his amusement, my reason for adopting those high-sounding military titles. We then stopped at the first respectable saloon, and took a hearty lemonade, with a powerful "stick" in it— dispensing with the lemons, water and sugar.

We soon returned, and, after supper at the hotel, walked out for another stroll about the city. At ten o'clock we parted, and I returned to the hotel, ready to retire.

"Colonels," said the clerk, "you drunks comes. We puts him in ze rooms for you."

"Very well; I will retire," I said. "See that I am awakened in time for the seven-o'clock train for Uniontown."

"Certainly, Colonels; we tends to dat. You vants to go to pet? I shows you de rooms."

He went with me to a double-bedded room on the first floor, where I found my trunk, (with a fresh dent in it,) and lighting the gas for me, and leaving the key in the door, he bade me a humble good night, as, with a cringing bow, he retired from my military presence.

It was after one o'clock before the mosquitoes consented to my going asleep, and I had not been asleep long, when thump, thump, knock, knock, knock, went some one at my door, breaking upon my slumbers most unpleasantly. They wanted to put another man in my room, and, as I did not concur in the arrangement, I lay still and let them pound at the door till their knuckles were sore. At last I heard some one say:

"There's no waking that fellow."

Presently a hurried footstep approached, and the well-known voice of the clerk who had assigned me my room, exclaimed excitedly:

"Vat you does dere? Dat's de Colonels! Mein Gott!"

And I was left in peaceable and untrammeled possession of the room.

I was awakened in due time in the morning; and, putting my rusty-looking clothes into my trunk and donning a more respectable suit, I came down to breakfast, and received such marked attention that I began to fancy myself a major-general, instead of a mere colonel. Immediately after breakfast, I paid my bill—($5.25)—found a carriage awaiting me at the door; and, having been bidden an affectionate adieu by the proprietors, three or four times, I rode to the depot.

I have not recorded this incident for the purpose of injuring the St. Charles Hotel; as it has since changed proprietors, and is now conducted in a creditable manner.

If you want to get along smoothly and comfortably while traveling, do not fail to make the clerks and proprietors of hotels believe you are something more than mortal : if you don't, you will find rough sailing. A very good plan is to knock down a porter or waiter now and then, by way of preserving your dignity. You will find it profitable.   Also, threaten to shoot the proprietor, occasionally, when you have a shadow of a pretext: that will never fail to establish your importance.   Above all, I enjoin you to register yourself as a senator, governor or military officer.

CHAPTER XXI.

COURTESIES OF TRAVELERS.

AFTER a ramble through the wild mountainous region of southwestern Pennsylvania, I returned to Philadelphia; and soon afterward started for Washington, to remain there a few weeks in the capacity of correspondent.

When I travel in a railroad car, I always prefer that end of the seat next to the window. My reasons for this are various. For one thing a person can get a little fresh air, when he wants it—and too much when he don't want it—he can get a far better view of the scenery without; and, besides, he can keep a look-out ahead for collisions, and jump out head foremost, if he sees another train coming from the opposite direction on the same track. Influenced by these considerations, I always manage to get to the depot a full half-hour before the starting-time of the train, and this course never fails to secure me my favorite end of the seat.

On this occasion, I was at the depot at Broad and Prime streets, in good time, and had no difficulty in locating myself on the train to my perfect satisfaction. When the car was nearly full of passengers, and it was within two minutes of the time for starting, a lady and gentleman came in, and began to canvass the interior in search of a wholly vacant seat that they might both occupy; but their search proved futile. Quite a number of the seats were occupied by but one passenger, each, but there was not one entirely vacant. Failing to find an empty seat, the gentleman concluded he would make one empty, and he therefore came to me, and said:

"Young man, won't you take a seat with another gentleman and give us this seat?"

"Very cheerfully," I replied, "if the other gentleman will allow me to sit by the window."

He regarded this as equivalent to a refusal, and became vexed.

"But," he said, rather petulantly, "don't you see I have my *la ly* with me?"

Until he said this, I had supposed her to be his *wife*.

"My friend," I returned, "I came to the station early for the express purpose of obtaining a comfortable seat, and I do not think it right that I should keep it this long, and then give it up to another. I therefore respectfully decline to relinquish my seat."

"I hope," said he, fairly grinding his teeth with anger and vexation, "that *you* will some day be traveling with a lady, and——"

"I hope so," I interrupted; "but I fear I will never be so fortunate."

"Well," he rejoined, changing his tactics, "I will see the conductor, and see if *he* don't make the arrangement for me."

"Very well," I retorted; "see the conductor. I

myself would like to see a conductor with the power
and authority to take this seat from me. That conductor would be a living wonder. Barnum would
pay handsomely for him."

"Young man," put in a gentleman behind me, who
was also occupying a seat alone, "why don't you
give them the seat? You can sit by me."

"Why don't *you?*" I retorted. "*You* can sit by
me."

"I like to sit by the window," he responded; "and
am not well."

"I, too, am partial to the window," said I, "and
have been at the point of death for a long time, with
the toothache and a bad cold. I am quite an invalid.
—Now, my friend," I went on, addressing the gentleman with his *lady,* "why did you come to me, the
first one. and ask me to move, when you see that I
am a cripple? There are others in the car who
occupy whole seats, and who could certainly move
more easily than I. Were I the only one, I would
willingly resign my seat, for the accommodation of
the lady."

"I think you shouldn't ask *him* to move," said a
gentleman who sat with another on an opposite seat.
"A man with but one leg ought to have some show
in the world."

This remark made the first gentleman a little
ashamed of himself, and he turned and said to his
lady:

"Come, let us try another car."

They walked to the car-door, and not one offered
to surrender his much-loved seat-by-the-window, to

accommodate them. Man is naturally a selfish creature, and nowhere is his selfishness brought out in so
strong a light as on a railroad car. Do not censure
me, gentle public, for not relinquishing my seat.
This was not the first or last time I was asked to
abandon a comfortable seat in a car, after taking the
trouble to go early and secure it. It seems that in
such cases, they always come right to me. I do not
know why. It may be that I look young, innocent
and verdant; and that they jump to the conclusion
that I am one of those persons who, as the poet
doesn't say :

> "Know *not* their rights ;
> And, knowing *not*, dare *not* maintain."

When I saw the two unfortunates about to leave
the car, I called them back.

"Come," I said; "you can have my seat. I cannot see a lady in a dilemma, when I can relieve her
by making so slight a sacrifice." And I arose, seized
my crutch and was about to walk out from between
the seats.

"No, no," said the gentleman who occupied the
seat behind me, and whose better nature began to
show itself, while, at the same time a dozen others
arose, ready to give up their seats. "No, *you* musn't
move. You're crippled, and I am not. They can
take my seat." And he jumped up, with an agility
that one could scarcely expect to see displayed by an
invalid, and took a seat beside me; while the gentleman and his *lady* returned, and took possession of the
vacated seat, without a single expression of thanks.

" Well," said I, addressing my companion, " if you
wish to take the end by the window, I will exchange
with you—at least, for part of the journey."

"O, never mind," he replied : " I am only going as
far as Wilmington."

Here, then, was a man who was only going about
twenty miles, who had at first refused to give up his
seat for the accommodation of the lady, and yet expected me to give up mine, which I had secured for a
ride of a hundred and forty miles.   O, the selfishness
of the traveler !

As I remarked before, there are always a dozen or
two of passengers who come aboard the car at the
eleventh hour, and have a time of it getting seated.
Among them there are usually two or three gentlemen
with their *ladies*, as in this case, and they always
come to me, the first thing, and ask me to give up
my seat.   I have long since, however, adopted a
course to pursue on such occasions, which, although
it involves a little fib or two—which are certainly
pardonable—spares me all controversy.   On being
asked to remove from my seat and take the wrong
end of another, I smilingly state that I would cheerfully do so if I were alone, but that unfortunately,
my wife and three little boys are out on the platform,
bidding some friends good-by, and will presently
come in to share the seat with me.   Of course they
don't detect the " white one " till the train has started,
and by that time, they have procured seats, by some
means ; and I don't care how much I overhear them
—as I often do—wondering " where that one-legged
fellow's wife and three little boys went to ?"

CHAPTER XXII.

"THE CITY OF MAGNIFICENT DISTANCES."

WASHINGTON CITY is styled the "City of Magnificent Distances," because it is laid out to cover a space four and a half miles long by two and a half miles wide, that is, eleven square miles. It is the Capital of the United States of America, and is composed of the Capitol building, the Treasury building, the Post-Office building, the Patent Office building, the Executive Mansion, War and State Department buildings, the Smithsonian Institute, Willard's Hotel and five thousand gin-mills. Such is the Capital of our country, the "City of Magnificent Distances:" and if it were a magnificent distance from the Country, the Country would be much better off and much more well-to-do in the world. I regret that a city which bears the name of that noble and pure man, George Washington, should be such a concentration of vice, corruption, intrigue, fraud and iniquity, as it has become of late years.

It was night when I reached Washington, and going to an hotel and registering my name, John Smith, Major U. S. Army—I never go below the rank of major—I received every attention. While there, my bill was only twenty-five or thirty dollars

a week, which they did not ask me to pay till I was
ready to leave, several weeks after, and then I paid
it without being asked. Meantime all the *attaches* of
the hotel were so attentive, obliging and polite, that
I did not find it necessary to kill a single one of them

The day following my arrival in Washington, the
weather being fine, I walked out to Tenallytown,
three miles from Georgetown, to visit the old ground
on which I had been encamped for several months,
while a soldier, early in the war. I found the ground
without difficulty, as well as a handsome earthwork
our division had thrown up while there, and which I
myself had worked on. It had been originally named
Fort Pennsylvania, but was now called Fort Reno.
Thinking I should like to walk in I approached the
entrance, and found it guarded by a negro soldier,
with musket and bayonet; while a sable corporal
stood talking to him.

"You can't come in dis place, sah," said the corporal,
with an insolent grin, before I was near enough to
solicit admittance.

I could not help feeling cut by such a greeting as
this, from a negro, at the entrance of a fort I had
helped to build. I smothered my rising indignation,
however, and with a sunny smile replied:

"No admittance, eh?"

"No, sah; guess not," was the taunting reply.

"I did not know that," I rejoined, still keeping
down my wrath. "I helped to build the fort, and
thought I would like to take a look through it.
However, I suppose you are ordered to allow no one
to enter."

"Guess we is. You helped to build it, eh?"

"Yes."

"You didn't tink den us cullud fellahs 'd git posses-sion!" he said, with an insolent laugh.

Without replying I turned and walked away.

I cannot imagine why this black brute should thus wantonly insult an inoffensive person like me, and especially a crippled ex-soldier who had walked all the way from Georgetown to see his old camping-ground: but I have given the words as he spoke them. I do not relate the incident because it will please or displease any political party: I simply tell the truth. No one will fail to admit that it was hu-* miliating and mortifying to me, after having helped to build the fort, to be insolently turned away from it by a coarse and ignorant negro. Had a white soldier been on post there, he would have received me cordi-ally, and if his orders not to admit any one had been very strict, he would have sent some one to his officer and asked permission to let me go in. There is always a certain sympathy between soldiers of one race; but I never yet saw any between white and black soldiers.

Although I had been in Washington many times, I had never yet ascended the dome of the Capitol, or visited the embryo "Washington Monument;" so, next day, I determined to visit both. In the Capitol, at the base of the stairway leading to the dome, the doorkeeper asked me if I had a pass to go up.

"No," I replied; "I was not aware that any was re-quired."

"Yes, visitors are not admitted to the dome without passes."

"If you will tell me where to get one ," I rejoined, "I will go and——"

"O, never mind," he interrupted. "I won't send *you* for a pass. But can you walk to the top?"

"O, yes."

"Go ahead then, and never mind the pass. Don't fall."

"Thank you," I replied, beginning the ascent.

I must say this much for my race—for this was a *white* man—that it is not made up entirely of selfishness. I frequently meet with little courtesies like this, and they are very gratifying to me: not for their intrinsic merit, alone, but because they show cheerful little gleamings of the bright side of the human heart.

When I reached the top of the dome, I felt a little tired; but probably not much more so than others who ascended. It is a fatiguing task for any one, to ascend to the height of three hundred feet, by means of a winding stairway.

That same afternoon I visited the unfinished monument erected to the memory of George Washington. This monument is beautiful in design. It was to have been five hundred feet high, surrounded at the base by a pantheon one hundred feet high and two hundred and fifty feet in diameter. But it has only reached the height of one hundred and seventy feet, having there abruptly stopped. It stands now a monument of the forgetfulness and ingratitude of the American people. Till it is finished—which I fear will never be—the whole land ought to be covered with one broad blush of shame.

The monument was commenced years ago, by a certain "Association" which collected large sums of money for the purpose; and for a short time the work went on so actively that had it thus continued till now, the grand column of stone would have pierced the clouds, and there would have been no way of getting at the top except by means of a balloon. It stopped short, however, at the height mentioned; and its square blunt-looking top is covered with boards, to keep the rain off; the poorly protected walls are cracking; and the stray swine are rooting and wallowing about in the mud at its base. Not seventy years have elapsed since George Washington, without whom we would probably never have been an independent nation, passed from earth, and now, alas! it seems that his memory has also passed from the hearts of his unworthy countrymen. Take John Smith's word for it, reader, a nation that can thus soon forget its father and founder, the very author of its being, must, at no very distant day, lose sight of itself. Byron says:

"There is the moral of all human tales;
    'Tis but the same rehearsal of the past;
    First freedom and then glory—when that fails,
    Wealth, vice, corruption, barbarism at last."

In the Revolutionary war we gained our freedom; in the war of 1812 we perpetuated it; in the Mexican war we gained glory; then followed wealth, in the acquisition of California, Texas and other territory; in the recent civil war, we almost reached the vice, corruption and barbarism.

Next day I rode out to Georgetown, in a street-car,
and then hired a riding-horse, to visit Camp Pierpont,
Virginia, several miles from the Chain Bridge, where
I had spent my first winter in the army. The proprietor of the livery stable, as he led the horse out,
saddled and bridled, said:

"You can ride a horse, eh?"

"With ease," I replied.

"How will you manage to get on?" he asked.

"This way," I replied; and I placed one hand on
the saddle and the other on my crutch, and sprung
up with ease.

He opened his eyes with astonishment.

"Whew! You get on a horse easier than I can.
But don't get thrown off."

"I won't," I replied. "Get up, old hoss!" And
touching the animal with a spur I had put on—I only
wear one, on ordinary occasions—darted away toward
the river at a brisk gallop.

I visited the old camping-ground, and had the
satisfaction of finding the exact spot—now lonely and
deserted—on which the cabin of our mess had stood
during the first winter of the war, and on which I
had slept many a night, with a thin blanket and hard
puncheon floor under me, a wood fire in the chimney
near my feet—I had two of the articles then—and my
knapsack, containing an extra shirt and pair of
drawers, a few writing-materials, letters and photo-
graphs of friends, under my head. How the old
scenes did come back to me! How vividly I saw, in
imagination, the forms and faces that have passed
away, and heard the merry voices that are hushed

forever! How distinctly I saw and heard around me
a hundred of the liveliest boys of my old regiment,
who sleep in unmarked graves before Richmond, at
Bull Run, South Mountain, Antietam, Fredericksburg
and Gettysburg! I had visited the old ground because
I thought it would be a pleasure, but somehow,
when the scenes of the past came crowding back upon
me, and I remembered so many of my jovial comrades,
now no more, a melancholy settled over me; and
when I turned away toward Washington, it was with
a sadness of heart that I cannot express.

CHAPTER XXIII.

Smith's Experience on a Skate.

I SPENT the ensuing winter in Philadelphia, the great city which was laid out by William Penn, Esquire, who took a checker-board—an article used in a game invariably played " on the square "— for a pattern, and, hence, laid it out in squares that were perfectly square, and have remained so to the present day.   Mr. Penn deserves great credit for his peaceable manner of acquiring the land on which the city is built.   Instead of going to work and killing the poor innocent savages, like others did, he pur-chased the land from them, at a good round price in buttons, keys, tooth picks, shoe-pegs, marbles, rum and the like.   This course, besides speaking well for the goodness of his heart, is also strong evidence of his superior judgment and foresight, as the Indians at that time were too numerous to be easily overcome.

One day, in the middle of the skating season, I concluded to go down to Eastwick Park, Mr. R. O. Lowry's popular resort, and amuse myself awhile by watching the skaters tumbling head over heels and cracking their brain-pans on the ice.   I always had a passion for seeing any one fall, especially on skates. There is a calm, quiet enjoyment about it—to the observer—that is not equaled by any thing else. "We always," remarks La Rochefoucault "have strength enough to bear the misfortunes of others," a saying which, however humiliating it may be to confess it, has a certain truth. The ancient Greek writer Isidorus puts it very bluntly when he says: "Nothing is more pleasant than to sit at ease in the harbor and behold the shipwreck of others," a sentiment which is repeated in an old English song:

> " I wander not to seek for more :
> In greatest storm I sit on shore,
> And laugh at those that toil in vain,
> To get what must be lost again ;"

to wit, their life. But to return to myself:

For the information of non-residents of Philadelphia, I will state that Eastwick Park is the largest skating-park in the world. It is a resort for pleasure seekers, both in the winter and in the summer: for skating and dancing in the former season; and dancing and rowing in the latter. It is something for Philadelphia to boast of, and for which she is indebted to the enterprise of the Park King, Mr. R. O. Lowry.

The smooth lake of ice was alive with skaters, of both sexes, and the scene was one of the gayest. I had not seen much skating since my return from the army, and, O, how this made me regret my inability to enjoy the delightful exercise. For the first time, I heartily regretted that I had ever served my country, and lost one of my nether limbs; and, in my vexation, felt that if I had it to do over, my loved land might go to the deuce before I would sacrifice a leg, and thus deprive myself of such delightful recreation.

"Never more," I muttered, "will my nimble feet glide over the smooth ice, and the bright, ringing steel of my skates sing gleeful songs behind me, while I fly like the wind! Never more shall I go it at the rate of twenty miles an hour, tumble heels over head on the dear, clear, smooth, cold ice, get my head cracked and my eyes blacked, and spring up and try it again, cheerful and happy! Ah, John Smith! John Smith! thy skating days are over! They are numbered with the things of the past, and with the things that were, and are not!"

Just then, the veteran skater, Colonel P * * *, an excellent friend of mine, came gliding gracefully along, to the shore of the lake, where I was standing, and seeing me, said, with his usual cheerful and jovial manner:

"How do you do, Smith? You are looking on as though you would like to try it."

"I wish it were possible, Colonel," I replied.

"Did you skate before you went into the army?"

"O, yes."

"Well, why don't you try it?"

"On a crutch?"

"Certainly—as active as you are, I have no doubt you could skate. Try it!"

"I would as soon risk another battle," said I. "Who ever heard of a man skating on one leg?"

"Have *you* never heard of the like?"

"I think not."

"I have then. Last year, I read of a one-legged skater in Boston. He was hard to beat too, it was said."

"Ah? Is that so?"

"I assure you it is. Go into the skate-room, get a skate and try it. There is a little nook of ice extending behind the buildings, try it there first, and if you find it a success, you can venture out upon the main body of ice."

"I believe I will," I said.

I went into the skate-room, and somewhat astonished the clerk by asking for "half-a-pair of skates."

"Are you in earnest?" he asked.

"Yes, by all means."

"Can you skate?"

"Yes," I replied, although I had never yet tried it in my present condition; "no mere amateur can beat me."

He gave me the skate, lent me a gimlet and file, and furnished me with a couple of nails. I drove one of the nails into the lower end of the crutch and the other into the end of the cane, and filed them off sharp about half-an-inch from the wood. I then put on the skate and went out upon the ice in rear of the row of buildings. With some misgivings, I stepped on the ice and gave myself a shove. I sailed out pretty nicely, and didn't fall. To my astonishment and delight, I discovered that I could skate nearly as well as ever. This discovery lent me confidence and vigor, and, without hesitation, I glided out upon the extensive lake of ice, among the throng of skaters, where I was regarded as a novelty; and, in a word, I created quite a sensation. I felt that I would much rather all the eyes turned upon me had been bullets aimed at me; but I "cheeked" it out, with all the "brass" I could muster, and glided around, apparently so much at my ease, that the observers might have fancied it was not my first attempt to skate on one leg, but that, on the contrary, I had skated many thousand miles thus. I soon met my friend, the Colonel, who was highly elated at my success.

As this was my first exercise of this kind, since my return from the army, I only remained on the ice about five hours that day: by the end of which time I felt as though I might travel two or three times around the globe on a skate.

I did get a fall or two, of course. In fact, I had not been on the ice fifteen minutes, when I got to skating too fast —my skate going so fast that I couldn't keep up—and the result was that I presently had the ice for a pillow, and lay there gazing at the clouds, with only one overhanging skate-clad foot to interrupt the view. Then, before I had time to stir from this novel position, a handsome young lady, who was trying the backward skating, endeavored to skate over me—a feat frequently attempted without success—and the result was, she violently took a seat upon my stomach and jobbed one of her elbows in my eye. She struggled up and said, "O, excuse me! Did I hurt you?"

"O, no; not at all!" I replied, although she had nearly knocked the breath out of me.

"I am glad of it," she said, skating away.

I recovered my crutch and cane, and arose, wondering whether she meant that she was glad she hadn't hurt me or glad she had fallen on me. I didn't feel glad about any thing.

This was my first skating adventure, on a crutch; but I have skated many times since. So, you see, th it after all, the loss of a limb does not necessarily deprive a man of such little enjoyments. Energy, will and self-confidence will work wonders. What I want to do, I do. I have swam in the Schuylkill, Delaware, Monongahela, Ohio and Mississippi rivers, and in all the lakes; skated hundreds of miles; ridden hundreds of miles on horseback; walked hundreds of miles—all with one leg. There are only two things I can't do, which another man can. One is to run; the other is to sit cross-legged. I do not say this to boast; for John Smith is modest. I merely mention these facts, that the public may know what a one-legged man can do, and that he's " a man for a' that."

CHAPTER XXIV.

OVER THE MOUNTAINS.

AS Spring approached, I resolved to take a western tour; and with that view left Philadelphia in February. For the sake of variety, having frequently traveled through Pennsylvania, I concluded to go to Pittsburg *via* Baltimore, Maryland; Fairmont, in Western Virginia; and Uniontown, Western Pennsylvania—certainly a circuitous route. I desired to visit some friends in southwestern Pennsylvania, however, and it was not much out of my way, after all, to take the Philadelphia and Wilmington, and Baltimore and Ohio Railroads.

One very cold day, I went from Philadelphia to Baltimore, and at ten o'clock that night left the latter place on the express train that was to run through to Wheeling—intending myself to get off at Fairmont.

On this occasion, just after taking a seat in the car, a gentleman sat down by me, and after regarding my countenance attentively for a moment, said:

" Pardon me: isn't your name Smith?"

I pardoned him, as desired, and told him it was.

" First name John?"

There was no denying it, and I replied in the affirmative.

"Delighted to meet you!" he exclaimed, as we shook hands cordially. "When did you leave Nashville?" "I never left it," was my response. "I was never there."

"No? Then excuse me: you cannot be the gentleman I supposed you, although your appearance and name strikingly correspond with those of a person I knew in Nashville a year ago—especially the name. He had also lost a leg, as you have."

"A remarkable coincidence," said I. "In the course of my own travels, I have met with a great many of me—in name."

My fellow-traveler was an agreeable and good-humored gentleman, and I related to him the following anecdote of Doctor B. Frank Palmer, of Philadelphia, the great manufacturer of artificial limbs. Receiving an order for a leg from plain John Smith one day, and being in a merry mood, the Doctor sat down and answered John's letter thus:

"Look here! What do you mean? I have already furnished you with five hundred of my patent limbs, and I don't think the Government allows you any more. However, I'll send this one yet, and if you continue so extravagant in the use of patent legs, I advise you to set up a manufactory for your own accommodation." * * *

The Doctor, who has manufactured thousands of artificial limbs for mutilated soldiers, once jocosely remarked to the writer that he found, by referring to his books, that John Smith had been literally hacked to pieces during the war. He had had his right hand cut off; his left hand; his right arm below the elbow; his left arm below the elbow; his right arm above

the elbow; his left arm above the elbow; his right
arm at shoulder-joint, with skin-flap; his left arm at
shoulder-joint, with skin-flap; his right toes; his left
toes; his right foot; his left foot; his right leg below
the knee; his left leg below the knee; his right leg
above the knee; his left leg above the knee; both
hands; both arms below the elbow; both arms above
the elbow; both feet; both legs below the knee; both
legs above the knee; the right arm and left leg; the
right arm and right leg; the right arm and both legs;
the left arm and right leg; the left arm and left leg;
the left arm and both legs; both arms and both legs;
et cetera. All that can remain of him now, it might
well be inferred, is about the size and shape of a sack
of wheat, though far less useful to himself and the
world.

The number of plain John Smiths on the Doctor's
book is quite astounding, to say nothing of the innu-
merable John A., John B., John C., John D., John E.,
John F., John G., John H., John I., John J., John K.,
John L., John M., John N., John O., John P., John
Q., John R., John S., John T., John U., John V., John
W., John X., John Y., and John Z., Smiths!

Things went on very finely through the night of
my journey over the snow-covered mountains of Virginia, and in the morning the train stopped at Cum-
berland, on the Potomac, where the passengers took
breakfast. Then we thundered on again among the
frosted hills. Within ten miles of Grafton, Western
Virginia, the wheels of the forward truck of the car I
was in, jumped off the track, and went bouncing along
on the ties beside the iron rails, in a way calculated to

startle the timid. I sprang from my seat, seized the bell-cord, and gave it a vigorous pull; but although I surely made the engine-bell ring, I could see no immediate diminution in the speed of the train.

I knew that this state of things could not last long before the car should break to pieces. The stove was soon shaken from its moorings, and fell over, scattering the fire about and filling the car with smoke and dust; several of the seats were also shaken loose, a deliberate crashing was heard; and, glancing around among the passengers, I saw as delicious a collection of pale faces as I had ever seen. The men all sprang to their feet, the women screamed, and some raised their windows, as though to squeeze through and drop out. I raised my window and thrust my arm out, so that I might thus cling to the side of the car, in case the floor should be shattered and torn out, as it must soon have been if the train had not been checked.

At last, the welcome sound of the whistle was heard, the brakes were applied and the speed of the train began to slacken. Just then, the axles of the front truck broke, the frame smashed up, and the floor of the car began to give way. With screams of horror the passengers all rushed to the rear end of the car; but in another moment, before any further damage was done or any one hurt, the train came to a full stop. Then the passengers all rushed out as quickly as possible, as though there were still danger within, and some of them got their ribs strained, squeezing through the door. I walked out and examined the wreck. Up to this time, I had not felt any trepidation; but now, when it was all over, and I realized what terrible danger we had passed through, I could not help trembling. Had the train proceeded fifty yards further, the car we were in must have been torn to pieces, and it would have been indeed a lucky passenger who would have escaped death or severe injury.

There was one car in the rear of us, and as the wrecked car could not be moved, the two were left standing, and all the passengers crowded into the three or four cars in our front. Thus we proceeded to Grafton, where other cars were added.

The Baltimore and Ohio Railroad is very well conducted, and accidents on it are not of frequent occurrence. It just chanced to be my luck to witness this. I heard the conductor say that it was the only accident of any kind that had happened to his train for three years.

At Fairmont, on the Monongahela river, I got off the train, and took the stage for Uniontown, which is forty-five miles from the above place.

After spending a few weeks in Fayette county, I went down the Monongahela river to Pittsburg, intending to remain there a few days, and learn whether the sun was to be seen there or not.

CHAPTER XXV.

DIFFICULTY WITH THE OWNER OF PITTSBURG.

I ARRIVED in the "Iron City," one morning, and having registered my name at an hotel on Grant street, I went down to the "Diamond," to see a friend of mine in a wholesale grocery there. Having had a talk with him and promised to call again before leaving the city, I bade him good morning; and, in a quiet, modest, unassuming manner, took my way up Diamond alley, toward Grant street, intending to return to my hotel. As I crossed Wood street, I observed a considerable crowd collected about the corner of that street and Diamond alley, and discovered that there was a fire in the vicinity, and that the house and goods of Openheimer & Co., were feeding the flames. A steamer was puffing away as usual, to try which could damage and destroy the most goods, water or fire. [This is a question which has never been satisfactorily decided.]

Feeling no curiosity to see the fire, I crossed Wood street, passed through the crowd, and continued up Diamond alley. I had not walked far, and was about clear of the crowd, when an insolent voice called out near me:

"Get out of the way, you! Do you hear? I'm
12

Chief of Police, and am here to keep the crowd away!"
And immediately, before I had time to look up, a
hand was laid violently on my shoulder, and I was
nearly snatched from my foot.

Now, fancying that I was a "free white male"
citizen of the United States, "of the age of twenty-
one years and upwards," I was quite otherwise than
delighted with this extraordinary treatment at the
hands of the arrogant chief of villains; and turning
upon him, and verbally apprising him of the fact that
he was a "scoundrel," I was about to "belt" him
"over the ear" with my cane, when a quiet gentleman
of prepossessing appearance, walked up to me, re-
strained me in a friendly manner, and said:

"Come, my friend, I will see you righted for this.
He has treated you shamefully. I suppose you have
been a soldier; I have, too. I am General P******,
I am also a lawyer. Come with me."

"Thank you," I said.

"It was an unprovoked assault," he pursued, as we
walked up Diamond alley. "That man is Bob.
H****, Chief of the Police. He is a coarse, ignorant, insolent, overbearing man. He insults every one
that comes in his way, if he happens to be a little out
of humor. You do not live here?"

"No, I live in Philadelphia. I thank you for your
kindness. If you will tell me where to find an alderman, I will have this fellow's case attended to."

"Go to Alderman B*****," said he; and he
directed me where to find it. "I will be a witness, if
necessary. Prefer a charge of assault and battery
against Robert H****, Chief of Police, and you

will find Mr. B ***** a man who will do you justice."

"Thank you; I will go at once."

And I went to the office of Alderman B *****, who did not chance to be any bosom friend of the Chief.

"Alderman," said I, "my name is John Smith, and I reside in Philadelphia. I come before you to prefer against one Robert H ****,—a fellow calling himself Chief of Police—a charge of assault and battery."

"What! Not assault and battery on you—a cripple!"

"Yes, sir, sad as the case is, it is true. I charge him with assault and battery. Please take my deposition. I have other witnesses. General P ****** is one of them. He saw it."

"Ah! He was present?"

"Yes, sir."

I was then sworn to tell "the truth, the whole truth, and nothing but the truth;" and I then made my statement—"in accordance with the *facts.*"

"Come to-morrow afternoon at four o'clock," said the Alderman. "I will have him here to answer at that time."

"I will. Thank you."

Next day I was at the Alderman's "on time." I had not been there long before Robert H **** stepped in. The Alderman had just finished making out a commitment for a lady, who had struck another in the face eight times with a broomstick for doubting her word, and saying so, pointedly; and he was now ready to attend to our case.

"Alderman," said Chief Robert, with his usual
arrogant air, "I want to get this trifling affair delayed
for a week, as all my witnesses are out of town. I
can't attend to it before next Friday. That will be
just a week from to-day."

"Alderman," I put in, rising from my chair, "I
respectfully object to any such delay. I am traveling,
and it is not consistent with my interests to remain in
the city beyond a day or two: and the *prisoner* knows
it."

On my styling the defendant the *prisoner*, he
scowled on me like a very demon, and I felt that it
wouldn't have been pleasant to have had my life in
his exclusive keeping, just then.

"Alderman," he said, fairly choking with malig-
nant anger, "it will be impossible to get my witnesses
soon, and you must give me a show."

"It is singular," I urged, addressing the Alderman,
"that I, who am a comparative stranger here, can find
and produce my witnesses so much sooner than the
defendant, who is an official here, and ought to be
well acquainted. I most earnestly object to any such
delay, as it would be scarcely just to detain me here,
on expense, especially when business calls me away
soon."

"Probably," insinuated the Chief, "the gentleman's
business is not so urgent—if he *is* a gentleman."

"Mr. H * * * *," said the Alderman, who was too
honest to allow any one to be insulted in his office,
"the plaintiff *appears* to be a gentleman. However,
it is not to be discussed here whether he is or not.
That is not to the point."

"Mr. Alderman," I remarked, calmly, "if our respective behavior here were taken as evidence, I think I could be proved quite as much of a gentleman as the defendant."

"We'll see about that by the time I get my witnesses," said Chief Robert. "*I've* been keeping an eye on him since he came to the city. *I* know——"

"Mr. H * * * *," interrupted the Alderman, "I cannot, and *will not*, allow any such talk in my office! For you, Chief of Police, to speak thus, is to insinuate that Mr. Smith is a suspicious character. There is nothing in his appearance to warrant such an insinuation. But let me not talk of that. Let us proceed with the case. This is Friday: I will postpone the hearing only till Monday. I think that will be dealing fairly by both."

"It will be no such thing!" vociferated the irate official. "You are not giving me a fair show! You are showing partiality toward——"

Mr. H * * * *!" interrupted the Alderman, peremptorily; "not another such word in my office! I shall ——"

"But I'll be——"

"Do you hear? Not another word! I shall send the case right down to court! You must go there and answer to the charge."

"Send it! and be——"

Boiling over with rage, the Chief had seized his hat, bolted from the office, banged the door after him, and thus prevented me from hearing the conclusion of his invective.

"The case will be tried in court," said the Alder-

man, to me. "Be at the court-house on Monday,
and give your evidence before the Grand Jury. By
Tuesday, then, it may be tried."

"I will; thank you."

Monday came, and I gave my evidence before the
Grand Jury, making the case against H * * * * as
strong as I could, without swerving from "the truth,
the whole truth, and nothing but the truth: s'help—"
etc.

A "bill" was "found" against him, in the brief
space of sixty seconds; and early next morning the
case came up before the "Criminal Court." It was such
a plain case against the poor cuss, that his counsel
advised him to plead guilty; which he did. He was
then severely reprimanded by the Judge, in a long
speech, in which he urged upon him the importance
of being careful about laying hands on an inoffensive
person, without a warrant, and mildly sentenced him
to pay a fine of twenty-five dollars, and the costs;
making in all, the handsome little sum of seventy-
three dollars and eighty-two cents: and what was still
more aggravating and humiliating to the dread (?)
Chief, he was immediately taken into custody, by two
tipstaves, and escorted into the sheriff's office, where
he had to pay the fine and costs, "on sight."

The affair cost me nothing. In fact, I gained by
it; for I was about that time commencing to write a
work of fiction, (since published), and I had been for
several days at a loss for some one to represent the
villainous character. This let me out, nicely. I
named my 'villain" Robert H * * * *, gave an exact
description of him, went on swimmingly with my

novel, and, at the conclusion, brought him to a terrible and tragic death.*

---

* The White Rocks; Or, the Robbers of the Monongahela. A thrilling story of Outlaw Life in Western Pennsylvania. By A. F. Hill, author of "Our Boys," etc., etc. 12mo. Cloth, price $1.75.

(John E. Potter & Co., publishers, Philadelphia.)

CHAPTER XXVI

PECULIARITIES OF TRAVELERS.

NEXT morning I took an early train for Wheeling, which city I desired to visit on my westward way.

On this occasion, about twelve minutes before the train started, two men came in, and, desiring to sit together and finding no seat wholly vacant, one of them had the incredible, the unparalleled, the unexampled, the unheard-of audacity to ask me to move and sit with another person—a thing I have refused to do even to accommodate a lady. It was not yet quite light in the car, as the sun was not up, and I pointed to my crutch, that stood leaning against the back of the seat in front of me, and stated that I had been badly shot in the knee the previous night, in a saloon difficulty, and that it was impossible for me to move with any sort of comfort or ease. Moreover, I observed, that my uncle was to accompany me on my journey, to take care of me, that he would of course occupy the seat with me, and that he had just gone to a neighboring saloon to get me a glass of ale and hand it in at the window. Otherwise, I said, I should accommodate them by moving to any part of the car they might desire, and take pleasure in it.

Taking all I said for the truth,—and thus making a wholesale mistake—they turned and went to the rear end of the car, where they urgently requested a respectable-looking negro passenger to get up and let them have his seat. But he knew his rights, and, knowing, durst maintain; and he maintained them after this manner:

"Guess not."

"O, come, now," argued one of the two passengers; "you might as well. You'll be just as comfortable some——"

"Well, now, I guess I won't leab dis yer, by golly!"

"You might have to," suggested one of the Caucasians.

"Hab to? Like to see de man——"

"For half-a-cent I'd move you!"

The darkey was now very much "riled," and being, besides, a little drunk, and naturally ill-natured and habitually profane in his language, he railed out thus:

"No, I'll be (profanity) if you does! (Profanity) my heart, if I jis' didn' fight fur dis (profanity) country, and I'll be (profanity, profanity, profanitied) if I ain't as good as any oder (profanity) man! I know what my rights is! I does! I'll be (profanity, profanitied) if I don't! (Profanity, profanity, profanity, profanity)——"

"Look here!" exclaimed the conductor, who had just entered the car, and was adjusting the bell-cord; "what the (here he made a concise and pointed allusion to a dark personage who wears a tail with a d rt on the end of it, and carries off bad boys that won't mind their mothers an l who run off and play base ball when sent to school) do you mean? What are you cursing that way for? Don't you see there are ladies in the car——"

" Dey wants my seat, and——"

"Well, they havn't got it, have they? You shall keep your seat, if you want to. No one is going to take it from you! Now, another word out of your black head, and I'll split it for you, and throw it out of the window, a piece at a time!"

The two troublesome travelers had, meantime, located themselves in separate seats, as near each other as possible; the darkey said no more, and quiet reigned for a moment or so.

Glancing out at my window, which I had raised, I presently saw two Irishmen—both drunk—approaching the car; and one of them was carrying a valise, a fiddle, a hat-box, a saw, a side of leather, an overcoat and an extra pair of boots. He was evidently going on a journey; but the other was in his shirt-sleeves, and had only accompanied him to the train to see him off.

"Good-by, Mike," said he in his shirt-sleeves. " Take gude care o' yer-sel."

"I'll do that, Zhammie," said the traveler, who was the drunkest of the two. " When'll'seeyez'gin, m'b'y?"

"I'll mate ye'n Whalin', Mike. Steek till the cause, me boy. Don't forgit the Fanians an' yer counthry!"

By this time, a number of the passengers who sat

on the same side of the car with me had raised their
windows, and were now listening to this dialogue,
much amused. The conversation was carried on in
loud, harsh tones.

"F'rgit m' counthry an' th' cause? Och! I shud
thaink naught," said the Milesian traveler, who was
now about to ascend the steps to the platform of the
car I was in.

He paused a moment, before blundering up, and
then struck up a patriotic Fenian song, the first verse
of which was something like this:

"Och! Kra! Kri mo kreeh! mee barry braugh,
    Augh quih-queeh, McQuairy, O!
Grah me Kreh! Grah me Kree! Ahkushlee! Hurrah!
    Mike graughin, Och borry bro!"

"Good me b'y!" exclaimed his friend, grasping his
hand. "Wull done, that! Now, good-by, Mike,
Tak care o' yer-sel!"

"Good-by, till ye, Zhammie. God be good till
ye!"

After shaking hands cordially, they parted. He
in his shirt-sleeves, James, by name, walked away,
with some sadness naturally engendered by the part-
ing; while Michael entered the car and took a seat
by the darkey—for all the rest were entirely occupied
by this time—his saw, as he sat down, accidentally
grazing the darkey's cheek, and coming within half-
an-inch of sawing one of his white eyes out.

" 'Scuse me, dairlint," said Mike; and he deposited
his luggage down among both their feet, threw himself carelessly back in his seat, with his cheek resting

on his dusky companion's shoulder, and soon fell
asleep.

The pleasant (?) time the conductor had waking
him, when he came round for his ticket, might be
described with excellent effect, by a professional
humorist; but let the reader picture it in his imagination.

CHAPTER XXVII.

McCULLOCH'S LEAP.

ABOUT eleven o'clock, A. M., the train arrived at the little village of Bridgeport, opposite Wheeling, where an omnibus was in waiting to carry over the river all passengers destined for the city. Between Bridgeport and Wheeling is an island, whose name I forget, and there are two bridges required for communication between the two places. That on the Wheeling side is a very excellent suspension bridge, ninety or a hundred feet above the water, with a span of one thousand feet. That on the Bridgeport side is a substantial wooden bridge with five or six piers. The steamboat channel is, as may naturally be supposed, on the Wheeling side of the island.

I and my trunk took passage on the omnibus, and I had reason to be pleased with the gentlemanly demeanor of the conductor, and with his moderate charges.

The first object of interest near Wheeling that I desired to visit, was the steep declivity down which the pioneer McCulloch made his fearful plunge on horseback, when pursued by the Indians. This, if my memory serves me correctly, happened in 1790

It was on a beautiful day, late in March, that I
arrived in Wheeling; and, having taken dinner at a
comfortable and tidy hotel, I walked into the sitting-
room where several gentlemen were seated poring
over the newspapers. I looked around me before
venturing to speak to any one, and was not long in
making up my mind as to which to address my inquiries to. •

This was a man of forty-five or fifty years, who was
in the act of folding up a paper he had been reading,
and whom I judged to be a resident of Wheeling.
Besides, his countenance was clearly the index of a
good mind, and a noble and congenial heart.

As I afterward learned, his name was Charles Cracraft—he was familiarly styled Charlie—an intelligent,
well-known and much respected citizen of Wheeling.
He and I became the warmest friends during the brief
week that I remained in Wheeling, and his society
delighted me.   He was one of those "gems" of which
Gray speaks in his "Elegy in a Country Churchyard."
A man better versed in history and general literature
I have seldom met. Few notable events ever happened in the world that Charlie could not tell all
about. Why he had never made his mark in the
world, I could not tell; but I felt sure he might have
done so.   In addition to his love of reading, and a
good memory, I found him possessed of most excellent
judgment, strong reasoning powers, an impressive
address liberality of views and an admirable knowledge of language and composition. With all his
gifts—gifts that would enable a man to shine anywhere—he was not known beyond his native city;

and that is why I regard him as one of those "gems" which Gray says are "born to blush unseen."

Well, it was to Charlie Cracraft that I addressed my inquiries regarding the place where McCulloch, under pressing circumstances, executed his celebrated equestrian feat.

"It is barely half a-mile distant," said Charlie. "Are you going to see it?"

"Yes, by all means," I replied.

"It is just outside the city. You go to the upper end of the city, and—however, I was just thinking of taking a walk myself, and I will accompany you, if you desire."

"I shall be pleased with your company," said I, "and I thank you."

We were friends from that moment. Charlie arose, and we left the hotel and walked up the street. Emerging from the upper end of the city we followed a pike for a few hundred yards, which led us to a considerable elevation, where I found laid before me about as grand a scene as I ever beheld.

"Here," said Charlie, "is where McCulloch rode down." We were standing with our faces toward the east; behind us, deep among the tall hills, flowed the Ohio river, and before us was a valley of great depth, through which Wheeling creek wound its way. This stream flowed directly toward the Ohio river, till it reached the base of the declivity immediately beneath us; then turning about, guarded away from the river, as it were, by the long, steep, intervening ridge, it flowed clear around Wheeling, and emptied into the **river below.** That portion of the creek which we

could see, hemmed in by a semicircular range of
hills on its right side, formed a path similar in shape
to a horse-shoe; only its principal curve was more
abrupt.

It was at this abrupt curve that the daring McCulloch plunged down the declivity. He had been pursued from a northerly direction, by the Indians, and
intended to gallop along the verge of the descent, and
turn toward the east, as the creek turned far below.
But just here he found himself intercepted by another
band of savages, and retreat in that direction cut off.
Behind him lay the Ohio river, three hundred feet
below, on either hand was a horde of howling blood-
thirsty savages, and before him was a steep descent
of several hundred feet, whose face was interrupted
by several perpendicular ledges of rock; and, in this
terrible exigence, he clutched his reins tightly, and
spurred his horse quickly over the brink and down
the fearful declivity. It is not really so steep as
some who have read the account suppose, for a line
drawn from the summit to the base, where the creek
flows, would form an angle with the horizon of only
between forty and forty-five degrees; but at intervals
there are precipitous ledges of rock, quite perpendicular, of from ten to twenty feet in height. That
the horse and rider plunged down over them in safety,
seems little less than a miracle.

This range of hills, or rather this ridge, is higher and
even steeper in some places than at the point where
McCulloch plunged down. Charlie and I walked
along the verge of the precipice, ascending gradually,
till we came to a point over four hundred feet above

the high-water mark of the river. From this point, we could see over many miles of Ohio landscape beyond the river.

It was at this highest point that, a few years ago, a man named Wheat, a citizen of Wheeling, actually drove over the precipice in a two-horse sleigh. Two other persons were in the sleigh with him, riding along the summit of the ridge, and on his declaring that he was going to eclipse McCulloch, they jumped out, and the fool actually touched up his horses and drove down the precipice. His name was *Wheat*, as I stated; but Charlie told me that *rye* had more to do with it than any one else.

Down tumbled Wheat, the sleigh and two horses; and only that good luck that ever seems to attend an intoxicated man could have saved him from a violent and speedy death. While the sleigh was dashed to splinters, and both the horses precipitated into Wheeling creek and killed, Mr. Wheat lodged among some stunted trees, about half-way down— badly bruised and "stove up," it is true, but still alive and in moderate *spirits*. He is still living, but has been a cripple ever since his mad and daring sleigh-ride.

Charlie and I returned from our pleasant walk, feeling as though we had been acquainted for years. We had considerable conversation, on various topics, and I will nevet forget a remark I heard him make. We were speaking of religion, and I found that he, like myself, was a dissenter from the orthodox faith. Speaking of the doubts and perplexities that always arose, when he thought on the subject, he said:

13

"If I possessed the wealth of the whole world; if
the lands, the houses, the gold, the gems, the king-
doms, and the thrones were mine; I would gladly
give them all to know the TRUTH!"

The reader has, no doubt, heard or read of a certain
cave among the rocks on Wheeling creek, in which
an Indian once concealed himself with a rifle, and,
by imitating the voice of a turkey, decoyed several
men from the fort in succession, and shot them.   His
strategem was at last detected, however, and a pioneer who was as shrewd as he, went in the night,
concealed himself in the neighborhood, and in the
morning saw the dusky savage go and ensconce himself in his usual hiding-place, and begin the song of
the turkey. The pioneer, who could see his dark visage
among the rocks, took aim with his rifle, and with
one shot silenced him forever.

Charlie pointed this cave out to me, and I went
the next day and visited it.   He would have accompanied me, but he was subject to rheumatism, and
was suffering considerably that day; so I went alone.
The cave is about a mile from Wheeling.   I had to
climb up the rocks fifteen or twenty feet, in order to
get into it, and I sat there awhile, aiming my crutch
at a stump beyond Wheeling creek, and imagining
myself the cunning but unfortunate Indian who personated a turkey and got shot for it.   The cave is not
large—in fact, one cannot stand erect; but half-a-dozen
persons could be stowed in it in a reclining position,
provided none of them were ladies in capacious
crinoline.

Returning from the cave, *via* McCulloch's Leap,

it was my lot to encounter one of the greatest bores
I ever met. He was one of those persons who, it is
said, can "talk a man to death." He made me think
of the celebrated lines of Pope:

> "No place so sacred from such fops is barred,
> Nor is Paul's church more safe than Paul's churchyard.
> Nay, fly to altars, there they talk you dead,
> And fools rush in where angels fear to tread."

He lived in a solitary house, by the creek at the
base of the declivity, and he happened to come out
just as I was about to make the ascent. He was a
fast talker, said a great many words in a few seconds,
and often spoke a good many seconds at a time.

"How do you do, sir? How do you do?" he said,
familiarly. "Fine day."

"Very," I said. "Quite pleasant."

I wanted to get back to my hotel, for my stomach
admonished me that it was fully dinner-time; and so,
I made an attempt to pass on and begin to climb the
hill. It was no use, though. He commenced by
asking me if I lost my leg in the army, then went on
asking one question after another—in such rapid succession that I only got each one about half answered
—till he had asked three times the number usually
proposed. He asked questions such as I had never
thought of before, and kept on so fast that I fancied
he asked them merely for the pleasure of it, and not
for the sake of hearing them answered. He not only
asked me if I was born in this country, where I was
brought up, what kind of saw-mills we had there,
and what barbers charged for cutting hair; but also
desired to know if I had ever looked at the moon

through a telescope, and if I thought corn as good a
diet for horses as oats. Every question that any
mortal man could think of in so short a time, he asked
me, till I finally felt that I must either move on, or
die. I moved on, in the midst of the conversation,
and looked back over my shoulder now and then to
answer questions, which he continued to ask.

"Are you going to walk up the hill?"

"Yes."

"Can you do it?"

"O, yes."

"Aint you afraid you'll fall?"

"No."

I began to ascend the acclivity, and he talked on.

"Did you ever go up such a steep place before?"

"Yes, steeper," I yelled back, thinking of Bunker
Hill Monument.

"And didn't fall?" he continued, as I took another
labored stride onward and upward.

"No."

"Wasn't you afraid of falling?"

"No."

"You must be plucky."

As this did not strictly demand any answer, I took
advantage of a momentary pause to say,

"Good day."

"Good——But say?   What regiment did you say
you were in?"

"Eighth Pennsyl——"

"Did you know a man in that regiment by the
name of—"

I had now ascended to the height of seventy-five

or eighty feet, when I stopped on a sort of shelf, to rest a moment, turned about and said:

"What was his name?"

"I forget—I was just trying to think—O, yes, it was—let me see—was it—no—was it—Harbertson?"

"I knew none of that name in my regiment," I yelled back; for the conversation now had to be carried on in a loud voice.

"I don't think that was the name," said he. "Now that I come to think of it, he was in a New Jersey regiment. I used to work with him, in ——"

"Well," said I, facing the hill again to continue the ascent, "I'll move on. Good ——"

"Wait a minute," he interrupted, coming up ten or fifteen feet to where it began to grow pretty steep, and there stopping. "What did you say your name was."

"Smith," I yelled. "Good ——"

"I have relations of that name in Pennsyl——"

"Ah, well, good-day," and I continued up the ascent.

"When will you leave Wheeling?"

"I have to leave on the two o'clock train," I sinfully replied, without pausing in the ascent.

"Where going?"

"To Pitt——, Cleve——, Cincinnati!" I replied, scarcely knowing what lie to tell.

"You'll have plenty of time," he yelled. "It isn't more'n twelve now." And thus he went on till he talked me clear to the top of the rugged height.

"Good ——"

"I was going to ask you ——"

"——— Day," I madly yelled, as I reached tho summit, and disappeared, half-fainting, from his view.

Of all the bores I ever met, this man was incomparably the greatest. If I ever visit McCulloch's Leap again, I will remain at the summit, and not go near enough the verge for that dread man, who lives in the lone cottage far below, to catch a glimpse of me!

CHAPTER XXVIII.

CINCINNATI.

IT was about the first of April, when the weather was delightful, and the nights were lighted by the full moon, that I left Wheeling for Cincinnati, on board the new little steamer "Como." I had a pleasant voyage of two days and two nights, and might write a good many pages descriptive of it; but that's old. Moreover, it is not John-Smithian.

As I wished to remain in Cincinnati for a month, I hired a lodging-room for that length of time, paying the money in advance, because it was not perfectly clear that I wasn't a "deep-dyed villain."

The landlady, for the sum of eighteen dollars, placed me in possession of a neat, tidy room, upstairs, and I there wrote and slept for one month; taking my meals at a neighboring saloon.

The proprietress of my lodging-house, who was a German lady—one of the Germanest I ever saw—accompanied me to the hall-door as I walked out to have my trunk sent up. On reaching the foot of the stairs in the hall, I noticed a room on the left-hand side, with the door standing open, and, involuntarily glancing in, perceived that it was handsomely furnished.

" Dat," said the landlady, whose knowledge of English, it will be perceived, was very imperfect, " is—is
—two—ah—ah—play-mens—actors, you knows. Dey
rent it from me. Dirty-five tollar pays."

" Quite reasonable," said I. " A nice room. Where
do they play ?"

" At de—de Deaters, you knows."

I had naturally inferred as much, but pretended to
receive this as a piece of extraordinary information,
and said :

" Ah ? Indeed ?"

" Yes. Dey gets—lots—great big much—vat you
call 'em—vages."

" O, yes. They get good wages?"

" Yes, von pig much tollars."

I had my trunk sent to my new quarters, then took
a leisurely stroll through the " City of Pork." I
first called on my friend Major J. P. Kline, on Sixth
street, and before I left him, he made me promise to
accompany him to the theater that night, stating that
Proctor was to play the tragedy of " Virginius," at the
I-forget-the-name-of-it Theater. I then took a further
walk, and in a couple of hours returned to my lodgings
and wrote a letter to an eastern paper, in which I gave
a great deal of valuable information concerning Cincinnati—considering my limited knowledge of it.

I accompanied my friend to the theater that even-
ng, and saw Proctor play " Virginius." He performed
his part well; but there was one actor, of lofty
mien, who personated Icilius in the tragedy, and
who attracted my attention and won my admiration
more than any other. He was perfectly majestic.

I thought he should have been born a king, at least.
He uttered every word with a loftiness and dignity,
and in clear, ringing, impressive, awe-inspiring tones,
that would have graced an emperor. Every word he
uttered he seemed to feel; and whenever he was on
the stage, I fancied I was looking on the genuine
Icilius, himself, and on those real tragic events that
occurred in the days of the Decemviri; instead of a
mere representation of them.

Virginius was cheered, applauded, encored; but
Icilius more than "brought down the house." When
he came out with the eloquent and brilliant passages
which it was his office to repeat, the effect was electri-
cal. The audience was dumb with admiration, and
seemed ready to rise up in the air on the wings of enthusiasm, bear Icilius to the skies, and have him en-
rolled among the gods!

That night, on reaching my "apartments" on Plum
street, (having loitered by the way,) I observed that
the ground-floor room I mentioned was lighted, and
that its occupants were at home. As I entered the
hall and closed the street-door behind me, I observed
that the room-door stood wide open; and I heard voices
within. One of them, who was standing at the center
of the room, adjusting the gas-burner, just then vexed-
ly exclaimed to his companion:

"Pshaw! Gol-darn it, Bill! Where's me pipe?"

Wondering if a person so harsh-spoken could be
one of the actors mentioned by the landlady, I involuntarily glanced in, as I walked past the door
toward the hall-stairs. The face of the speaker, who
continued to growl about "me pipe," was toward the

door, and the glare of several gas-burners shone full
upon his visage.

Ye mythic gods! Ye gods, Grecian and Roman!
Ye gods, from great Jupiter down to the nude little
cuss with the bow and arrows, inclusive! It was
Icilius! Where now his gallant bearing—his majestic mien—his glittering armor—his proud helmet—
his waving plume—and the burnished sword I had
seen him flourish, as though it were a king's scepter?
Where!! Where, too, was that noble look of defiance with which he had confronted Claudius Appius?
Where that expression of more than mortal anguish
that had settled upon his god-like face when beautiful
Virginia, loved Virginia, *his* Virginia, was slain with a
butcher-knife by her own father, to avert dishonor?
All gone! Gone!!

"Dash it, then, give me a cigar," I heard him say,
as I passed the door.

He was in his shirt-sleeves, his shirt was unbut-
toned at the collar, and carelessly thrown open to let
the air in upon his manly breast, after his exertion;
and, instead of the "raven locks" he had worn that
night, his head was covered with short, stiff, reddish
hair—*locks* not so easily broken. Still, in his eyes,
features, and voice, with all his change of dress and
bearing, I recognized Icilius! "How are the mighty
fallen!" Was it for him I had that night stamped,
clapped my hands, and screamed "Encore?" I felt
small, and said, to myself, "Icilius! I-cili-us! I
silly ass! To think how I yelled, cheered, and *encored* this night for such a worm as thou!" I then
went up to my room, resolving never to applaud an

actor again, without knowing him to be a "star." It is perfectly safe then, for we seldom see *them* in dishabille.

Next day Major Kline and I visited a pleasant resort on the river shore, several miles above the city, known as "Ohmer's Zoological Gardens." "Pete" Ohmer, the proprietor, was a friend of Major Kline, and he cheerfully accompanied us through his pleasant grounds, showed us the numerous animals which he had on exhibition, and explained their peculiarities. They were all in cages, because some of them were dangerous, while the others might run away.

He had one "gentle" bear that was a perfect pet, and would fondle upon one like a dog. (That sentence is ambiguous. I do not mean that he would fondle upon one who was like unto a dog, (the son of a female dog,) but that he would fondle in a manner similar to that of that sagacious animal.) I put my hand in his mouth, and he playfully closed on it with his excellent teeth, just enough to make the blood come: no more. After that, I patted him affectionately on the head and left the cage. As I did so, he left the marks of his teeth on my crutch, and growled a pleasant "good-by."

Another cage we visited contained an animal which I thought looked fully as good-natured as the pet bear.

"What animal is this, Mr. Ohmer?" I asked, as I walked up to the cage, and was about to thrust my hand through the bars and pat the gentle-looking creature on the head.

"That is the Cal—— Look out! Don't put your hand in! Were you going to?"

"Yes: he looks so pleasant, and——"

"O, it's well you didn't. You think him a good-natured fellow, eh? That's what we call a California Tiger. Watch me stir him up, if you think him a pleasant fellow."

He picked up an iron rod, thrust it into the cage, between the bars, and gave the creature, which had the honor to hail from California, an abrupt poke on the ribs. The result fairly startled me. The animal, which had appeared as docile as a kitten a moment before, now sprang up, uttered a growl as fierce as thunder only ten yards distant, displayed a mouthful of sharp white teeth an inch long, and fastened upon the iron rod with its savage jaws. At the same time its eyes glared like balls of fire, and seemed ready to dart out at me. Altogether, the savage creature looked as though it could bite a man's leg off without noticing that there was a bone in it.

"What if you had put your hand in?" said Major Kline.

"It would have bit it off, I suppose," I returned; "and I couldn't well afford to lose it."

"Yes," said Pete Ohmer, "he could snap your hand off in a second, and eat it up; and it would only give him an appetite to eat the rest of you."

I could not help congratulating myself on my narrow escape, and resolved never to trust my hand to an unknown animal, merely because I liked its gentle appearance.

CHAPTER XXIX.

FALLS CITY AND CAVE CITY.

EARLY in May, I left Cincinnati and went to Louisville, Kentucky, one hundred and fifty miles down the river. I took passage on a splendid steamer—one of the finest on the Ohio or Mississippi. The fare was only two dollars, and each passenger was furnished with two excellent meals by the way, and a state-room berth when night came. It will naturally be thought that this was remarkably cheap; and so it was. But it was the result of competition. "Opposition" boats were at that time running between Cincinnati and Louisville, and the fare —usually four or five dollars—had crawled down to two. Certainly "Competition is the life of trade."

This, however, does not quite equal, for extreme consistence, the rates of fare on the Hudson river boats some years ago, when an "Opposition line" from New York to Albany was established. The distance from New York to Albany is about the same as that from Cincinnati to Louisville; and the fare got lower and lower, at one period, till any weary traveler could go from New York to Albany—or *vice versa*— for twelve cents—meals *not* included. Nor did the freaks of competition end then. One of the lines, at last, concluding that the difference between twelve cents and nothing was but a mere trifle, reduced the fare twelve cents, and carried passengers a week or two for nothing. Not to be outdone, the other line not only carried all for nothing, but promptly paid ach passenger a premium of six cents for riding from one place to the other. It will be naturally supposed that they could not make much at such rates, but it is said that the number of passengers was so great that they did a better business then than they had done when the fare was two-and-a-half dollars.

Louisville is the largest city in Kentucky—its population being now about ninety thousand. It is a great tobacco market, and has some of the most extensive warehouses, for the storage of that weed, in the United States. The principal business street in the city is called Main street, and it is one that would do no discredit to any city. It is wide, perfectly straight, about four miles long, and is lined with fine large buildings occupied by merchants. A well-con-ducted passenger railway is laid on this street.

Louisville is also called the "Falls City," because the Ohio river there takes a considerable fall, so that steamboats, except at high water, are compelled to pass through a canal with several locks. The Falls of the Ohio at Louisville, are not abrupt, but extend with a gradual descent, over two or three miles. Oppo-site Louisville is the town of Jeffersonville, Indiana; and three miles below, on the Indiana side, is the city of New Albany, with a population of about sixteen thousand. Of course I visited those places.

From Louisville I determined to go on a visit to

the celebrated Mammoth Cave, a very considerable and extraordinary hole in the ground, situated about half-way between Louisville and Nashville—that is to say, nearly one hundred miles from each place. I was informed at the Falls City, that I should take the Louisville and Nashville Railroad, and get off at Cave City, whence I should take a stage for the Mammoth Cave, ten miles from the railroad.

Leaving my trunk at my hotel in Louisville, I took the five o'clock evening train, and arrived at Cave City—a small village that isn't a city at all—by reasonable bedtime, where I retired to rest for the night in a good but rather expensive hotel. I was put in a double-bedded room with another passenger from Louisville, who also intended to visit the Mammoth Cave next day.

The clerk having conducted us to our room, withdrew from the chamber and closed the door after him.

"I wonder if there is a lock on the door?" said my companion.

"There ought to be," I replied. "We should secure it by some means, at all events."

"Yes," he remarked, "I always make it a rule, when traveling, to see that every thing is secure.— Yes, here is a lock and bolt," he said, as he walked to the door and examined it. He turned the key and shot the bolt. "Are you going to the Cave tomorrow?"

"Yes, that is my object."

"Did you come on the train from Louisville?"

"Yes; did you?"

"Yes, I too. I am from Missouri: and you?"—
"I am from Pennsylvania."
"Were you engaged in the war?"
"Yes."
"Federal side, I suppose."
"Yes; and were you also—"
"Confederate."
"Exactly. Well, we are fellow-citizens and country-men once more, and let us congratulate each other that the strife is over. If you are going in the stage in the morning, we will be traveling companions, and, I am sure, will prove agreeable to each other, notwithstanding that we have been fighting in opposing armies, and possibly shooting at each other."

"I agree with you," he replied, "and was about to make such a remark myself. True soldiers never carry animosities home with them, when the contest on the field is over."

My Confederate companion was a young man of prepossessing appearance, twenty-five or twenty-six years of age, intelligent, affable and polite; and, as the lamp was extinguished and we retired to our respective beds in opposite corners of the room, I congratulated myself on my prospect of having an agreeable companion to join me in my visit to the Mammoth Cave on the morrow. Nor was I mistaken. My new acquaintance proved to be all that he appeared—a perfect gentleman.

With a confidence I seldom feel while a stranger is sleeping in the same room with me, I fell asleep, and enjoyed a good night's rest, after my ride on the train from Louisville.

CHAPTER XXX.

John Smith's Absence from the Face of the Earth.

NEXT morning, having taken breakfast, we got into the coach, and departed for the Mammoth Cave, which we reached after a not unpleasant ride of ten miles, over a hilly and wooded country. It was one of the pleasantest days of the year, and the conversation between my companion and myself was of such an agreeable nature, that when we reached the hotel near the cave, I fancied we had scarely traveled half-a-dozen miles. The length of time we had been on the road, however, indicated that we must have traveled fully ten miles. It was about ten o'clock.

We each paid two dollars for the services of a guide; and the latter providing three lanterns, and some combustible material for temporary lights at certain particular points, accompanied us into a deep valley near by: and in this valley, in so obscure a place as to be almost hid from the eyes of men, we found the entrance to the renowned Mammoth Cave.

It is not my intention to give a general description of it. Many a graphic account of the great cave has been furnished by tourists; and yet, as in the case of Niagara Falls, no one has ever given an adequate

14

description, and no one can form any proper conception of it without having seen it. However, I'll
mention a point or two that may prove interesting or
amusing to the " gentle reader."

Once within the cave,—which we entered without
striking our "brows" on the overhanging rocks at
the entrance, where a little cascade sings away its
happy life—the guide lighted the three lamps he carried. It is customary to give one to each visitor, on
entering the cave; but as I could not have carried one
conveniently, the guide, having given one to my Confederate friend, carried two himself.

We then walked on, following a straight and narrow passage for a quarter of a mile; by which time
we began to feel quite independent of the sun. It
would be natural to suppose that dampness would
predominate in this cave, but such is not the case.
On the contrary, quite the opposite state of things
prevails. Except near the subterranean streams, the
cave, both over-head and under-foot, is as dry as one
could wish the paper on which he writes—and you
know that isn't sloppy.

The temperature of the atmosphere within the cave,
at all seasons of the year, is about fifty-nine degrees;
and chemists have decided that the air is purer there
than without—that it contains a far less proportion of
carbonic acid gas.

The first point to which the guide respectfully directed our attention—for he was very polite—was a
place called the " Rotunda," situated at the first turn
of the passage—or rather at the junction of this passage with another running off toward the left, nearly

at a right angle. The "ceiling" of this "Rotunda"—so-called from its resemblance to the interior of a dome—is about one hundred feet high, and eighty feet in diameter. Over the floor are still strewn some of the wooden pipes, used by the miners in 1812, at which time saltpeter was taken from the cave in large quantities.

Turning to the left, we soon passed a small stone hut, and, somewhat surprised, we asked the guide what it meant to see a building thus far under ground, half-a-mile from the light of the sun.

"That," said he, "and another similar one, which we shall soon pass, were built ten or fifteen years ago, for residences for consumptive patients, who, it was thought, would be benefited by the mild and regular temperature of the air."

"And is it possible that any came in here to live, and thus shut themselves up from the light of day," I asked.

"Yes," returned the guide, "a number tried the experiment."

"And with what result?" asked my companion.

"Not a very satisfactory one. Several of them died in here, and never saw the sun again; while nearly all who lived to be taken out, died within a week or two after. When they reached the light again, it was discovered that all their eyes were perfectly black, no matter what their original color had been."

This fact, my friend and I silently doubted; but subsequent inquiry convinced us that it was true. **Any** person who desires black eyes can acquire them by a residence of a few months in the Mammoth Cave. If any of my lady readers are afflicted with eyes of celestial blue, and are tired of them, they can have them promptly dyed black by taking apartments for three months in the Mammoth Cave. I don't advise them to do it, though, for I—John Smith is but mortal—have a weakness for blue eyes that I cannot overcome.

A few hundred yards from the Rotunda, the passage widens out into a spacious apartment, styled the "Methodist Church." It is so-called because a congregation of Methodists used to hold "divine services" there. A good idea; for if they *were* a little noisy in their adorations, they did not disturb any one; and their prayers could as easily ascend through the two hundred feet of earth above them, as through a slate roof, with a tall spire to point out the way.

A little further on we saw a huge rock which had evidently at some time or other fallen from above— I mean from the roof of the cave—which, to look at it from a certain position, is a most perfect semblance of a coffin. It is termed the "Giant's Coffin," as the guide informed us. It is forty feet long, twenty feet wide and eight feet deep. It would make a good sarcophagus to bury some great politician in, some day.

Just beyond, the guide called our attention to some huge figures on the ceiling above. They represented the outlines of several persons of immense size. He informed us that they were styled the "Giant, his Wife and Child;" and I just wondered, but didn't ask him, if they were to be put in the "Giant's Coffin," when they should die? These figures had been formed by some dark substance that had apparently oozed from the rocky roof.

Soon after passing them, we emerged into another spacious apartment, called the "Star Chamber." It is so called, because the ceiling, which is there of a dark hue, is covered with white spots; and when we gazed upon it for a moment, in the meager light of the lanterns, it looked like the mighty heavens studded with stars.

"Now," said the guide, "sit down on those rocks there a little while, and I will take all the lamps and retire into a recess, where you cannot see a single beam of them. You can then see what perfect darkness is."

We sat down, and the guide, taking all the lamps, walked away, descended into a kind of pit, and disappeared in a small sub-cavern; and every ray of light soon vanished. The darkness was indeed perfect; and it occurred to me that if a man intended to remain in such a position, he might as well have his eyes sewed up and covered with black sealing-wax.

Neither my companion nor myself spoke. The darkness was so absolute, and the silence so profound that strange thoughts came into my head. I thought of the busy world without—fancied I saw the thronging multitudes of all the cities and towns of the globe; and the moving men and women scattered over the broad land; the ships with their crews, tossing about over the breasts of the great oceans; and I asked myself: "Does the eye of the great unknown, incomprehensible, Almighty Being who created and who governs the Universe, take note of all these, and still peer into this silent and secret place ?"

" There is a light !" exclaimed my companion, after a minute or so of black darkness and grave-like silence.

Silence? No—all the while I had heard the beating of my own heart, although I was almost un-conscious of it as I sat musing, and the very absence of sound caused a singular imaginary ringing in my ears that I had never experienced before.

I looked and saw our guide approaching from a different direction. He had traversed a small passage not known to visitors, and emerged from it some forty yards distant.

"Now, gentlemen," said the guide, when he reached us again, "I am ready to accompany you further."

"I presume we will see the 'Bottomless Pit,' by and by," observe l my Confederate friend, as we arose

"Yes," returned the guide, while we walked on " That is a mile from here. We will pass over it."

"And the river Styx," said I—" where is it ?"

"About two miles from here," responded the guide.

The *nonchalance* with which the guide would speak of miles of distance in the cave was very remarkable. He would say of such and such a point, " Why, that is two-and-a-half (or three or five, as the case might be,) miles from here," just the same as one in the out-side world would say, " You will find the Cross-roads about two miles from here;" or, " The village is just four miles distant." I remember his once telling us that some point—I forget what—was "five miles from here." **Five miles underground! Think of it.**

However, that is not the extreme. Persons who go in to spend the whole day, travel as far as nine miles from the entrance. We only went three or four miles from the entrance that day, but we visited a great many intermediate passages, *etc.*; so that we probably traveled ten miles in the aggregate.

In half-an-hour, after having seen many curiosities by the way, we reached the celebrated " Bottomless Pit." Much curiosity regarding this pit prevails among those who have only heard it spoken of: therefore, I will remark that its very name is a contradiction in terms. A pit, in order to be *bottomless*, must have no bottom at all; but this pit has one bottom, in a very good state of preservation, and, therefore, cannot be bottomless. If the word *bottomless* is an adjective of the comparative order, I would say of the " Bottomless Pit;" " There are no doubt bottomlesser pits in the world than it is, but it is the bottomlessest pit I ever saw."

Directly over the Pit is constructed a wooden bridge, which—for every thing is named there—is called the "Bridge of Sighs." It might be termed the "Bridge of rather small Size," for it is not much wider than a darkey's foot.

We stepped upon this structure—which the guide assured us was perfectly safe—and stood directly over the center of the yawning pit. While we stood there he lighted a piece of peculiar paper he carried with him for the purpose, and dropped it from the bridge. Away it went, glaring, flaring, blazing, fluttering, down, down, down, till it reached the bottom of the pit that has no bottom. I do not mean to make light of it—in fact, it is too dark and gloomy to be made *light* of—for it is grand and terrible even as it is. Its depth is probably one hundred and fifty feet. It is round, like a well, and about twenty feet in diameter. Water a few inches deep stands silently on the bottom, and the loose stones—probably such as have been cast down from time to time—can be seen peeping above the surface.

The guide showed us another pit called "Side-saddle Pit"—so named because to see into it one must thrust his head through a small aperture, the lower part of which is in shape very similar to a side-saddle. This pit is very little wider than an ordinary well, and is, we were informed, more than one hundred feet deep.

Not far from this we arrived at a wide place in the subterraneous passage called "Revelers' Hall;" because it is customary for visitors to stop there awhile, rest from their rambles and drink each other's, or somebody else's health—if they have anything to drink it with. I happened to have about my person somewhere—say in the breast pocket of my coat, for example—a willow-encased receptacle containing a strong unmixed toddy, without water or sugar. I produced it, and my companion, the guide and I imbibed all our healths, the healths of all other visitors, the healths of distant friends, the health of the owner, and finally of the Cave itself, with all its curiosities and wonders. If I had thought of it at the time, I would, moreover, have proposed Horne Tooke's regular after-dinner sentiment: "All kings in h—l; the door **locked**, *the key lost !*"

We soon after visited the river "Styx," which, unlike the Styx of mythology, we can cross without arriving in Erebus. We went over it on a natural bridge of rock, with a single arch through which the dark river flows, and found the other shore about the same as this—either being gloomy enough to represent Erebus, on a small scale. We descended to the water's edge on the opposite shore, and embarked in a small boat, which the guide propelled with a long pole, and rode a few hundred yards on the bosom of the awful stream. As we went gliding along through those gloomy passages that frown in everlasting silence, our figures barely seen in the dim light of the lamps, and the black walls grumbling at each sound, and echoing it back and forth, I thought that nothing in the depths of the earth could be more like the fabled mythic river over which Charon ferries his passengers to Hades. Certainly, the subterranean stream could not have been more appropriately named.

In some places we passed under dark arches that hovered over us so closely that they seemed ready to close upon us and crush us in their dismal grasp; and in other places we passed through narrow passages, where there was no path on either shore, and we were hemmed in on both sides by perpendicular walls of sombre rock. The stream is from twenty to fifty feet wide, and is not very deep, except in some noted places. The guide assured us that it is inhabited by fish without eyes. I have heard doubts expressed on this point, but there can be no reasonable doubt about it. In fact, why should they need eyes there? What material eye could penetrate the awful gloom?

While gliding leisurely down the dusky river, the guide struck up a song; and whether his voice was sonorous or not, or the words beautiful, I thought I had never heard anything sound so majestically musical. The dim dark walls took up the words and echoed them again and again; and they rolled along the passages, like half-tamed thunder, and returned to us again from remote pits and recesses.

O, what's the use for humble John Smith to attempt to describe those scenes of awful and gloomy grandeur! Let me desist, and escort the reader from the grandly dismal labyrinths, the yawning pits and frowning recesses, to the bright day again! As we go toward the entrance I will mention a few other things that I saw. The guide conducted us into an avenue—I forgot what he called it: some "arcade," I think—which was adorned with innumerable stalactites and stalagmites, and many grand columns that seemed placed there to support the ceiling, which had been formed by the meeting and blending together of stalactites and stalagmites. The stalactites form like icicles. They are carbonate of lime, i e., limestone. The carbonate of lime, mingled with some other chemical substance, has oozed from the ceiling, and, as the other substance leaves, it hardens into suspending columns, as water freezes into icicles when the cold air carries away the caloric from it.

In one place, four columns arise in a kind of cluster, so that one can stand among them. They constitute what is termed the "Altar." The guide told us that a marriage ceremony was once performed there. A young lady had promised her mother during the latter's dying moments, that she would " never get married on top o' ground ;" but as time rolled on, and the dear creature concluded that it was not good to be alone, she and her " intended," accompanied by a minister, entered the Mammoth Cave, repaired to this novel place, and were married *under* ground. Literally, she kept her promise, but scarcely in spirit. It looked like " whipping the—' ould one—round the stump." I do not censure her, though ; nor should I, even if she had got married on the " cloud-capped" crest of Mount Hood ; for, " a bad promise is better broken than kept."

It was three o'clock when we emerged from the cave, an I experienced the blinding influence of suddenly returning daylight. Without delay we repaired to the hotel and took dinner—for which we had acquired a good appetite—then got into a coach and returned to Cave City. My Confederate friend wanted to travel into Tennessee, and cordially bidding me good-by at Cave City, he left on an evening train. I had to wait till twelve o'clock for a train northward ; and I passed the interim very agreeably, playing " All-fours" with an ugly gentleman who wore spectacles, and begged on three trumps.

Although this work is no " Traveler's Guide," as I have mildly insinuated before, I will favor the reader with a tabular statement of the cost of visiting the Mammoth Cave, making Louisville the starting-point :

From Louisville to Cave City...................... $4.00
Supper at..........."....."...................... 1.00
Night's repose at...."....."...................... 1.00
Breakfast at........."....."...................... 1.00
Coach from Cave City to Mammoth Cave,.......... 2.00
For guide, (paid to proprietor,).................... 2.00
Trifle presented to guide as mark of esteem,....... 1.00
Dinner at Mammoth Cave Hotel,................. 1.00
Coach back to Cave City,....................... 2.00
Supper at......"....."...................... 1.00
Playing "All-fours" with ugly gent. for lemonade,.. 1.00
Train back to Louisville,....................... 4.00
Incidentals,.... .... 5.00
Other incidentals,................................ 2.00
                                            _____
                                              $28.00

That was what it cost me, and I'll venture to say
that anyone, by being economical, can visit the Mammoth Cave from Louisville for the same amount.

CHAPTER XXXI.

THE NIGHTINGALE.

IN the course of my stay in Louisville, I had the pleasure of an introduction to George D. Prentice, Esquire, the well-known editor of the Louisville Journal ; and I found him as agreeable and good-natured as he is witty. He was engaged in writing a scathing article denunciatory of Parson Brownlow, at the time my friend and I entered his sanctum, and was in excellent spirits.

Perhaps no one of the many who have heard of the witty journalist, and read his writings, but have never seen him, has ever formed any correct impression of his personal appearance. He is quite homely, does not look half as bright as he really is, is noble-hearted, kind, affable, polite, and exhibits a partiality for grain products in a liquid form, at all seasons of the year. But this is nobody's business but his own.

About the middle of May, or a little later, perhaps, I took passage on the steamer Nightingale, for Saint Louis. The steamer was a stern-wheel one, pretty well loaded, and did not make very fast time ; but the weather was delightful, every thing on board was comfortable and pleasant, and, as I was in no hurry, I

could not have complained if the journey had occu
pied a week.

Fellow passengers on board a steamer soon make
themselves acquainted with each other, and I had not
been aboard twenty-four hours before the faces of all
were as familiar to me as though I had known them
for years. With but few exceptions they were agreeable persons. The captain was a handsome man of
twenty-eight or thirty, and one glance at him was
enough to convince any one that he was a true gentleman. All the *attaches* of the boat, including the
bartender and porter, were just what they should be.

Among the passengers was a fellow of twenty-
seven or twenty-eight, who called himself a Doctor.
He told me he was from New York, and was going to
Saint Louis to establish a practice for himself.

"I don't care," said he, "whether I am successful at
first or not. I have five thousand dollars in my
pocket, and that will keep me a year or so without my
doing much. By that time, I'll get myself worked
into a practice, no doubt."

"Certainly," I agreed.

He was not a fine-looking man, but he was obviously a vain fool, and one whom I thought I should
not like to trust further than I could throw a comet
by the tail. Every one called him "Doctor," and he
seémed to like it. I will say more of him by and by.

The sharer of my state-room—he occupied the
lower berth—was a venerable man of eighty years, a
native of Missouri. He was a man of finished education, and, by profession, a physician. He and I were
so much pleased with each other, that we have since

corresponded; and I have found his acquaintance truly edifying, as well as agreeable. His name was Crele.

Dr. Crele told me a sad tale of his troubles in Missouri during the war. He resided in Lafayette county, of that State, where old feuds held carnival during the desolating civil war. He had taken no part in the contest, in any way, he told me; and he said that his nearest and best friend on earth had lately been an only son of thirty years—whom he pictured to me as all that was manly, noble, pure, honorable, and worthy of a parent's fond affection. This son, he said, had studied for the ministry, had acquired a rare education, and, like himself, had taken no part in the war. But one bitter night, when he himself was seriously ill, and his son was sitting by his bedside, a party of armed men, headed by an old enemy of his family, abruptly burst into his house, and shot down that son—the last prop of his old age. One of the reckless and deluded men was going to shoot him, as he lay in bed, but another interrupted him, saying:

"Never mind the old white-headed reprobate. It isn't worth while. He'll soon die, anyhow."

So, sparing him a few dim years of bitterness, they ransacked the house, carried off all the valuables they could find, damaged much of the furniture, set the building on fire, and departed. The flames were extinguished by friendly neighbors, who came to his assistance, and who lifted up from a pool of blood the lifeless form of his son.

There were tears in the old man's eyes as he told

me this; and no wonder. His hair was white, his hand trembled, and his step was unsteady with age. He must have felt alone in the world.

I will not state which cause the villains professed to be attached to, who murdered the Doctor's son, and left him a blank and desolate old age. There were wrongs and outrages committed on both sides during the war. No reasonable person will fail to admit this. A civil war gives a horrible license to bad men; and God forbid that our land should ever be blighted by another.

Gambling was not allowed on board the Nightingale, but there was a good deal of euchre-playing, for amusement, during the voyage. At Evansville, Indiana, a flourishing town of eight thousand inhabitants, we landed for half-an-hour, and, while there, several passengers came aboard; among them was a well-dressed young man, with what I considered a bad countenance. He had cold, gray, almost expressionless "windows" for his "soul," to look out at, a smooth, beardless face, and a mouth with an unusually crescent-like shape.

This person had not been aboard very long— in fact, the boat had barely backed away from the landing and begun to move on down the river, when he suggested to a green-looking fellow that they should get up "a little four-handed game of euchre—just for amusement." Mr. Greeney assented; and inducing two other passengers to join them, they began to while away the time, as we glided down the river, "passing," "taking it up," "turning it down," "ordering it up," "assisting, "making it," "going it alone," and the like. If I remember correctly, Mr. Greeney and Mr. Sharper—I take the liberty of providing these names for them—were " partners."

Well, a game was played through, pleasantly enough, and another commenced: and, by and by, it was Mr. Sharper's deal, for the third time. There is something magical about that number *three.* "The third time is the charm," it is said. The third time a man does any particular thing, something unusual is sure to happen. This was no exception.

" My hand would be a good one if we were playing poker," observed Mr. Sharper, carelessly, as he took up his cards.

I chanced to be standing behind Mr. Greeney at the moment, and lo! as *he* picked up *his* cards, he, too, held no trifling poker hand: four kings and a seven-spot.

" I myself," said Mr. Greeney, " haven't a bad hand on poker."

" A pity we're not playing it then," Mr. Sharper lazily rejoined. " Well, what will you do ?" He addressed this pointed inquiry to the player on his left.

" I pass," replied the latter.

" I pass," said Mr. Greeney.

" I pass," repeated the player on Mr. Greeney's left and Mr. Sharper's right.

" I turn it down," said Mr. Sharper, adroitly whirling the face of the trump card downward. " Who will make it ?"

" I won't," said the player on his left.

" I won't " said Mr. Greeney. " But—but—"

15

"Well, what is it?" said Mr. Sharper, in a tone
barely tinged with impatience.

"Why," rejoined Mr. Greeney, with a frankness
that spoke better for his heart than his head, "I just
wish it was poker!"

"Why?" asked Mr. Sharper.

"Because, I'd bet some—"

"Well," suggested Mr. Sharper, with a careless
yawn, "we might get up a little bet on our hands,
anyhow, just to pass away the time. I've felt dull
for the last half-hour, I'd risk something on my hand,
if I were *sure* of losing. But I warn you, it is not a
bad hand. Have you all any thing like poker hands?
Come: a pair of deuces——"

"I haven't," said his left-hand man, interrupting him.

"Nor I," said his left-hand-man's partner, who sat
on his right.

"Well, darned if *I* haven't, though," said Mr.
Greeney.

"Have you, really?" responded Mr. Sharper.
"Well, I'll bet five dollars on my hand, win or lose."
And he carelessly threw upon the table a crumpled
five-dollar bill, which he took from his vest pocket.

Mr. Greeney got a little excited at this demonstration, laid his cards on the table, faces downwards,
of course, thrust his hand deep into his right-
hand trousers pocket, and nervously drew forth his
pocketbook.

"I'll cover your five dollars, and go five dollars
better," he said, with firmness, as he laid down a ten-
dollar bill.

Who wouldn't have ventured something on four

kings—next to the best hand in the pack—that had thus come out by chance, while playing euchre for amusement?

"You do?" said Mr. Sharper, glancing up and down the cabin. "Now, the captain wouldn't allow—however, he isn't about. I didn't think of risking more than five dollars, but I guess you are trying to bluff me. I'll not back out. Here's fifteen dollars more, and that makes the bet twenty." And he produced the amount specified.

"Ten dollars better still," said Mr. Greeney, promptly, as he laid down twenty dollars. It was quite clear he had played poker before.

Mr. Sharper hesitated. "Thirty dollars," said he. "I—no, confound it!—I'll put fifty on the top of it, and that's all I *will* risk!—No—or, yes; I've said it now, and will stick to it. It won't make me a bankrupt, if I *do* lose." Thereupon, he produced three twenty-dollar bills and laid them on the table—making the bet eighty dollars.

"I call you," said Mr. Greeney, eagerly, as he counted out five ten-dollar bills and threw them down upon the table.

"*Four aces,*" said Mr. Sharper, as he smilingly displayed the hateful four that can't be beat. "What have *you?*"

What could he have, in a case of that kind?

"Only four kings! Darn the luck!" poor Mr. Greeney exclaimed, in unfeigned vexation. Then he said, "Pshaw!" "The deuce on it!" "I'll be!——" and several other words, better and worse; while Mr. Sharper, with a calmness, complacence and benignity that one could not but admire, raked down the "pile," and stowed it away in his pocket.

"Well, whose deal is it?" said Mr. Sharper, who seemed to devote no further thought to the trifle he had won.

They finished that game of euchre—for amusement—then Mr. Greeney, with a most extraordinary expression of countenance, arose from his seat at the table, and, in a rather husky voice, said he believed he wouldn't play any more: he seemed to have lost all interest in the game : and he walked away *whistling.*

Whistling? Yes. But, O, what a dull, dry sort of a whistle he made of it! The sudden loss of eighty dollars is not very elevating to the spirits of a person in moderate circumstances; and who can say what the poor dupe suffered? Notwithstanding all his attempts to appear unconcerned, and to emit a forced whistle, it was plain that he was suffering no ordinary mental torture.

How remarkable it is, that when a man feels right bad, and don't want the fact made public, he tries to turn it off with *whistling!* There seems to be something soothing in a strain or two of this species of music, if only executed with any skill; but a man who is suffering inward "pangs," can rarely get the right "pucker" on his lips. Poor Mr. Greeney made a miserable whistle of it, and if he had wept aloud for his lost cash, he could not have more clearly exhibited his anguish to the unsympathizing spectators.

The game being ended, Mr. Sharper purchased a good cigar at the bar, lighted it, and, taking an armchair out upon the cabin deck, seated himself, rested his polished boots on the railing, and laid back in his chair, quietly smoking, and at the same time regarding the picturesque shores of the river, with a calmness and self-satisfaction that must have been agonizing for poor Mr. Greeney to look at.

When the Captain learned what had happened in the cabin, he went to Mr. Sharper, and told him he must leave the boat at Cairo, as soon as a landing could be conveniently effected, as he could not tolerate a gambler on his boat.

Mr. Sharper coolly replied that he had not intended to go further than Cairo, anyhow; but, if he had——

The Captain interrupted him with a friendly warning against any thing bordering on defiance or insolence. He remarked that he had not picked a blackleg or thief up by the neck and heels, and pitched him into the river, for nearly a year, and that he was beginning to feel marvelously like taking a bit of such exercise; and that he would assuredly do so, if so much as one more articulate sound should escape him (Mr. Sharper). The latter appreciated the warning, and during the remainder of his stay on board the Nightingale, maintained a commendable silence.

At Cairo, where the Ohio river empties into the Mississippi, we landed, and laid for a couple of hours, before proceeding up the broad Mississippi; and Mr. Sharper promptly left us.

Cairo is a city of about twelve thousand inhabitants, and but for the unhealthy nature of the low country surrounding, it would eventually become one of the greatest cities of the Mississippi Valley. Its geographic location is one of the best in the country, being, as it is, at the junction of two noble rivers. But in that vicinity, the land is so low that it becomes inundated for many miles around; so that the air, especially in the summer season, becomes fraught with miasma. Cairo itself is built on very low ground, and but for the high levee, that stands as a perpetual sentinel before the gates of the city, the river would be continually staring in at all the doors and windows in the place. Even the levee is overflowed sometimes, and the streets become navigable for boats of moderate size.

I went up to a periodical store, on the principal street, and purchased several newspapers of a late date. Among them was a Louisville Journal; and, on casting my eye over it, what was my astonishment to run across a very flattering notice of myself, which Mr. Prentice had inserted. It stated that "J. Smith, Esquire, the celebrated author and poet, who had lost a limb in the civil war, was making a tour of the Western States; had honored both him and the Mammoth Cave with a visit, and had just departed for Saint Louis, on board the steamer Nightingale!!!"

This really alarmed me, and I fancied that every one who looked at me recognized me as the redoubtable John Smith, the "celebrated author and poet," who was "making a tour of the Western States."

Fearing that some enthusiastic demonstration might be made by the citizens of Cairo, who had probably read of my approach, and that I might be called upon for a speech—and I hadn't as much as the framework of one ready—I hastily returned to the boat, and shut myself up in my stateroom, and did not sally forth again till the Nightingale was steaming gallantly up the Mississippi.

Nothing worthy of note occurred during our voyage up the river, except that the mosquitoes tormented us in a style entirely new to me. They were about the first crop of the season, fresh and vigorous, and they attacked the boat in numbers amounting to millions of millions. O, the misery of that night! How the little fiends tormented me! Warm as it was, I shut myself up almost air-tight in my stateroom and tried to defy them. I thought I would rather be smothered to death than eaten up alive. But even there they found me. They came in through the keyhole, in two ranks, military order, and at once began the attack. I fought bravely, but it was of no use. Faster than I could cut them down, they received reinforcements through the keyhole—while, to utterly dishearten me, and drive me to despair, I could hear myriads of them still without, knocking at the door, and impatiently waiting their respective turns to file in at the key-hole and drink some of me.

I could not stand it. I opened the back door and fled—fled to the cabin deck—to the hurricane deck— to the boiler deck—up stairs and down—and down and up—and back and forth, and forth and back, half crazed—I knew not, cared not, where! I had half a mind to jump into the river, and take refuge from these and my other woes in the bosom of the Father of Waters—but didn't.

They pursued me everywhere; some of them, I believe, went in advance of me, to be ready to meet me at any new point I should flee to. My eyes, ears,

mouth, nose, cheeks, chin, neck, hands and wrists
were covered with them; and, while thus tormenting
me, they sang musically in my ears, even as Nero
played "Hail Columbia, happy land!" on a banjo,
while Rome was burning. O, the agonies of that
night! The thundering cannon of battle, the shriek-
ing shell, the hissing bullet, and glistening bayonet,
are mere toys compared with these fiendish tor-
mentors! How I ever got through the night I cannot
remember distinctly. It seems like a kind of long-con-
tinued dream to me. I have a vague recollection of
standing at the bar and asking the bar-tender if he
had "anything calculated to keep the mosquitoes
away?" This scene recurs to me as having been repeated several times that night; but I think it only
originated in the imagery of delirium—for I must
have grown delirious.

The next night, for some reason, they "let up" on
us a little, and I got some sleep; and early on the
second morning after leaving Cairo, we arrived at the
"Mound City," Saint Louis, the chief city of the Mississippi Valley. It was a charming morning, not too
warm, and leaving my trunk on board, I walked up
into the city for the purpose of securing lodgings for
a month. Before I did so, the passengers had all bid
each other good-by, and were beginning to go their
different ways, wondering if any two of us should
ever meet again.

My aged companion bade me a cordial farewell,
and took passage on the steamer "Post Boy," bound
up the Missouri river.

The vain *young* "Doctor," whom I have mentioned,

went to the Southern Hotel—one of the grandest and most aristocratic in the country—and registered his name, stating that he would remain a couple of weeks. That I may not be troubled to speak again of so worthless a fellow, I will here state, that, a week after, I met another fellow-passenger in Saint Louis, who told me that the " Doctor" had stayed four days at the Southern Hotel, and then absconded without paying his bill. This most pretentious and presumptuous of the passengers of the Nightingale, proved to be an unworthy loafer and a base fraud. Such is life !

CHAPTER XXXII.

SMITH'S EXTRAORDINARY ADVENTURES IN THE "MOUND CITY."

WE had landed at the foot of Pine street, which I followed directly up into the city. I was just about to cross Third street, when my attention was irresistibly attracted to a very beautiful girl of eighteen, who came walking down Third, on the lower side, and turned to cross and go up Pine street but a few feet in advance of me. I was just thinking how happy a man her husband would be, in case she should ever take it into her head to get one, when, as she reached the opposite corner, a man standing in the door of a periodical store near the corner, called to his dog, which had strayed across the street. The dog was a fine, large, sleek, spotted, good-natured, intelligent-looking fellow, dressed in a burnished brass collar. He wore a pleasant smile on his sagacious face, and looked as though he wouldn't harm a flea that was biting him. With all the ready obedience of the faithful animal, he came bounding toward his master just as the young lady in question arrived opposite the door. It appeared that she had not observed the owner of the dog, or heard him call to his property; and seeing the animal come bouncing toward her, she

"She uttered a musical scream, whirled around and came in direct contact with me, the shock nearly knocking me down."—*Smith in St. Louis. Page 235.*

naturally imagined that the sagacious creature was "going for" her—and how did she know but that he was afflicted with chronic hydrophobia? On the impulse of the moment, she uttered a musical scream, whirled around to rush back across Third street, and came in direct contact with me. It was so sudden, and unexpected, that the shock came near knocking me down under a cart-wheel as the heavy vehicle went jogging by, near the curbstone; and, to make the matter worse, she slipped on a bit of orange-rind, and we came near falling down together, all mixed-up. To prevent this catastrophe, I instinctively clasped her waist in my encircling arms, while she, on the spur of the moment, threw her plump arms confidingly around my manly neck! And there we stood, at one of the most public street-corners of Saint Louis, unconsciously embracing, like two gentle lovers that hadn't seen each other for a month of Sundays.

"O!—O!—O-o-oo-oo!" she exclaimed; "excuse me! I was so afraid of that dog!"

"He shall not hurt you," I gallantly replied, as I released her from my protecting arms, and picked up my cane, which had fallen in the confusion.

"I declare!" she said, blushing confusedly,—I have always thought this was because she perceived that I was young and handsome—"I might have pushed you over! I'm sorry! Did I hurt you?"

"O, no!" I replied warmly, wondering at the same time whether she meant she was *sorry* she hadn't pushed me over; "I was only anxious on *your* ac-

count. I am happy that it was my privilege to save
you from falling, when you slipped."

"Thank you; but it wouldn't have hurt *me*. If
you had fallen, though—and you—you"—

She was going to allude to the trifling circumstance that I lacked one of the usual number of legs,
but, with some delicacy, hesitated.

"O, it wouldn't have hurt me," I said, coming to
her relief; "there isn't so much of me to fall now
and I, therefore, don't fall so hard as others."

As we were both going up Pine street, we walked
on, side by side, and I had the pleasure of her company for four squares. We walked slowly, too. I
could have walked four hundred squares, if she had
kept on; but when we reached Seventh street, she
told me she lived just around the corner. Thereupon, we bade each other an affectionate farewell and
parted.

I crossed Seventh street and walked about half
way to Eighth, when, thinking that the young lady
had had time to get out of sight, I retraced my steps.
After I had gone a little way below Seventh, I des-
cried a card on a door, containing the following
notice :

"FURNISHED ROOMS TO LET."

I rang the door-bell, was soon shown in, and,
stating that I desired a lodging-room for three or
four weeks, was shown a neat, well-furnished room
on the second floor, which the landlady said was
worth five dollars a week, and would be very suita-
ble for a gentleman and wife. I stated that I would
occupy it alone, gave the landlady twenty dollars for

four weeks' possession of the room, then went down to the boat and sent my trunk up by an express wagon.

I was again walking up Pine street, and once more crossing Third, when some one tapped me on the shoulder, and a voice behind me exclaimed,

" Why, Smith! is this you?"

I turned, stating that it was—for I never ignored my proud name—and beheld a familiar face. It was that of one whom I had known when a boy, but had not seen for some years. His history is somewhat remarkable. When I knew him in my youth, he was a young man of twenty years, and quite proverbial for his piety. He was often pointed out, to the profligate youth of the village I lived in, as a shining example of Christianity, and he was, in truth—or seemed—so sober, honest, and good, as to put ordinary young fellows to shame, by comparison.

His name was Albert Hague. His occupation was that of salesman in a dry-goods store ; and such confidence did he ever command, that his employers trusted him implicitly with everything about their stores—safe-keys, cash accounts, and the like. By and by, however, much to the astonishment and amazement of all who knew him, he actually stole ten thousand dollars from his employer, and absconded. From that time forth, nothing, to my knowledge, had been heard of him in the old neighborhood; and this was the man I unexpectedly met in Saint Louis.

" Why, Bert!" I exclaimed, shaking hands with him—for I was truly glad to meet any familiar face in a strange city—"is this you? Where do you come from?"

"I am living here," he said. "I saw you crossing the street, and did not know whether to hail you or not. I fancied that, after what you know of me, you would not speak to me."

"Then you do not know me," I replied. "You never injured me, if you did commit a grievous offense. It is a great mistake to cast every one down as soon as he commits an error. It is no way to recover him. It only discourages him, and renders him indifferent about reforming.—I have just hired a room on Pine street. Come with me, and tell me all about it."

We walked up Pine street, and were soon sitting in my room. There he told me all that had happened to him. He had eluded the law, and fled with his ill-gotten ten thousand dollars to California, where, he said, he saw no rest, day or night. He declared that when I knew him as a pious young man, he was all that he appeared to be; but said that, by and by, he began to be tempted to take advantage of the excellent opportunity he had to acquire a large amount of money; and, in an evil moment, yielded.

He did not remain in California three weeks, he said, before his conscience compelled him to return to Pennsylvania and restore the ill-gotten cash to its owner; which, he said, he had recently done.

He had now determined, he remarked, never to yield to temptation again, and was resolved to atone for the past by a future life of integrity and uprightness; he now had a position as salesman in a wholesale house in Saint Louis, and was doing well. He gave me the name of the house, and asked me to call and see him. He remarked that he could freely confide in one who had so readily overlooked his former disgrace.

I replied that, as a matter of course, it would injure him for his employers to know his past history, that I believed he was sincere in his good resolution, and that he need not feel apprehensive that I should ever cast a stumbling-block in his way.

The strictly "pious," with the blindness that too often characterizes them, may censure me for not warning his employers; but let them do so. Do they think, that when a man commits one crime, he is necessarily lost, forever? Suppose I should have regarded it as a duty to go to his employers and tell them what I knew of Hague? He would have been discharged at once, because they could never have relied on him. He would then have despaired of recovering from the effects of that one error; and no matter how good his intentions might have been, while his prospects were bright, he would, probably, have turned a rogue again, on the first opportunity, because he had no other alternative.

It is a fearful mistake to thrust a man down at once, for his first crime, instead of taking him by the hand and lifting him up: it is that unchristian-like policy that fills our penitentiaries, and gives such frequent employment to the hangman. Frown on vice as much as you please; but do not frown on all who once yield to temptation. If you hope or wish to save them, display some forbearance. Remember we all have our faults. And we are all only too apt to

"Compound for sins we are inclined to,
By damning those we have no mind to,"—

as Hudibras says.

"There is none good: no, not one." We have all
committed bad deeds, of some kind or other, whether
they come within the pale of the law or not. If you
demand strict *justice*, look to yourself. "Use every
man after his desert," says Hamlet, "and who shall
'scape whipping?"

My pious friends, remember that none of you are
quite perfect. Remember, that if there is a God,—
"And that there is, all Nature cries aloud!"—His
eye is upon you; and if you cannot tolerate your
fellow-creatures, simply because their sins happen to
be of a different class from yours—though probably
no worse—how can you expect Him to bear with
you?

I did not remove from Saint Louis for four weeks,
and during that time made a number of little excur-
sions into the interior of the state, and also into the
state of Illinois, which lies on the east side of the
river.

I liked the "Mound City" very well. As it may
not be generally known why Saint Louis is styled
the "Mound City," I will state that it is because the
ground on which it is built was once occupied by
numerous artificial mounds, supposed to have been
built by the Indians.

It may not be out of place, either, to say a word
regarding the pronunciation of the name of the city.
I observed that all the citizens give it the old French
pronunciation—that is, Saint Loo-ee—the final "s" not

being sounded. It should be so pronounced by all, as the citizens of a place are generally accepted as authority in such matters. I observed the same fact in Louisville, Kentucky. The citizens there pronounce it Lou-ee-ville. It would sound harsh to them to hear it pronounced as it is spelled—Lou-is-ville. The sibilant sound of the "s" would make the drums of their ears quiver.

I was not at first favorably impressed with the water in Saint Louis; but I soon became fond even of that. The water is taken from the Mississippi river, and is always very muddy. Let an ordinary bucketful of it stand awhile, and an inch of "mire" will settle on the bottom. This muddy state of the fluid is owing to the turbid Missouri river, which empties into the Mississippi twenty miles above Saint Louis. Chemically, however, this water has been pronounced, by scientific men, the purest in the country. It is said to be perfectly free from all deleterious minerals, and, when the mud is taken from it, is as nearly pure water as can be produced.

The fire arrangements in Saint Louis, as in most western cities, are very imperfect. While there, it was my luck one day—and I had had the same luck in Louisville, where I made the same observations—to stand in the immediate presence of a destructive fire, when it first broke out. A heavy volume of black smoke rolled up toward the blue sky, the flames burst out through roofs and windows, and leaped for mad joy, walls crumbled down at their leisure, and I think that twenty-five minutes or half-

16

an-hour elapsed before any steamer or hose-carriage made its appearance. I do not attach so much blame to the firemen themselves—although they are not so active as New York or Philadelphia firemen—as to the deficiency of the force. On this occasion I was told that the same firemen had been working all the afternoon, at a fire in a distant part of the city, and I could not wonder that they were a little tardy. Their force should be at least doubled—but I think they will realize this ere long. Louisville and Saint Louis are now fast recovering from the paralyzing effects of the recent unhappy war; they do not lack enterprise; and I predict that in a few years their arrangements for protecting property against the flames will be equal to those of the eastern cities.

CHAPTER XXXIII.

ʜOW NOT TO ᴏPEN A ᴘATENT ʟOCK.

WISHING to visit some portions of Iowa, I started up the Mississippi in June, on a boat running regularly between Saint Louis and Keokuk, an Iowa town or city with a population of eight thousand, situated at the mouth of the Des Moines river. It is two hundred and twenty-four miles above Saint Louis.

Only one funny thing happened during my voyage from Saint Louis to Keokuk, and, probably, one of the parties concerned could not, have been led to agree that even that was funny. It occurred during the day following our departure from Saint Louis, while the boat was lying at the landing at Quincy, a city of twenty-five thousand souls, on the Illinois shore.

The boat laid there for half an-hour; I know not what for, as no freight was being shipped or put ashore. During that brief half-hour, two sharpers came aboard. They were confederates, or "pals," but pretended not to know each other. In fact, one of them, whom I shall style Number One—although they were both *number one* rogues—came aboard a few minutes before the other, whom I shall call Number Two. He did not go up to the cabin deck, but stood on the boiler deck, talking with the deck-hands —most of whom were darkeys—and asking such questions as were calculated to convince any one that he was badly green.

By and by, Number Two, Esquire, came aboard, carrying a kind of padlock in his hand, and, with a respectful manner, said to Number One.

"My friend, can you tell me how soon this boat will go up the river?"

"No, sir," replied Number One; "I just came aboard."

"She go up de riber in a little bit," put in one of the darkeys that were lounging idly about the bulk-head.

"Thank you," said Number Two, who appeared to be a perfect gentleman. He was walking up the steps leading to the cabin deck, when Number One called out:

"Stranger—excuse me—but are you the gentleman I saw up in town with the new patent lock?"

"Yes," returned Number Two, pausing on the stairs: "this is it."

"Would you be kind enough to let me look at it?"

"Certainly," returned Number Two, with an obliging air, as he descended the stairs.

"Perhaps," suggested Number One, "you are in a hurry, and—"

"O, no," replied Number Two; "not at all. I intend to take passage on the boat, and I can go up to the office at any time and pay my fare." And he handed Number One the lock.

"I believe I heard you say," observed Number

One, as he began to inspect it, "that this is your own invention."

"It is," replied Number Two.

"Have you a patent for it?"

"Yes, it was patented but lately."

The deck-hands and several passengers, who happened to be strolling about the lower deck, now collected around and gazed on the lock with curious eyes.

"Did I understand you to say," queried Number One, "that no key is used to open the lock?"

"Correct. No key is required, I can simply take it, shoot the ring-bolt into its place, and I'll bet any man a hundred dollars that he can't open it."

The spectators looked on with increased interest.

"Lock it for me," said Number One, handing it back to the owner. "I would like to try it."

"Certainly." Number Two took the lock—a spring-lock, apparently—shot the bolt into its place, with a snap, and returned it to Number One. "There," said he, "you'll be the sharpest man I ever saw if you open it."

The spectators now gathered around closer, and looked on with an interest that was intense.

Number One took the lock, inserted his finger in the ring-bolt and took a dead pull on it.

"It won't come open that way," he remarked, as he pretended to scan it more closely.

"No," replied Number Two; "you might as well pull against two yoke of oxen."

Presently, Number One appeared to discover a slight,—almost imperceptible,—protuberance, which looked as though it might connect with a secret spring; and pressing this slyly, he opened the lock, and handed it back to Number Two, with an air of triumph.

"There," said he; "when you invent another lock, bring it to me and I'll open it for you."

A loud laugh went round at the expense of Number Two, who seemed much disconcerted.

"Ha, ha, ha," laughed an ebony deck-hand. "If all de locks was dat easy opened a fellah's prwopehty wouldn't be very safe."

"*You* can't open it," retorted Number Two, a little irritated.

"What'll you bet?" said darkey.

"I'll bet a hundred dollars you can't," said Number Two, whom discomfiture seemed to have rendered reckless.

"Will you bet *me* a hundred dollars that *I* can't open it?" asked Number One, boldly.

"No," returned Number Two. "You have opened it once, and know how; or else I would. Why didn't you bet before you tried it? you would have won then."

"I'm sorry I didn't now," said Number One.

"O, pshaw!" said the same darkey who had spoken before. "I seen how him opened it!"

"Well, *you* can't open it," retorted Number Two, banteringly.

"An' will you bet me a hundred dollahs I can't?" said the darkey, on whose black face I could read *enterprise*.

I happened to be sitting by the railing of the cabin

deck just above, and could look down and witness the whole scene.

"Why—I—yes—yes, I will," stammered Number Two, with well-feigned hesitation.

"You'll lose then," Number One said, in a low tone, as though speaking to himself.

"Will you put up de money?" pursued the darkey.

"I—why wouldn't—yes, I will. I won't be backed out, even if I lose. I'll put up the money in the hands of this gentleman or any one else." When he said "this gentleman," he pointed to Number One.

"You had better not trust me with the stakes," said the latter jocosely, "I might run off."

"O, no fear of that," replied Number Two. "We'll trust you. I know a *gentleman* when I see one."

"By golly!—I—I bet," said the darkey, decidedly. And he produced a fifty-dollar bill and some odd tens and fives amounting in all to one hundred dollars; and he handed the money to Number One, who was to act as stake holder.

"Come, now," said another darkey, to Number Two, as the latter hesitated. "Don't back out. Put up your money."

"Confound me if I'll be backed out!" he said, as he took out his pocket-book, counted out one hundred dollars and handed it to the stake-holder.

O, that money was in precious hands!

"Now," said the darkey, who had made up his mind to win or lose one hundred dollars, "fix de lock fur me."

Number Two "fixed" it.

The darkey took it, and first, merely as a matter of

form, took a pull at the ring-bolt. It would not open, of course. Well, no matter: *he* knew where that "secret spring" was. You bet! He easily found the little protuberance, and pressed on it with his thumb. But it wouldn't open. He pressed harder. No go. He pressed harder still, and pulled harder at the ring-bolt, at the same time. Bootless. He pressed harder still and pulled harder still. Vain efforts. He got a little apprehensive and a little desperate. The sum of one hundred dollars was at stake. The lock *must* be opened. He inserted the ring-bolt between his white teeth, placed his thumb on the imaginary spring, and pulled and pressed, and pressed and pulled, with the energy of despair. The lock was firm : his efforts futile.

A laugh now went round at the poor darkey's expense; and he trembled, perceptibly, while his face assumed a sort of lead-color, with a greenish tinge. His thick lips also became quite void of moisture, and he spoke in a husky voice.

"Dun'no—dun'no—wedder I kin open him or not."

"I don't think you can," said Number Two, calmly.

The poor darkey saw that his "stamps" were gone. Still, he tried it once more. He shook the lock—and something loose within rattled with a taunting sound, tapped it against the capstan, pulled at the bolt, pressed the delusive spring, pulled and pressed, again and again. All was in vain. He gave it up; but, O, with what a poor grace! and handed the lock to Number Two.

"I b'lieve dah's som'in' wrong about it," said he.

"It seems, I've won the money," Number Two ob-

served, carelessly; and Number One handed him the
two hundred dollars.

Another laugh went round. O, the heartlessness
of human beings! What they would regard as a grave
misfortune, if it happened to themselves, they look
upon as an excellent joke when another is the victim.

"Dat's nuffin," said the darkey, trying to appear
unconcerned. But, O, how poorly he succeeded!

"Nothing, when you get used to it once," observed
one of the spectators, soothingly.

"But it takes a fellow a deuce of a time to get used
to it," put in another unfeeling passenger.

Poor darkey turned away, as sad a picture as I ever
saw, went and took a seat on the capstan, and tried to
whistle a careless tune. But his clumsy lips were
dry and unsteady, and he couldn't get them puckered
in any sort of shape.

"Confound if I haven't come near forgetting my
valise, with this fooling," said Number Two, abruptly,
after he had stowed away his money. "I left it up in
Quincy, and must go and get it." So, he walked
down the .gangway plank, up the wharf, and disappeared in the city.

"I wouldn't be surprised if that fellow were a
regular rogue," observed Number One, gazing after
him. "I intend to keep my eye on him." And he,
too, went ashore.

Soon after, the boat backed out from the landing,
and proceeded up the river; but neither Number One
nor Number Two were among the passengers.

CHAPTER XXXIV.

A GAME OF CHECKERS.

IN traveling up the Mississippi river, I could not help remarking that the Illinois shore was, with but few exceptions, very low—in many places not more than a foot or two above ordinary water, and, in some places, even submerged; while the western shore—that of Missouri and Iowa—was, with some exceptions, reasonably high.

Illinois is a low, swampy State, nearly all over. I have visited all portions of it, both the borders and the interior; and, excepting the vicinity of Peoria, and some few bluffs along the Mississippi river, the ground is low, flat, marshy, and evidently anything but salubrious. The soil, however, is as rich as any in the world; and things grow there in a way that would be quite novel to an eastern man. By and by, it will be drained, grow more healthy, and, perhaps, become the richest and most desirable State of the Mississippi Valley.

The most beautiful land I ever saw any where, was in Iowa, between Davenport, on the Mississippi shore, and Iowa City, in the interior. It is difficult to look upon that garden-like land, when clothed in its dress of summer, without actually breaking forth in words of admiration. It is slightly rolling—just enough so to relieve it from excess of water—the view is little obstructed by timber; and one can stand on a somewhat elevated point, and see for eight or ten miles in any direction—see the smooth green fields spread out before him, like the face of the ocean, till they fade in dimness and kiss the blue sky at the distant horizon!

But, in winter, stay away from these regions, with all their beauty, unless you are fond of being frozen; for the winter winds there can split a tough white-oak into rails, in no time, and fire itself couldn't stand it long out-of-doors, without being frozen into icicles. Even their thermometers cannot stand it out-of-doors. They are obliged to hang them by the stove or fire-place—where they make it a point to keep the temperature of the air as high as twenty-five or thirty degrees *be'ow* zero.

But this is a digression I did not intend.

At Keokuk, I stayed all night, and, next morning, took an early train for Fort Madison, a flourishing town situated at the head of the Rapids, twenty-five miles above Keokuk. Not every one is aware that the navigation of the Mississippi is obstructed for some miles above Keokuk, by extensive rapids, in the course of which the water falls considerably. Yet such is the case. To obviate the difficulty, a railroad has been constructed from Keokuk to Fort Madison, where the traveler takes another boat up the river. When the water is high, however, boats of any size go over the rapids, as they do over the Falls of the Ohio at Louisville.

In the car, a gentleman, who was a native of Iowa, occupied the same seat with me. Noticing that I had a checker-board in my hand, which I had taken out of my trunk while on board the boat, the previous day, he said :

" Do you play checkers ?"

" A little," I replied. " Do you ?"

"I don't often get beat," was his modest (?) rejoin-der.

" Will you take the boat at Fort Madison ?"

" Yes."

" Then, if you desire, we will play a game or two, when we get aboard."

"I was just about to make the same proposition," he returned.

The train had not proceeded far, when, as we were passing a saw-mill, we saw a man, who had charge of a yoke of oxen, standing, with open mouth, gazing upon the train, and staring the very locomotive out of countenance.   He was one of the homeliest men I ever saw.   My companion and I had had some con-versation with two lively young ladies, who occupied the seat in front of us, and one of them remarked :

" What a singular-looking man !"

The other laughed.

" He isn't a very pretty man, is he ?" said I.

" No," retorted my male companion, who probably thought this (because he knew me to be from Penn-sylvania,) a thrust at Iowa generally, " he looks like a Pennsylvanian." This, he certainly meant for a hit at the old Keystone State.

I said nothing, however, but silently determined to

have revenge at checkers, when we should get on the boat—unless my companion should prove to be a remarkable player.

So, when we had embarked at Fort Madison, and were gliding up the river. I saw the Iowa gentleman sauntering through the cabin, and said:

" Are you ready for that game of checkers?"

" O, yes," he replied; "I was looking for you."

We sat down by one of the tables, arranged the board and " men," and went at it. He moved with much circumspection, and was very careful lest he should make a blunder. But, with all his caution, he soon made one, which I quickly saw; and I gave him one of my men, took three of his in exchange, and hopped into the king-row.

" Pshaw!" he exclaimed, in a tone of vexation. "I wasn't watching!"

I soon won that game, and he didn't get a king.

" Let's try it again," said he. " I will do better next time."

" I hope so," I replied, as we replaced the men— but I *didn't* hope so.

This time he moved with more care than ever, and succeeded—in getting beaten as badly as before.

He tried it again and again, till we had played eight games, and I had won two-thirds of a dozen of them.

" I will not play any more," he said, petulantly, as he arose from the table. "I never met with such a player."

" I play the Pennsylvania game," I complacently observed.

I landed at Muscatine, Iowa, that evening, where I remained all night. Muscatine is about thirty miles below Davenport, and is called a city. Its population is eight or ten thousand.

Next morning, I took an early train for Wilton, a flourishing town situated at the intersection of two railroads, in the interior of the State. I visited some relatives there, and passed a week or two with them very pleasantly.

CHAPTER XXXV.

JOHN IN CHICAGO.

EARLY in July, having visited various sections of Iowa, I started one evening for Chicago, where I arrived next morning about daylight—the distance from Wilton being a little over two hundred miles.

Chicago is styled the "Garden City," because handsome private gardens are attached to many of the residences. There are other cities, however, which, for the same reason, are equally entitled to the sobriquet.

Chicago is much the largest city of the northwest. It has sprung up faster than any other, and has now a population of about two hundred and ten thousand. It is situated in North-eastern Illinois, on the shore of Lake Michigan. It is one of the liveliest cities in the country, and must always be the largest city of the Mississippi Valley, except Saint Louis, which will naturally stand number one, on account of the numerous advantages of its position.

An appropriate sobriquet for Chicago, I think, would be "City of Boards"—because it is built chiefly of boards. Most of the houses are frame buildings, weather-boarded; the sidewalks are nearly

all composed of thick pine boards; and the streets
are paved with the "Nicholson pavement." The
sidewalks are raised some feet above what was once
the original height of the ground, leaving many dirty
caverns beneath—an arrangement highly gratifying
to the rats. The rat population of Chicago is supposed to amount to about one hundred to each in-
habitant of the *genus homo*, which would make their
whole number about twenty-one millions. As Josh
Billings remarks, " This shows at a glance how many
waste rats there is." They are very playful, especially about eleven o'clock, when one is going home
from the theater. One night, returning from Crosby's
Opera House, I counted all I saw on my way to my
lodging-house. I had but three or four squares to
go, however, and therefore only counted eighteen.
Of these, I succeeded in knocking only two over with
my cane, by way of amusement.

As I had done in Cincinnati and Saint Louis, I
hired a lodging-room, and took my meals at a restaurant. The room was a very good one, in a house on
Dearborn street, opposite the Post office.

I spent some weeks quite pleasantly in the " Garden City," during which, the only very funny thing
that happened to me, was my nearly getting drowned
in Lake Michigan. My love of rowing led to this.
On a beautiful moonlight evening, two young ladies,
and a young gentleman who lived in the same house,
went down with me to the lake, and we hired a row-
boat.

We seated ourselves comfortably in the boat—I
taking the oars—glided away from the shore, and

were soon outside of the breakwater, where the full moon, rising in the eastern sky, made an endless path of quivering and shining silver over the limpid waves. The air was still, balmy and pleasant on the water. But the wind had been blowing that day, the waters were agitated, and the waves rolled considerably. When we were two miles from shore, we lay-to for a time ; and while the waves rocked us about, in a playful manner, the two young ladies and the gentleman—I never sing—sung a beautiful song, which, the murmuring of the lake blending with it, and the beauty of the evening, rendered quite enchanting. When they ceased singing, one of the young ladies said :

" I wonder if I could row ?"

" I have no doubt of it," I responded; " did you ever try it ?"

" No, never."

" Then," I rejoined, " it is possible you are an excellent rower, and have never given yourself an opportunity to discover it. Will you try it ?"

" I'm afraid," she said, timidly.

" Nothing to fear," I urged; " the oars are stationary in the row-locks, and you cannot lose them. Moreover, there is no wind or tide, and the boat cannot run away with you."

Thus encouraged, she said " I believe I'll try it."

" Then let us exchange seats," said I.

" Well."

She was sitting aft, and as we moved to exchange seats, we awkwardly attempted to pass each other on the same side of the boat thus throwing too much

17

weight on the port gunwale, and destroying the equilibrium of the boat and all the crew. Just then, too, a fine, fresh, unusually large wave came rolling along. The lady caught at the side of the boat as she lost her balance, but missed it, and pitched out! The boat dipped; the wave swept over, nearly filling it with the pure waters of the lake; and a wild scream of terror from the other lady lent interest to the scene.

I seized the unfortunate one in time, dragged her into the boat and called quickly to the gentleman to go to bailing, and never mind the price of hats. He wore a fine silk castor that held a gallon or so, and it was refreshing to see the way he began bailing with it. I hastily turned the head of the boat toward the waves, and we rose with the next one. Managing to keep her straight with one oar, I took my "beaver" in the other hand, and went to bailing for dear life. Meantime, the two ladies were trembling with terror, one of them coughing, sneezing and strangling, too—and uttering brief impromptu prayers, such as "Lord, save us!" and the like.

I assured them there was not the slightest danger—that the water was not deep there anyhow, that I could reach the bottom with an ordinary poker—I meant by jumping out and diving with it, though—and I succeeded in restoring their nerves to something like composure.

As we were all soaking wet, from top to toe—and especially the young lady who had taken an involuntary dive into the deep-green waters—we began to steer for the "Garden City," which we reached with thankful hearts, wet clothes and hats utterly ruined.

As the others stepped out of the boat before me, I observed that, with the exception of my person, it was entirely empty, and said :

" Where in the deuce is my crutch ?"

" Isn't it in the boat ?" responded the young gentleman, who stood on the shore.

I will never forget the picture he presented, as he stood there in the moonlight. His ruined hat was on his head, and it had lost all its stiffening, the nap was no longer sleek, smooth and shiny, but was rumpled and crooked, and stuck out in all directions; while the now pliable crown was crushed down till it rested on his cranium, like a wet dishcloth laid on the top of his head, and looked as though it had been beaten down by a terrific hail-storm. The dull, lifeless, lead-like way in which his garments hung about him may be imagined.

" Your crutch ?" said he. " Can it be possible that it fell out when the boat tipped ?"

" Blazes !" I exclaimed. " How will I get home ?"

I might have hopped all the way—four squares— but that novel mode of locomotion would have attracted public attention and placed me in an undignified light.

" Here it is," said one of the girls, laughing. " I took it out when I left the boat." And, much to my relief and delight, she handed it to me.

The other young lady also handed me my cane, which she had picked up on leaving the boat.

" You had better believe I was glad, if you are fond

of being correct in your opinion, for I was just making up my mind to row out upon the Lake again, and look for my crutch, as I thought it possible I might find it floating about somewhere. I would have had a wide bit of territory to canvass.

CHAPTER XXXVI.

TRAVELING COMPANIONS.

ABOUT the middle of July, I resolved to return to Philadelphia before completing my tour; and one evening I took an express train for Pittsburg, *via* the Pittsburg, Fort Wayne and Chicago Railroad. The train was not crowded, and each passenger in the car I was in had a whole seat to himself.

We had traveled about a hundred miles, and were rolling across the State of Indiana, in the darkness of night, when two persons got on at a station, some-where, came to the middle of the car, and one took a seat beside me, while the other sat immediately in front. I glanced casually at my companion, and had not the slightest difficulty in making out that he was a sharper.

"This is a fine evening," he said to me, politely, as the train thundered onward.

"Very," I replied.

Let it be borne in mind, however, that he had no special reason for stating, nor I for agreeing, that it was a "fine evening." On the contrary, it was dark and cloudy, and looked like rain.

"How far are you going?" he asked.

"To Philadelphia," I frankly replied.

"Ah? So am I."

"Do you live there?" I queried.

"No; but I have an uncle there—a merchant——"

"What street?" I asked, pertly.

"Why—I—O, yes! Market street." He then changed the subject, and said: "I see you have lost a leg."

"Yes," I assented.

"In the war, I suppose?"

"Yes."

"Ah!" he pursued, with earnestness, "many noble youths have made this sacrifice for their country, and I hope they will never be forgotten."

"I hope so, truly," I replied.

"I know," he went on, "that you must find it very inconvenient traveling, in your condition—especially when it comes to changing cars, and the like—and I was going to suggest that I would remain with you till we reach Philadelphia, and render you any assistance——"

"Thank you," I interrupted. "The truth is, I used to get around very clumsily, when I had two feet to take care of; but now, having got rid of one of the encumbrances, I get about astonishingly well. If you knew how convenient it is to have but one leg to take care of, you wouldn't retain both yours a week. You'd have one of them sawed off, sir. You would indeed."

Mr. Sharper began to see that I wasn't his man, and he presently got up and took a seat just in front of his pal. On the same seat was a young man who evidently had not made a regular business of traveling, and with him Mr. Sharper struck up an animated conversation, soon gaining his confidence. By and by, he introduced a very curious puzzle, with two cups and ivory balls, which he said he had bought that day from an Italian peddler with one eye, who had lost a brother and two wives in a storm at sea, on his way to this country. I was not near enough to see the exact construction of the cups and balls; but it was not long before he got up a bet about them, with the green traveler. His confederate, sitting on the seat between him and me, still pretending to be a stranger to him, made a sham bet of thirty dollars, and the other man on the same seat—also a man who had never been sharpened on the grindstone of experience—bet fifteen dollars. The money was put up in the hands of a passenger, and, of course, Sharper won. He and his confederate got off at the next station, each about twenty dollars "in;" leaving a couple of foolish passengers so much poorer, and, it is to be hoped, so much wiser.

Reader, in your travels, beware of friendly strangers. John Smith always bewares of 'em, and it pays.

A description of a forty hours' ride by railroad, would prove as tiresome to the reader as the ride always does to me. It is a delightful thing, in fine weather, to take a ride of fifty or a hundred miles on a train; to see the fields, and houses, and gardens, and barns. and woods, and fences flying past you, and to feel that lightning would get tired before it could catch you: but when you have to ride a thousand

miles, as I have often done, the thing becomes fright-
fully monotonous, and is any thing but a pastime.

Especially when night comes does the ride grow
tiresome. As for sleeping-cars, I have long since
vetoed *them*, as far as I am concerned. I decide that
they are a nuisance, and I believe the majority of
travelers will ratify and endorse my decision—and
thus render it legal. I never slept in one yet, that I
did not suffer all the time, either from heat or cold.
Such a thing as an even or moderate temperature, I
never experienced in a sleeping-car. Then the space!
To be stuffed, as tight as the wad in a pop-gun, into
a narrow cell, which they honor with the appellation
of "berth," a cell so narrow as to evoke unpleasant
contemplations of the anticipated long and narrow
home we must all go to; so narrow and contracted
that you haven't room for your elbows; so narrow that
you can't turn over without getting out upon the floor
for the purpose; so narrow and close that, as you lie
on your back, you are afraid to wink, lest you should
scrape your eyelids against the ceiling above you and
break the lashes off: to be crammed into a place like
this, I say, with an implied promise of repose, is the
opposite extreme of extraordinary felicity!

However, occupying a seat in a car, for a whole
night, is no delicacy, either; although I prefer it to
the "berth." How frequently one consults his time-
piece on such an occasion! I look at my watch, and
find it, say, twelve o'clock, P. M. Then I recline on
my seat and try to steal a little sleep. At first, I feel
quite comfortable, and fancy I can sleep in that position for several hours. But scarcely have I time to

draw a breath, before I find that my head does not rest quite comfortably against the window-sill or the back of the seat; I move it slightly; then I find that my arm is going asleep; I move it; then my ankle is twisted; I move it; then I find that my whole body is out of shape; I move, turn round and lie with my head the other way; then I close my eyes, and doze; I wake, presently, with a start; find my nose itching, and my leg asleep and beginning to tingle as though ten million insects were swarming in it; I then rub my eyes, think an hour has passed, look at my watch, and find it thirteen minutes after eleven. Find I made a mistake of an hour when I looked the other time.

At last, the night has dragged itself away; and, O, how welcome are the tips of morning's "rosy wings," as they flutter upon the horizon among the hills or over the plains! How welcome are the gray streaks that play in the east, ushering glorious morning upon the skies! How welcome the green fields again, as the curtain of the gloomy night is lifted from the face of Nature! I involuntarily exclaim with Shakspeare:

> " Look what streaks
> Do lace the severing clouds in yonder East!
> Night's candles are put out; and jocund day
> Stands tiptoe on the misty mountain top."

CHAPTER XXXVII.

MILWAUKEE AND THE LAKES.

I REMAINED in Philadelphia a month, then returned to Chicago, in order to begin where I left off and finish my tour. I only remained in the "Garden City" long enough to give my old friends there a call, and to get a slight attack of cholera; then moved northward. I went by railroad to Milwaukee, Wisconsin, a city with a population of sixty thousand, situated on the shore of Lake Michigan, about ninety miles from Chicago.

Milwaukee is remarkable for at least three things. First, it is built, almost exclusively, of a kind of yellow brick that presents a neat appearance I much admire. Second, the German element predominates in the population. In fact, I believe that fully three-fourths of the inhabitants are Germans. Third, the lager-beer there is of a superior quality. So superior is it, that it deserves more than a passing remark. It is everywhere conceded among intelligent persons, that Milwaukee produces the best lager-beer that is made in this country. It has such extraordinary "body." It has none of that resin-soap-and-old-boot taste, which we frequently have the misfortune to discover in beer; but is the pure, unadulterated, unsophisticated lager-beer, even such as nature intended it should be, when she produced the grain, hops and water to make it of. Beside, they give a fellow such a large glass there for five cents! The glass holds about a pint. I confess that I felt conscience-stricken whenever I took one, and only paid five cents for it. That was the price, however. I would have offered more, only I feared that I might be thought verdant; and John Smith does not desire to rest under such an imputation.

Early in September, I embarked for Detroit, Michigan, on the *St. Louis*, a handsome lake propeller, running between Chicago and Buffalo. Our route was *via* Lake Michigan, Fort Mackinaw, (in the straits,) Lake Huron, the St. Clair river, Lake St. Clair and the Detroit river. If you will take the trouble to glance at a map of the United States, dear reader, you will perceive that Lakes Huron and Michigan are two parallel lakes running north and south, and that they curve round and intersect each other at the north, forming an inverted letter U.

I look back upon my voyage on the Lakes, as the pleasantest of my life. Our vessel was a first-class steamer, the passengers were all jolly and good-natured, taken collectively; the ladies were amiable, affable and beautiful; and the gentleman were sober, intelligent, agreeable, and good judges of beer.

I will never forget my first evening on board the *St. Louis*. We were steering N. N. E. the western shore had just faded from view, and the sun was sinking into his rosy couch. A few light clouds hung over the horizon, like crimson and purple curtains, as the god of day sunk into his luxuriant bed of rest, reminding one of McDonald Clark's beautiful lines :

"Now twilight lets her curtain down
And pins it with a star."

The lake was nearly smooth, and the red light, making its lengthy paths over the wide waters, from west to east, looked like myriads of playful little flames chasing each other over the crests of the waves.

The sun rose next morning and smiled on us over the north-western shore of the State of Michigan, and we found ourselves approaching Mackinaw Straits. That afternoon the vessel laid for a couple of hours at an island in the Straits, and the passengers all went ashore. We discovered the earth to be about as nearly barren as any soil could be. Late as it was in the season, September, we found a few stunted raspberries, that were just making a feeble effort to ripen.

While the propeller lay there, half-a-dozen of the male passengers, I among them, hired a sailboat, and, accompanied by three or four of the lady passengers, took a pleasant sail of an hour. I think I never saw such clear water anywhere as I saw there. A pin could have been distinctly seen at the depth of twenty feet. I was so charmed with the limpid water, and the white sand and pebbles at the bottom, that I fancied it would have been almost a luxury to be drowned there.

That night we stopped for an hour at Fort Mackinaw.

Next morning—Sunday morning—we found ourselves in Lake Huron. Another beautiful day passed away in perfect harmony and happiness on board the *St. Louis*, and another night came. All this time the propeller glided along so smoothly that one could scarcely believe, at times, that she moved at all, till he should go out, look over the side, and see the green waters rushing by, and the waves receding from the prow on either side. I never slept anywhere more tranquilly than on board the *St. Louis*.

Next morning, we found ourselves in the St. Clair river, which runs north and south, and connects Lake Huron with Lake St. Clair. On its eastern shore is Canada, and on its western the State of Michigan.

About nine o'clock, we landed at the town of Newport, Michigan, the home of the captain. Being assured by him that she would lie there several hours, another passenger and myself went ashore and walked up into the town, with the view of hunting a billiard-table and playing a game or two. Some others also went ashore for a stroll.

We found one, and played one game. I do not remember who won it. What happened shortly after was calculated to rub out trifles from one's memory.

"Now," said I, when we had finished the game, "we had better go. Something tells me we will not have time to play another."

"O, pshaw!" replied my companion. "Didn't the captain tell us the boat would lie here several hours?"

"True, but I cannot help feeling uneasy."

"O, nonsense! let's play another."

We commenced another game, and had each made

fifteen or twenty points, when another fit of uneasiness seized me.

"Come," said I, something tells me the boat is ready to leave; I'll give you this game. Let us go."

"O, there's no danger of the boat's going," he replied. "It will whistle first, anyhow."

We played about seven minutes longer, when a boy came in.

"Bub," said I, "is the *St. Louis* lying at the landing yet?"

"Why," he replied, "did you 'uns, intend to go on her?"

"Yes," said I.

"Yonder she goes!" he said, coolly, as he pointed out the window looking down the river.

Yes, the *St. Louis* had gone, and was just disappearing round a bend nearly half a mile distant.

If the reader wants to know what pure, unalloyed anguish is, I can tell him that I experienced it on this occasion. There I was, fifty miles from my destination, and the propeller, on which I had spent several such happy days, gliding away and disappearing from my gaze, bearing from me the many good friends I had made among the passengers, whom I should now never, probably, see again, depriving me of the melancholy pleasure of bidding them good-by, and also of taking the address of a handsome young lady I fell in love with—to say nothing of my trunk, and some other articles I prized highly, scattered about in my state-room.

"I told you so," said I to my conscience-stricken companion.

He gazed from the window, threw down his cue, and pronounced a great many words, in rapid succession, which, if found in the Scriptures, are not found exactly in the same order in which he uttered them. His case was worse than mine. His destination was Buffalo; and should we fail to reach Detroit ere the propeller should leave there—and we had little hope in that direction—he would lose four hundred miles of his ride. Besides, he had left his overcoat and revolver in his state-room, and who should answer for their safety?

As for me, my trunk was checked to Detroit, and I felt sure that it would be put off there; but in my state-room were left my chess-board, a set of chessmen, and other property, amounting in all to the value of about fifteen dollars—and what hope had I of ever seeing them again? *Kein!*

" Well," said I, " let us make the best of it."

" Yes, we might as well finish the game now," said he, ruefully.

" First," I proposed, " let us drown our sorrows in a glass of beer."

" Agreed," said he.

And we did.

" There'll be another boat along soon," observed the boy.

" How soon ?" we both asked, eagerly.

" It ought to be here by eleven o'clock; that's its time."

" Does it run to Detroit ?"

" Yes; it's a little side-wheeler."

" Then we'll watch for it."

"If you will give me a glass of beer," said the boy, "I'll watch for it, and tell you when it comes."

"Very well, watch for it. Whenever you see it coming, run and tell us, and we'll give you the beer."

In less than half an hour, sure enough, we received the welcome intelligence that the boat was coming; and, giving the boy his beer, we hurried down to the landing, and reached it as the little steamer came up. We went aboard, and paid our fare to Detroit—another net loss of two dollars—and she soon moved on after the *St. Louis.* But we soon saw, with sinking hearts, that her speed was not equal to that of the propeller.

When we reached Lake St. Clair—a lake as round as a dollar, (or the city of Boston,) and twenty-five miles in diameter—we fancied we could see the *St. Louis* just sinking beneath the southern horizon. If we did, we never saw her again—at least *I* never did. When we reached Detroit, she had been gone half an hour. My trunk was there, but my other articles were clearly forfeited.

My companion and I got on the ferry-boat, went over to Windsor, Canada, just opposite Detroit, and inquired when the first train would depart for Buffalo. We were informed that an express-train would go at seven. He determined to go, and did so, no doubt, arriving at Buffalo a dozen hours in advance of the propeller. I have never heard of him since. I told him, when we parted, to go to my state-room when he should reach the propeller, and take possession of my chess-board, et cetera, remarking that I "willed" them to him; and I presume that he did so.

The ci*y of Detroit, where I remained a week, is about the size of Milwaukee, Wisconsin, and is the largest city in Michigan. It was there that Hull surrendered to the British, during the war of 1812 ; and it was there that the Fenians crossed into Canada and frightened the Canadians in 1866. So much for its historical importance. Its *sobriquet* is, " The City of the Straits." Its location on the Detroit river—which is, more properly, a *strait*, connecting Lake St. Clair with Lake Erie—gives it this name. Detroit is a French word for *strait*.

18

CHAPTER XXXVIII.

SMITH IN SEARCH OF HIS UNCLE.

FROM Detroit, I went, by railroad, to Toledo, Ohio, distant eighty or ninety miles. I stopped there with the view of visiting an uncle of mine, whom I had never seen, and who resided near a little village called Holland, nine miles from the city. I inquired a whole day for a village of that name, but no one knew where it was. I began to think of offering a reward for it; but at last went to the post-office, where I gained the desired information. I was told that Holland was a little place on the Air Line Railroad, and that it was also—and, in fact, regularly— called Springfield. I was furthermore told that the first train would go at ten o'clock that night.

As I did not contemplate remaining long at my uncle's, I left my trunk at an hotel in Toledo, and went out to Holland, *alias* Springfield, on that ten-o'clock train. It happened to be a naturally slow train, and, besides, it met with a little accident on the way; so that it was eleven o'clock when we reached Holland, which I found to be a little village, comprising a couple of dwelling-houses and a small grocery-store.

When I got off the train, it moved on, and I found

myself standing beside the track, alone—a "stranger in a strange land," at night-time. What was I to do? The village appeared to be wrapped in sleep, and not a light was to be seen. Presently, however, I looked toward Toledo, and saw a man—obviously an employé of the road—approaching me, carrying a red lantern in his hand.

"Good evening," said I.

"How do you do?" he returned, sleepily. "Did you just come up?"

"Yes—just got off the train."

"How did you—O, I thought it was Simon McCann," he said, as he drew nearer.

"No, I am not Simon," I replied. "On the contrary, my name is Smith—first name John. Do you know any one of that name here?"

What a question to ask anywhere in the world!

"O, yes; half-a-dozen families. There's old John, and——"

"Do you know William Smith?"   .

"Yes—quite an old man, is he not?"

"Probably he is. I never saw him. He moved here twenty-five years ago."

"From Pennsylvania?"

"Yes."

"Are you from Pennsylvania?"

"Yes; can you——"

"I see you've lost a"—I began to tremble now— "leg."

"Yes, can——"

"In the army?"

I shuddered at the thought of having to stand

there and answer four or five hundred questions, at
that time of night; and I determined, as I perceived
he was getting into a regular train of army questions,
to make a desperate attempt at insulation.

"Yes, can——"

"What battle?"

"Antietam where does——"

"What reg——"

I had already begun to ignore commas, and I now
saw the necessity of throwing out the spaces between
my words; and I hurriedly replied:

"Eighthpennsylvaniareserveswheredidyousaywil-
liamsmithlives?"

The spell was broken, and he responded, like a
white man:

"About two miles from here."

"Is there no hotel here?"

"None."

"No house of entertainment?"

"No."

"Is there any chance then to get a conveyance?"

"None that I know of."

"Then I must walk it.   Will you direct me to his
house?"

"Yes; you go——"

He gave me the directions, and they appeared so
plain that I fancied I could find my uncle's house
with my eyes shut.

The moon was just up, the night was beautiful and
pleasant, and the roads surpassingly muddy; and I
had a walk that night that, I think, will never "slip
my memory."   The land in this portion of Ohio is

low and flat, the soil black, loose and soft—very fertile, too, so far as that is concerned; but a man isn't particular about rich ground to walk on with a crutch—and the soundings were from three to thirty inches.

At the first cross-road, I went astray—took the wrong road, traveled half-a-mile on it, and, beginning to grow apprehensive, stopped by a gate, yelled, waked somebody's neighbor, and asked if that was the road to William Smith's?

"Did you come from the station?" was the response of the neighbor, who was in his night-dress.

"Yes."

"Then you are on the wrong road. You should have kept on toward the south at the cross-roads. It is at the next cross-road after that. Then you turn to the——" I thought he said—— "right."

"Thank you," I said. "Good-night."

"Good-night."

The door closed, and I was alone. I retraced my muddy way, followed closely by a large savage dog belonging to the owner of the house, while—the soil being unusually pliable there—my crutch sunk in eighteen inches at every step.

Before reaching my uncle's that night, I got off the wrong road, and on it again, five times, did two miles of superfluous walking and two miles of the requisite article, waked whole dozens of neighbors, and alarmed whole battalions of dogs. These faithful creatures barked furiously as I approached, and set others to barking, in response, at a distance, and *they* barked and set others to barking at another distance,

and they others, and so on, and so on, again; till I
must have indirectly and innocently aroused or disturbed the greater portion of the population of Ohio
that night. Cleveland, Sandusky, Steubenville,
Columbus, Dayton, and Cincinnati, all heard from
me through the dogs.

At last, worn and weary and covered with mud, I
found the place, and not without apprehensions of
getting shot for a robber, approached the door, and
knocked.

As intimated, I had never seen my uncle, and how
did I know what kind of man he was, or what sort
of reception awaited me? Suppose he should be ill-
natured, being disturbed at that time of night, and
make me feel as though I were not welcome? Such
misgivings suggested themselves to me, as I stood at
the door.

I knocked a couple of times, without getting any
reply, and began to fear that my uncle supposed me
to be a burglar and was getting his gun ready to
shoot through the door. I therefore stepped aside,
and yelled:

"Hallo!"

I heard a movement within, but no reply.

"Hallo!" I repeated: the somber echoes of my
voice rang through a gloomy wood near by; and I
was a little afraid it might stir up a panther or wild-
cat, and tempt it to come out and eat a piece of me.

"Who is there?" came from within.

"Does William Smith live here?" was my non-
committal rejoinder.

"Yes."

"I am his nephew from Pennsylvania, John Smith, Junior," said I, in a distinct voice.

The whole house shook, as my uncle sprung from the bed and alighted on the floor of the little old-fashioned farm-house.

"Wait one moment," said he, in a voice that was musical with welcome.

There was a hasty fumbling among garments for a moment, and a glad little light sprung up within, and peeped slyly out at me from crevices about the door. Then the door opened, and before me stood a strong old man of seventy-three, with snow-white hair and beard.

"Is this my uncle?" I asked.

"Yes," he replied, cordially grasping my hand. "Come in, my boy! You are my nephew John?"

"Yes."

"And have lost your leg. Too bad!"

"O, I don't mind that any more, uncle," I said, as I walked in.

Never have I been received anywhere with such open-hearted welcome, as by this aged uncle. It was nearly two o'clock; my aunt—only two years younger than he—soon made her appearance, and welcomed me as cordially as he had done: ten thousand questions were asked and answered, and the early morning would have found us still in conversation, but that my uncle, by and by, observed that I must be tired, after my walk, and said I had better take some rest.

That I had walked from the station with my crutch and cane, lost my way several times, and wandered about over some portion of the State of Ohio, was a matter of marvel to him.

Not to tire the reader with family affairs—however interesting a general history of the Smith Family might be—I will silently pass over the brief and happy period I spent with my good uncle and aunt.

I took a propeller at Toledo, for Buffalo, and after a pleasant voyage of two nights and a day, on Lake Erie, arrived at that city.

I spent a few days there among my Cold Spring friends—in the course of which I had but one narrow escape from drowning, while out on the lake on a pleasure-excursion—then returned to Philadelphia, *via* the New York and Erie, Northern Central, and Pennsylvania Central Railroads.

CHAPTER XXXIX.

SMITH'S KNOWLEDGE OF GERMAN, ET CETERA.

IN the fall, I determined on another western tour, which I accomplished. In this tour, I visited the following places: Columbus, Dayton, and Cincinnati, Ohio; Indianapolis and Lafayette, Indiana; Springfield, Decatur, Bloomington, El Paso, and Peoria, Illinois. I had intended to go on into Iowa again, but winter came on, and it began to get too cold for me. So, I returned to Philadelphia shortly before Christmas, *via* Logansport, Fort Wayne, and Pittsburg.

During this tour, not much happened that would interest or divert the reader. I might briefly mention one or two amusing incidents that came under my notice.

Often as I had passed through Lancaster, Pennsylvania, I had never stopped there; and, on my way west, I determined to drop off for twenty-four hours. In Lancaster every one talks English and German, (or Dutch, as they call it there,) with equal fluency; and it is not unusual for a person relating an incident or making some remarks, to begin in English and end in Dutch; or *vice versa*.

While I was sitting in my hotel, not far from the

depot, a Lancastrian, who lounged in, got to telling
the proprietor a very interesting story, of an adventure he had recently met with while hunting ducks.
He was relating the story in English, and I listened
with interest. The purport of the story was that he
and another man had shot at a duck simultaneously;
it had fallen, and a dispute had arisen as to which
had brought it down. Just as he reached the crisis
of the story, where the dispute was about to be decided, against the other fellow, of course—and there
seemed some funny circumstance about it, for they
laughed immoderately—he jumped off the track, as it
were, and finished in Dutch, something like this:
"Undsehrichtienochtuchuherkroshomlustienblosterb
hionmemmtebtebtchtchch-h-h—h-h-h—h——h——h
—— ——h— — —h— — —h—cht—AUGH!"

Imagine how tantalizing this was to me. My
knowledge of German or Dutch is very limited. Beyond *Lager Bier und Schweitzer Kase, ein, swei drei* I
simply know nothing of any of those Teutonic languages; and I, therefore, do not, to this day, know
the *dénouement* of the Lancastrian's story.

While in Lancaster, I took the liberty of calling
on two prominent men of opposite political parties,
both of whom have since passed away. I allude to
James Buchanan and Thaddeus Stevens. Each received me cordially and conversed with me in an easy
and pleasant manner. From the citizens of Lancaster,
I learned that they were kind-hearted and noble men,
and that their private characters were above reproach.
Those two public men were regarded with some bitterness during their lives; but whatever may have been

their errors, I believe they were errors of the head and not of the heart. They are at rest now, and I earnestly ask the whole people of our Country to join me in saying—"PEACE TO THE ASHES OF BOTH!"

I shall never forget the extraordinary courage I saw displayed by an hotel clerk, in Columbus, Ohio, while sojourning there during the little tour in question. I was in the sitting-room, one day, when a large, rough-looking man, in a state of inebriation, came in, took a seat in one of the arm-chairs, and manifested symptoms of slumber. The clerk soon saw him, went promptly to him, and gave him to understand that that state of things wouldn't do.

"Come," said the clerk, "this won't do. You must get out of this. We don't want a man to come in here drunk, and sit around half asleep."

"Wha-at?" growled the inebriate.

"I say you must get out of this." said the clerk, laying his hand on his shoulder. "Come!"

He said this in a decided tone, as though he expected the drunken gentleman to get up and be led out. But the man made no move toward getting up, and, moreover, didn't appear to be much afraid of the clerk.

"Did you hear what I said?" demanded the latter, shaking him slightly.

"Well, s'pose I did? What then?"

Such impudence to an hotel clerk!

"What then! I'll show you what then! Now, you get out o' here!" And he seized the inebriate's shoulder.

Thereupon the latter arose slowly, and I supposed

he was going out; but when he got straightened up, he turned defiantly on the clerk, and raised his fist as though about to strike "from the shoulder."

"Clear out, you darn cuss!" he said, to the frightened clerk, who retreated with agility. "Don' come layin' yer hands onto me, or I'll batter the nose off o' yer face!"

"Well, you've got to get out of here," said the clerk.

"You can't put me out," retorted the intoxicated gentleman, defiantly.

"You'll see pretty soon," said the clerk, who, however, kept at a safe distance. "I'm not going to allow a fellow that's been somewhere and got full of rum to come in here and sleep it off! You got nothing to drink in *this* house."

"I would if I'd 'a' wanted it."

"You would, eh?" The clerk now walked toward the door, and, in doing so, was obliged to pass within a few feet of the intruder; and the latter, not knowing what his intentions were, turned round slowly, as if on a pivot, so as to keep his face toward the clerk till he went out. In about three-quarters of a minute the latter returned, and exclaimed:

"What! Haven't you gone yet?"

"No—nor aint a goin' till I'm ready. An', look out!" he exclaimed, as the clerk approached him again. "Don't ye come near me, or I'll *spiller* ye!"

I do not know exactly what he meant by this remarkable word, as I have searched in vain for it in the lexicons of several languages: but I suppose he meant something dreadful.

The clerk, however, did not seem inclined, as yet, to make any aggressive movement: he merely walked past him, as before; and again the pugnacious gentleman stood on the defensive, and personated a first-class pivot. Strange as it may seem, I could not help fancying that if I had been in authority at the hotel, as the clerk was, I would not have trifled quite so long with an insolent drunken man.

While these sage thoughts were revolving in my mind, the clerk seemed to grow all at once inspired with extraordinary courage. Starting suddenly from where he stood, he walked briskly toward the intruder, saying, decidedly:

"Now walk out of here in less than a second!" And he actually laid hands on the big fellow.

The secret of the matter was that two policemen entered at that moment, having been sent for by the clerk at the time of his brief absence from the room; and that was what raised his courage so wonderfully. The two officers walked the pugnacious inebriate out, and the clerk followed him to the door, saying:

"Confound you! You won't come in here loafing around! Next time you try such a game, I'll kick you out!"

"Go to——" The sound of the loafer's voice died away, as he was trotted out by the preservers of the peace, and I am unable to record what the rest of the sentence was.

While at Decatur, Illinois, I heard a conversation between a traveler and an hotel clerk, that strikingly exemplifies the irregularity of western railroad trains.

"What time does the train go to Springfield?" he

inquired, at the counter, about eight o'clock in the evening.

"At twelve," replied the clerk.

"Then," rejoined the traveler, who was evidently posted, "give me a room, and wake me at about one. That will be time enough."

He was right. The "twelve o'clock train" from Lafayette, going through to Springfield, did not come along till about fifteen minutes after one. In the winter time, a traveler in the west can always count on a train about one hour after its time, unless some unusual accident has delayed it.

At Logansport, Indiana, I got taken down a little. The way of it was this: On the train from Peoria, I made the acquaintance of a gentleman who kept an hotel in Logansport, and, in the course of the morning, as we neared that place, I borrowed a literary paper from him, which I forgot to return. Having an hour or two to wait for a train to Fort Wayne, where I should be obliged to change cars again for Pittsburg, I went into the hotel of the gentleman mentioned, for the purpose of getting breakfast. Having taken breakfast, I thought of the paper I had borrowed, and not seeing the landlord, and desiring to return it to the owner in person, and thank him for the favor, I asked the clerk where he was.

"He is out at the stables," returned the clerk.

"Will he be in soon?"

"I don't know. He went out to show a man a horse that he has for sale."

"Then I will go out; shall I go through this way?"

I asked, pointing to a path leading from the rear of the house to the stables.

"Yes, go right out that way. But be careful. There is a dog out in the yard that is a little cross sometimes, and——:"

"O," I interrupted, carelessly, "no dog bites *me*. I am not afraid."

The fact is, I have ever prided myself on the "charm" I can exercise over the canine race, and have often taken the most ill-natured dogs in my hands, picked them up bodily, and even put my hands invitingly to their mouths, and they have not harmed me. The reason is simply that I never shrink from them, or exhibit any fear; which demeanor inspires the sagacious creatures with respect for a fellow.

It was a large, and beautifully-spotted black-and-white dog, and, as I pursued my way to the stables, it came trotting out from a kennel it occupied, and looked at me as much as to say:

"Are you afraid of me, sir?"

I looked calmly down upon the animal, as if to reply:

"Sagacious creature, I am not."

To prove that I wasn't, I paused to admire it, and fearlessly laid my hand upon its head. Thereupon, it capered around me, joyfully, and made a succession of springs upon me as though to kiss me. Just then three juvenile canines, that I had not observed before, came running from the kennel; and their resemblance to the adult one was so striking, that I had no difficulty in making out the fact that a near relationship existed between and among them. I stooped down to pat one of the little beauties on the head, and just then, the big one made another playful spring at my face, not with any intention of biting me,—I'll be sworn to that,—when one of its confounded, awkward teeth struck me just below the eye and penetrated to the cheek-bone; and the crimson "gore" flowed from the incision.

It was a most provoking circumstance, for the clerk was looking from the window, and the landlord and another man just then appeared at the stable-door, all thinking that the dog had bitten me; which placed me in a ridiculous light, in the eyes of the clerk, after my boast that dogs were not in the habit of biting me. Although the dog did not purposely hurt me, and was still capering about, playfully, I execrated its awkwardness, and felt that I could have knocked the top of its head off with my crutch—had no one been looking. It was a female dog, too, and I told it so, very concisely, in my vexation: which was all the satisfaction I had.

Traveling incessantly for forty-eight hours, I reached Philadelphia on a winter night, when the wind was howling and the snow falling fast. I had slept very little on the trains during the last two nights, and it might well be surmised that an individual like John Smith (or "any other man") would feel like "turning in," under the circumstances. Such a conclusion would be but rational.

But it is said that, "Man is a creature of circumstances;" and that adage was fully exemplified by my remarkable experience on that memorable night.

I had already instructed the baggage-agent on the Pennsylvania Central train to send my trunk to my residence, and I was just stepping forth from the depot, at Thirty-first and Market streets, with the view of walking home through the jovial snow-storm, when a familiar voice accosted me with:

"Hallo, Smith! Where have you been this long time? Where are you going?"

I recognized a young friend named Feeny, who was standing near a sleigh, to which two handsome and spirited horses were attached. In the sleigh sat another friend named Aaron, who also said:

"Why, Smith! How do you do? Glad to see you. Where have you been?"

"In the West," I replied.

"Going home?"

"Yes."

"Not going to walk?"

"Yes."

"O, don't do that! Get into the sleigh with Feeny and me, and ride."

"By all means," urged Feeny.

"Are you going directly home?" They lived near my residence.

"N—no—but that need make no difference. We were just taking a little sleigh-ride. You don't mind a ride of an hour before you go home?"

"I am rather weary," I replied. "I have been rattling along in the cars for two days and two nights. Have come all the way from Peoria, Illinois."

"Well, jump in. We will at least take a little

19

drive down Darby Road. You must feel chilly. Here is something to warm you."

This was an article of glassware, containing a genial fluid, designed for the interior of mankind. Having availed myself of this blessing, I sprung into the sleigh ; Feeny jumped in after me ; and we dashed away in the blinding storm.

"We were just at the depot to meet a friend we expected," said he, "but he did not come."

Away we went out Market street, defying even the wintry wind to outstrip us. Instead of turning down the Darby Road, as proposed, we kept on out Market street.

"We'll take a little ride out this way first," said Mr. Aaron, "then we will return, go down Darby Road, cross Gray's Ferry Bridge, and go home."

"All right !"

We had an extensive ride through West Philadelphia ; and candor compels me to say that some of the proprietors of hotels in that vicinity lost nothing by it.

At last, we found ourselves dashing down Darby Road : the noble steeds still fresh and vigorous, and we three "jolly boys" suffering nothing at all from the malady known as "depression of spirits."

Rest! I thought not of it now. I remembered not that I had slept none for two nights. Away we went in the snow-storm; the wide fields of snow my imaginary bed, the murky clouds my curtains, the wind and sleigh-bells singing a merry song in concert to lull me to—wakefulness and mirth.

We approached a certain toll-gate. What hour it

was, I can never know; but any one supposing it to be earlier than the beginning of another day, would subject himself to great ridicule among the " posted."

" Wonder if the toll-man's up?" said Feeny.

" Doubtful," responded Aaron.

" We'll wake him, of course," said I.

" Certainly—if we can yell loud enough."

We dashed onward. So far from tiring, our horses seemed to gain new strength and energy just then. The toll-gate and the little house there situated, were very near.

We did not slacken our speed.

" Toll !" yelled Feeny, in a loud voice.

" Toll! Toll !" shouted Aaron, as we reached the gate without stopping.

" Toll! Toll! Toll !" I shrieked, in a jolly mood as we dashed by.

Alas! the keeper of the gate never had the felicity to receive that "toll." He did not get his *due;* but we got plenty of *snow.*

" Get up! Get up!" screamed Aaron, addressing the horses.

The animals " flew. "

The snow-covered road rushed away behind us so fast that I fancied we were leaving the whole earth behind, and plunging away into space.

" Hurrah! Hurrah!" shouted Feeny.

" Hip-Hip-Hoowee !"

We reached the road leading to Gray's Ferry Bridge, and Mr. Aaron, who had the lines, drove recklessly " round the corner."

The result may be imagined. The centrifugal force

overturned the sleigh in about the sixteenth part of a second; we were all spilt; Aaron was hurled into a fence-corner; Feeny was scattered along the road behind the sleigh; I, with my crutch and cane strewn all around me, was "chucked" into a snow-bank at the road-side, in an inverted position—fairly buried in the cold snow, and my lonely foot pointing up toward the clouded heavens: and in the midst of this scene of general confusion, our conveyance dashed away through the winter night, and —we had to pick ourselves up and walk home, a distance of two miles and three quarters!

"I was chucked into a snow bank and fairly buried in an inverted position, my lonely foot pointing up towards the clouded heavens."—*On the Darby Road.* *Page 292.*

CHAPTER XL.

Ნ ON THE OCEAN WAVE, AND
ON THE ROLLING DEEP."

FOR some time I had projected, for the spring of 1867, a voyage to San Francisco, *via* Cape Horn. My friends advised me, if I wanted to go to California, to take a steamer and go by way of the Isthmus; but, for the novelty of the thing, I determined to take passage on a sailing-ship and double Cape Horn, South America, where the Patagonians live, who eat up all the unfortunate sailors driven on their shores. [It's a pity Cape Horn should ever be *doubled*, for there is too much of it now.]

When March came, and it began to get windy and stormy, I went to New York, with the intention of taking passage on the first sailing-vessel that should clear for San Francisco.

My friends again gave me a little wholesome advice, and endeavored to dissuade me from attempting the voyage till after the stormy season, but I replied that I didn't mind seeing a storm at sea, that, in fact, I rather desired it: so, I went.

Some of the merchants, ship-owners and underwriters of New York, have occasion to remember the clipper-ship BREWSTER, which sailed from New York for San Francisco, on the fourteenth of March, 1867, with a fresh north-west wind and under good auspices, generally. I, John Smith, was that ship's only passenger. She was not a passenger ship; but I was allowed to take passage on her, because I wanted to go round Cape Horn. Captain Collins, the master of the vessel, asked me whether I thought I could stand up on my crutch, when the ship should come to be tossed about on a rough sea: I replied that I didn't know about that, but that I was quite skillful at falling down.

As before hinted, we sailed on the fourteenth of March; and as a powerful little tug towed us out of the harbor, past Forts Richmond, Lafayette and Hamilton, and I looked back and saw Trinity Church steeple fading from view, I pondered on the long voyage of four or five months before me, and wondered when, if ever, I should see New York and the Atlantic coast again.

That day, and the day following, the weather was so extremely cold, that the salt water of old Ocean, as it splashed over the bulwarks, froze into a nasty uncomfortable slush, upon the deck. On the third morning —that of Saturday, the sixteenth of March—the air was much milder, and I began to entertain the liveliest hopes that we were to be favored with pleasant weather, that I might sit by the low bulwarks of the forecastle deck, and watch the blue waves foaming and splashing as the ship plowed its way through them.

Captain Collins was an excellent fellow, a lively and agreeable companion, and a perfect gentleman. The two mates, Messrs. Trufant and Gorham, were unexceptionable; I was soon on the best terms with them, and anticipated a pleasant voyage.

But, somehow or other, these three gentlemen were a little morose on this pleasant Saturday morning. It was quite unaccountable to me.

"What can be the reason?" I asked myself. "Can it be that they don't like pleasant weather, and would prefer it cold and stormy?" I had heard such things, of sea-faring men. [Reader, when *you* hear it said that sailors enjoy stormy weather, don't believe it.]

About ten o'clock the first mate, Mr. Trufant, after several earnest consultations with the Captain, came out of the cabin,—while I was standing on deck enjoying the pleasant breeze and the fine view I had of the waste of waters—and called out:

"Steward!"

"Ay, ay, sir," responded the steward, from the galley.

"Get up a few barrels of potatoes, and what other things you may need from the after-hatch: we're going to have a gale o' wind."

[That was what the matter was. The barometer was getting low.]

"Ay, ay, sir," said the steward.

The wind was still N. W., and glancing in that direction, I perceived that some solid-looking, lead colored clouds were rising above the horizon.

"Going to blow, is it?" I said, to the mate, as he walked by me.

"Yes, a little," he replied, as he proceeded to give some order to the sailors.

A couple of hours passed by, and I saw nc indications of a storm. It had grown a trifle cloudy; and the wind had increased but little.

"We won't have that gale, after all, will we?" I remarked, as we sat at dinner.

The captain laughed. "Give it time," said he. "The barometer usually warns in advance. If you don't see a fresh breeze before morning, there will be a big change in the weather somewhere."

I said no more.

After dinner I was on deck, and, observing that the sailors were working the pumps, I said to Mr. Gorham, the second mate:

"The ship leaks a little, does it?"

"O, yes," he replied, indifferently: "all ships leak more or less."

"I hope ours will leak *less*, then, if we get in a gale," I said.

"So do I," he returned; "but I fear it will leak *more*."

The ship was rocking somewhat, but I had not yet grown sea-sick. In fact, persons who have once been sea-sick are not quite so easily or so severely affected the second time.

I walked to the bulwark, scanned the north-western horizon, and perceived that it was beginning to wear a threatening aspect. The wind was stronger, the waves rolling higher, and the sailors grave and thoughtful.

It was no easy matter for me to stand, without holding to something: and hatch-houses, masts, bulwarks, ropes and belaying-pins came quite handy to brace myself against, or cling to with one hand.

In another hour, the wind was blowing hard, the waves were running high, and one of them jumped over the bulwarks, and wet everybody on deck—myself included. That is what sailors term, "Shipping a sea."

"You had better stand within the cabin," observed the second mate.

I thought so, too, made my way to the door, and stepped in. The cabin was built on deck; but a high sill at the bottom of the door-way kept the water from running in.

I then stood at the cabin-door for a couple of hours, grasping each side of the door-way to brace myself, and watched the rising gale.

CHAPTER XLI.

J. SMITH'S CURIOSITY TO SEE A GALE MORE THAN SATISFIED.

ANOTHER heavy wave dashed over the bulwarks, and fell upon the deck, with a thump that made the ship tremble. The wind rose higher, and was soon howling among the rigging with a fierceness entirely new to me. Wave after wave swept over, and the deck was continually washed with the agitated waters. Evening came and I had no appetite for supper.

Night came, darkness frowned on the furious sea, the wind increased in violence, and fairly screamed among the ropes, shrouds, masts, and yards; we were indeed in a gale.

The ship tumbled about so, that I got sick; but determined not to give way to it. I stood by the cabin door, leaned over the high sill, and contributed my dinner to the waters of the ocean.

The sails had all been taken in but the three lower top-sails, and with those still unfurled, we had been running before the wind. These were now taken in —except the lower main top-sail, which is always left unfurled, in order to control the ship—and the vessel was hove to: that is, turned with her head to the wind, her bow a point or two off, in order that she might rise on the waves.

When these measures had been taken, it seemed to me that the wind just tried how hard it could blow; and to do it justice, I must say, that it blew much harder than I had ever before thought it could. Wave after wave—every successive one seeming to run higher and higher—struck the ship, which was continually trembling, and straining, and "working," as though it might at any moment break to splinters.

Ah, I began to realize that a storm at sea is no luxury! Reader, if you have not seen one, you are fortunate. If you ever start on a voyage, pray earnestly for smooth weather, and if your prayers are answered be very thankful.

I retired to my room at last, and "turned in." That is the nautical phrase for "going to bed." You never hear a sailor say he will "go to bed." He never "goes to bed." Such an expression would sound very odd at sea. "Turn in," is the proper term there. If a sailor should hear a man talk about "going to bed," he would think that man had actually never been out of sight of land in his life.

I "turned in," and slept. When I awoke again, the ship was tumbling about so that I wondered I had not been pitched out of my berth. Seeing one of the mates pass through the cabin, I accosted him with—

"How is it, without?"

"Blowing a regular gale," he replied.

"What time is it?"

"Seven bells."

At sea, they never say eight, nine, ten, eleven, or half-past eleven o'clock. There is a large bell at the forecastle, which is tapped every half-hour. At half-past twelve, it receives one tap; which is called "one bell." At one o'clock, it is tapped twice: that is, "two bells." At half-past one, it is tapped three times: that is "three bells;" and so on, till four o'clock, which time is "eight bells." Then at half-past four "one bell" is struck again; at five o'clock, "two bells;" and so on, up to eight o'clock, which is "eight bells," again. Commencing at half-past eight, "one bell" is again sounded, "two bells" at nine; and so on till twelve, when "eight bells" is reached once more. So, when the mate told me it was "seven bells," it will be perceived that it was half-past eleven.

I tried to sleep again, and succeeded. How long I slept, I could not tell; but when I awoke again, the vessel was tossing about fearfully, and the waves dashing over her fore and aft, with a fierceness that threatened to burst her to pieces. But the wind had suddenly lulled. Not a breath of air was stirring; the lower main top-sail was flapping idly about; they had lost control of the ship, because she would no longer steer when the wind ceased; and so, falling fairly into the trough of the sea, she could not struggle up over the billows; and there she lay at the mercy of the waves, being buffeted by them without any mercy at all.

It was indeed a perilous time. The captain, with his many years of experience at sea, knew our danger; but what could be done? Should this state of things continue long, the ship must inevitably be beaten to pieces. All hands had been called on deck; and I got out of my bunk and struggled to the cabin-door. I opened it a little way, but a fearful sea swept over and dashed it shut in my face. I could hear the voice of the captain giving hurried commands to the sailors who were at work securing the rigging. The shrouds were growing slack, and it was every minute expect-ed that the masts would be carried away.

No breeze came; and probably the angry sea would have crushed us down then and there, but that the clouds gathered thickly over, and a heavy rain came pattering upon the agitated waters—a very unusual accompaniment of a north-west wind.

It may be wondered, by the uninitiated, how a heavy shower of rain could help us. It is not gener-ally known that rain has a soothing effect on the angry sea. Yet, such is the case. No matter how fiercely the waves are running, let the wind lull, and a brisk rain of an hour will take all the rough edge off them. It is the dashing and breaking waves that sailors dread. A regular swelling wave, no matter how high it towers, will do no harm, as a vessel will rise with it, and ride lightly over.

This rain of twenty-five or thirty minutes, so far soothed the turbulent waves as to place us out of im-mediate danger; and not long after, the wind sprung up again, command of the ship was recovered, and so the night passed—and the morning of Sunday, the seventeenth of March, St. Patrick's Day, dawned upon the wide ocean.

The wind was still blowing freshly, but the sky

was clear, the sun shining brightly, and the waves of the sea rolling within the pale of moderation. They still washed the deck at intervals, but I had got used to that, for the deck had scarcely been free from the briny water since the middle of the previous day. The officers and sailors all wore high rubber boots, and oil-cloth hats and clothes. But still, the water dashed over them so violently, that they were wet to the skin all the time. If any one ever asks you, dear reader, whether a sailor's life is a pleasant one or not, say " No !"

      *   *   *   *   *   *   *   *

A strong breeze blew all day, and as night approached, it increased to a gale again. I had hoped the storm was over; but a storm at sea seldom subsides entirely within twenty-four hours.

What we had experienced on Saturday night, was not to be compared with the terrors of that memorable Sunday night. I have suffered much, and undergone much danger in my time, but I never, either before or since, passed such a terrible night.

The gale grew fierce again—fiercer even than before—and the lofty waves thundered over us so, that much of the time it was difficult to determine whether we were still floating or not.

But the most fearful time was about midnight. Light clouds were hurrying over, driven by the mighty wind, while, at intervals, portions of the sky grew clear, and the moon shone down upon us. It was an odd sight—such an awful tempest seen in the moonlight. The wind blew with such violence that the ship was nearly the whole time on her beam-ends, that is, lying over on her side. At intervals she would struggle up for a moment, but the fierce blast would soon hurl her over again. On one occasion, while she stood up for a moment, the pumps were sounded, and the captain soon after called out,

"Starboard watch to the pumps!"

The fact was, the ship was found to be leaking badly, and the hold already contained about four-and-a-half feet of water! One of the mates informed me of this. I had requested him to be frank with me, and to let me know the full extent of any danger; stating, that if it became necessary for us to die, I would do my share of it with as good a grace as possible under the circumstances.

The crew of a vessel is divided into two watches—one called the Starboard, and the other the Port. The port watch is commanded by the first mate, and the starboard by the second. [The port side of a ship is the left-hand side, the starboard the right.] While the starboard watch worked most energetically at the pumps, the port watch went aft with the captain and first mate, and proceeded to heave cargo overboard.

All that was cared for now was to save our lives, and to do that, the ship must be kept afloat. What cared we now for stores of wealth! The wealth of the whole world would not have been more highly regarded than an old rusty nail! What cared I for my trunk, my clothes, my books, money, papers, manuscripts, and little valuable and favorite trinkets! I could have seen them all, and a million times more, swept overboard into the dashing sea, without giving them another thought.

How faithfully those sailors worked! both at the pumps, and at the after-hatch, where the valuable cargo was being dashed from the ship, as though a sacrifice to appease the wrath of the billows! How quickly and submissively they sprung to execute every slight command! There was no tardiness now. They were working for dear life, and it was only necessary for them to know *what* to do. The commands of the officers were merely instructions. There was no cursing the sailors by the officers. [As for the captain, *he* seldom swore at the sailors; but the mates could do so, in mild weather, with a skill that no reasonable person could impeach.]

There was no longer any distinction between officers and men. All appeared equal. All labored for a common end. Death, which lays every one low, with an impartial hand, was apparently near us, and we were comrades now. Kings and emperors, had they been aboard that seemingly doomed ship, must have felt that they were only men!

I remained at the cabin door, most of the time, watching, at times—as the receding sea would allow me to open the door a little way—the second mate, Mr. Gorham, and his watch, working at the pumps, and the phosphorescent sparks chasing each other over the deck and out at the ports and scuppers. I could also see long lines of gleaming phosphorus on the crests of the waves far out upon the dreadful sea.

The steward, who had been helping at the pumps, made his way into the cabin for some purpose, and said to me,

" Passenger, don't you think we're gone ?"

His voice indicated that he had already abandoned all hope.

"Things look rather gloomy," I replied.

"Well," he rejoined, "we have but once to die. If we go down, it will soon be over; we won't suffer long."

This was all the consolation any of us had. The water in the hold did not decrease—the storm raged with unabated fury—and the question now, was not, "Shall we go down?" but, "How soon?" It seemed but a question of time. If we had a spark of hope left, it was merely as one compared with one hundred. The mate told me it was *possible* the ship could be kept afloat till morning, and that then it was *possible* some vessel might be in sight and come to our assistance. But these vague possibilities were worse than no hope at all. They were too tantalizing. I should really have felt better if I had known, beyond a doubt, that we should go down in ten minutes.

Still, it is natural for man to cling to any hope that is held out to him, however slight. Probably, hope, faint as it was, saved us on this occasion. Had all given up, and sat down, with the conviction that we were lost—although no one on board was really of any other opinion—the ship would have filled in an hour, and we must have gone down to our dismal graves in the depths of the Gulf Stream.

In this awful extremity, I could not help remembering certain verses from Byron's "Don Juan" which were very applicable to the occasion. I quote them:

20

"It may be easily supposed, while this
　　Was going on, some people were unquiet;
That passengers would find it much amiss
　　To lose their lives, as well as spoil their diet;
That even the able seaman, deeming his
　　Days nearly o'er, might be disposed to riot;
As, upon such occasions, tars will ask
For grog, and sometimes drink rum from the cask.

　　　*　　　　*　　　　*　　　　*　　　　*

"Then came the carpenter, at last, with tears
　　In his rough eyes, and told the captain he
Could do no more; he was a man in years,
　　And long had voyaged through many a stormy sea,
And if he wept, at length, they were not fears
　　That made his eyelids as a woman's be;
But he, poor fellow, had a wife and children—
Two things for dying people quite bewildering.

"The ship was evidently settling now
　　Fast by the head; and, all distinction gone,
Some went to prayers again and made a vow
　　Of candle to their saints—but there were none
To pay them with; and some looked o'er the bow,
　　Some hoisted out the boats: and there was one,
That begged Pedrillo* for an absolution,
Who told him to be d——d, in his confusion."

The night passed—I scarcely know how—and, contrary to our anticipation, morning found us still afloat.
The storm was yet raging, and the sailors were still
busy pumping and heaving cargo overboard. I took
my position at the cabin door again, standing in
water six or eight inches deep—for the water had
made its way into the cabin, where my trunk was

---

* Pedrillo, a licentiate who accompanied Don Juan, and was
his tutor.

leisurely soaking. I heard the first mate tell one of the sailors to climb up to the mast-head and keep a look out for a vessel. Shortly afterward he came to the door, held it a little way open and said:

"Mr. Smith, just glance out! There is the wildest sight I ever saw, during all my experience at sea!" And he pointed to windward.

I looked; but how shall I describe that sublime and awful picture! The sun was shining brightly, the wind blowing so fiercely that it shattered the green waves, lifted up the waters bodily and dispersed them into a thick spray, so that I could not discern where sea and sky met. The next moment we were enveloped in such a cloud that we could not see thirty yards around us; the heavens grew black and it began to look like the dusk of evening. A minute later, the clouds had swept over, and the bright sun burst once more upon that scene of fearful grandeur. Never did the god of day shed light on a wilder picture! It was grand—majestically grand—awfully grand, beyond the expression of human tongue! Notwithstanding our prospect of speedy death, I was lost and swallowed up in momentary admiration. How vividly came to my mind, as I stood there gazing on the tempestuous scene, those sublime words from the one-hundred-and-seventh Psalm—words that I had never before properly appreciated—

"They that go down to the sea in ships, that do business in great waters;   *

"These see the works of the LORD, and his wonders in the deep.

" For he commandeth, and raiseth the stormy wind, *which lifteth up the waves thereof.*

"They mount up to the heaven, they go down again to the depths; their soul is melted because of trouble.

" They reel to and fro, and stagger like a drunken man, and are at their wit's end."

Presently the whole wild picture was again wrapped in gloom, and I was only conscious of the thunder of the waves beating over the ship, of the howling wind and dashing, blinding spray; a moment of gloom: then the clouds were dashed away by the wind, the sun burst out and the wild day shone round again.

We were in the Gulf Stream, which is of a warmer temperature than the other waters of the Atlantic in the same latitude; and the cooler wind seemed to grasp the water up and dash it into the sky; so that, at times, as the spray mounted up and formed in clouds, the sea and sky appeared to leave their places, rushing about through space and commingling in unutterable confusion.

In the midst of all this, how frail did our ship seem!—so frail, that I fancied it lived only because the battling elements did not deign to notice it, or think it worth their while to crush it, as they might have done with a breath!

But now, a beam of hope dawned on us; and it could be seen shining on the faces of all. Every countenance was radiant with it. There was, at last, after eight hours of constant pumping, a perceptible decrease of water in the hold. Sixty or seventy tons of cargo had been thrown from the after part of the ship; the carpenter had gone down and succeeded in patching up one of the rifts: and, to our joy, it was found that the pumps were now capable of throwing the water out a little faster than it ran in. Although the gale was still blowing, and many planks had been torn from the bulwarks by the waves, imminent death no longer threatened us, and we felt compara- tively happy.

All that day, (Monday,) that night, and a portion of the following day, the storm raged. But on Tuesday afternoon it gradually lulled, and on Wednesday morning the sun smiled cheerfully on a nearly smooth sea. A slight breeze was blowing, the sky was clear and blue, the air perfectly charming; and I began to forget the terrors and dangers of the storm through which we had passed. After all, now, it was pleasant to be at sea.

Of course, such a thing as proceeding on a voyage of fifteen thousand miles was not to be thought of; and the captain put back for New York, which was now about seven hundred miles distant, as we had drifted a long way during the north-west gale.

That beautiful morning, as I went up on the after deck—a deck, usually called the poop deck, which surrounds the cabin, and is raised about three or four feet above the main deck—I met the captain walking to and fro, and he said:

" Well, Mr. Smith, taking into consideration our recent gale, what do you think of the man who wrote 'A life on the ocean wave?'"

" One of two things," I replied: " he was either a

lunatic, or else never saw the 'ocean wave.' In the latter case, he was, at least, a fool."

"That," rejoined the captain, "reminds me of· a certain Doctor—a friend of mine—who once took a voyage with me. He was much elated with the idea of going to sea, and, as we sailed from port, and he gazed out upon the endless expanse before us, he was perfectly enraptured. But, by and by, as we got out where it was a little rough, he became sea-sick—terri· bly so—and I found him aft, in a little while, hanging over the bulwark, and ready to turn inside out. O, wasn't he sick! 'Hallo, Doctor,' said I; 'not sick, I hope?' 'O, Lordy! yes,' said he. 'O, dear!' Then I thought his stomach itself would come up. 'What do you now think of the man who wrote, "*A life on the ocean wave?*"' I was cruel enough to ask. 'Think!' said he. 'I think—bawk!—think he was a d——d fool! Bawk! Bawk! O, Lordy, O!'"

CHAPTER XLII.

MORE OF THE DREADFUL SEA.

WITH Thursday morning came an east wind: it was moderate, at first, but freshened up, and blew positively strong; the sky became heavily overcast with clouds, the rain fell—so did the mercury in the barometer—and there was every indication of an easterly gale.

Still, as night came on, and it had not yet amounted to a gale, the ship was kept running before the wind under her three lower top-sails, and we made pretty good time toward New York.

I retired that night not quite at ease, but still sufficiently so to rest well; and as the vessel was kept before the wind all night, and did not rock much, I didn't tumble out of my berth, as one may reasonably expect to do when the vessel rolls heavily.

I am not in the habit of paying any attention to dreams, or of relating them; but one that visited me that night was so inexpressibly ludicrous, that I must "out with it."

I dreamed that I, in company with a very black African, armed with an axe, was in a deep, thick wood in California, looking for a pole to make sled-soles of, when a big bear made his appearance, and immediately "went for" us. The darkey dropped the axe, sprung upon a stump near by, and squatted on the top of it, trembling with terror; but I, not being in a condition to retreat with speed, caught up the axe, threw down my crutch, balanced myself on my foot, and as the bear came on and reared up to hug me to death, I aimed a blow at his head. But it missed his head and cut off one of his fore-paws—a bear has *four* of them, you know—the blood spurting forth from the stump, in a way that was quite gratifying to me. He was not placed *hors du combat*, however, but persisted in his attack on me with extraordinary vigor. I aimed another blow at the seat of his intellect; but, singularly enough, missed it again, and cut off the other fore-paw. As I did so, the axe flew from my hands, and fell at the foot of a big tree, thirty feet distant. The bear, not yet discomfitted, growled savagely, showed his teeth, and came dancing at me, holding up his bloody stumps, as though still determined, even with them, to crush me. Finding myself unarmed, and without so much leisure time as to pick up my crutch, I turned about and made a hop toward the stump on which the darkey sat. The bear hopped after me. I had thought of climbing up on the stump, but the frightened darkey occupied all the space there; so I just kept on retreating round the stump, hopping as fast as I could, and close at my heel came the bloody bear, hopping, too, as fast as *he* could.

The whole picture, with the scared nigger on the stump in the center,—his thick lips mumbling unintelligible words of fright, and his white eyes starting out so that they could have been knocked off with a

club, without touching his flat nose—was so unprece-
dentedly ludicrous, that terrified, as I fancied I was, I
laughed outright, in the very midst of my visionary
peril; and so awoke.

It was daylight; the roar of the agitated sea struck
on my ear; the waves were dashing over the stern
of the ship and rolling over the roof of the cabin; the
winds were howling without; the ship was plunging
and pitching, rising in the misty air and sinking into
the depths among the waves: it was blowing a regular
gale. I got up and was making my way toward the
cabin door, when the captain entered.

"Good-morning," said I. "How are things now?"

"O," he replied, in a tone of vexation, "about as
bad as they can be, this side of the bottom. We have
an easterly gale to contend with, and the ship is still
before the wind. I wanted to run as long as I could,
in order to get out of this cursed Gulf Stream. Now,
I am half afraid to heave the ship to, lest it should
strain her. Every thing goes wrong. This is the
most unlucky voyage of my life. I have followed
the sea for twenty years; I have been in innumerable
gales; I have had ships burnt under me; I have been
shipwrecked on coasts; I have run upon icebergs,
and been attacked by pirates; but never had such
continued ill-luck. I hoped the other gale would
have been enough for one trip. We got out of that
by barely a hair's-breadth; and now, in our crippled
condition, before we have time to get out of the Gulf
Stream, we have a black, blustering easterly gale
rushing upon us. If it lasts as long as the other, we

must either go to the bottom or be driven upon the coast. Nothing can save us."

"Too bad," said I, taking advantage of a momentary lull, to attempt to walk across the cabin.

But just then the ship gave a fearful lurch, and I was dashed violently back upon a sofa, striking, upon the back of it, that leader in the elbow commonly styled the "crazy-bone," and temporarily paralyzing my arm.

"Are you hurt?" asked the captain.

"Only my arm," I replied, grasping the back of the sofa with my other hand to keep from rolling off. "Only my arm. It, I am inclined to believe, is broken."

"I hope not."

My arm was so paralyzed that I could not move it for a quarter of a minute; when, as it began to recover from the benumbing effects of the shock, it tingled in a way that was agonizing. It was not broken, however, but badly bruised.

"I think," said the captain, "you must be the *Jonah* of this ship. It is said when ships are unfortunate, that they have a Jonah on board. Hadn't we better throw you overboard?"

"If you will insure me a safe voyage to land in a whale's stomach," I replied, "you may do so. If it will take me to New York in three days and three nights, I think I will reach land much sooner than this leaky old ship."

"I don't know," he rejoined. "We may reach the nearest point of land much sooner."

"Where is that," I asked.

" 'The *bottom*."

The gale did not grow so fierce that day as our northwestern gale had done; but still it was a bigger gale than any man need wish for.

Two of the men were severely injured at the wheel, and had to be conveyed to the forecastle and stowed away. Moreover, one or two others had fallen ill, from sheer exhaustion; and as the crew only numbered twenty-three, including officers, steward, and carpenter, this was a considerable diminution of force. The ship leaked as badly as ever, and the pumps had to be kept going continually.

That night, in the midst of the gale, the wind hushed suddenly, as on the night of the sixteenth, while the sea was running high, and left us again struggling in a trough of the sea.

> " At mercy of the waves, whose mercies are
> As human beings' during civil war."

However, it was soon blowing again, and the captain, who wanted to get across the Gulf Stream as soon as possible—for the sea is always more turbulent there than elsewhere—put the ship before the wind, determined to run her "as long as she would float."

CHAPTER XLIII.

JOHN SMITH'S END IMMINENT.

BY morning—Saturday, the twenty-third of March —a fearful gale was blowing, and the weather was so heavy that the dismal, misty clouds seemed to float on the bosom of the sea.

The ship was leaking worse than ever, the water in the hold was actually gaining; and the second mate, who was on watch, told the captain that unless the vessel was hove to soon, she must go down, as it was impossible, with the gale astern—the chief leakage being aft—to keep her from filling. The captain told him to call all hands on deck at once; and he came to the cabin door and called the first mate.

Mr. Trufant, the first mate, "turned out" hastily, put on his water-proof clothes, and stepped forth on deck. Just then a heavy sea swept over and carried him off his feet, dashing him against the starboard bulwark, where both his feet slipped under one of the spare spars that was loosely lashed there, and was floating on the water. As the wave receded, and the the water ran off through the rents in the bulwarks, the spar settled down again, its immense weight resting on one of his legs, which he could not withdraw in time. He uttered an exclamation of pain, and Mr.

Gorham and the sailors at the pumps, hurried to his assistance. They could not move the heavy spar, and the unfortunate man was obliged to lie there, suffering the most excruciating pain, till another sea swept over, half-drowning him, and floated it again.

Then Mr. Gorham and the sailors hastily dragged him from the bulwark, and carried him, groaning and fainting, into the cabin. His leg was broken about five inches below the knee.

Here then was another important portion of our force rendered useless; to say nothing of the depressing influence their officer's misfortunes and sufferings had on the sailors, who, like most seamen, were superstitious, and were heard declaring that the BREWSTER was an "unlucky ship." Mr. Trufant was an exemplary seaman, and could have handled the ship as well as the captain.

At this most distressing time, the gale grew more violent than ever; heavy seas swept over from stern to stem, in rapid succession; the main hatch-house was stove to pieces; both galley doors were stove in, and the sea dashed through, putting out the fires, washing away provisions and important utensils, and hurling the steward out against the bulwark, and almost overboard; nearly all the remaining planks of the bulwarks were torn away; the wheel-house began to go to pieces; the lower fore top-sail was blown to ribbons; and the ship broached to—that is, came round into the trough of the sea, and lay with her side to the wind and waves.

The captain hurried out upon the after-deck, had the lower mizzen top-sail taken in, and ordered the

lower main top-sail to be braced so that the ship
should lie close to the wind, and steer over the waves.
This done, he returned to the cabin, and he and I
"set" Mr. Trufant's broken leg—and a dence of a
"set" we made of it. I had read "anatomy" in my
ime, and fancied I knew something of surgery and
the general construction of the human frame; but,
tossing about as the ship was at that time, the most
skillful surgeon could scarcely have done justice to
the case.

Only the *tibia*—that is, the large bone of the leg—
was broken, and we applied three splints to it, bound
it too tightly, with too much bandage, and fancied we
had "reduced the fracture," in a scientific manner.
When we arrived in New York Harbor, nine days
later, and the mate was taken to the Brooklyn City
Hospital, the surgeons there had to set it over again,
and attach a forty-pound weight to the foot to keep
it in its place.

Our troubles were not over when Mr. Trufant's accident occurred. Another man at the wheel had his
shoulder dislocated, and was carried to the forecastle.
Every wave that swept over did some additional
damage—crushing in a panel of the house on deck, or
tearing a plank from the bulwarks. Mr. Gorham told
the captain that the water in the hold was increasing,
and that one of the two pumps was out of order. The
rigging grew slack again; the shrouds had endured
such a strain that some of them were beginning to
give way and were flapping loosely in the wind: and
it began to be pretty clear that the main-mast would
soon go.

The sky was not quite so heavy as it had been; and the captain went aft with his glass and anxiously scanned the horizon. There was a schooner in sight, three or four miles to windward, and as she rose on the waves we could see her distinctly. So, he went into the cabin, got an odd-looking flag from his private state-room, took it out and hoisted it at the mizzen-mast. It was a *signal of distress.*

"Mr. Gorham," he shouted, "don't give it up! Keep the pump going! She may not see us!"

"Ay, ay, sir!" responded the brave mate. "I will not give it up!—Work away with a will, men!"

The remaining effective pump was worked with unusual energy for half-an-hour; during which time, I climbed up the companion-way, went out on the stormy after-deck, clung to a rope with which the wheel-house was lashed, and anxiously watched the schooner. She was standing several points off, and did not change her course. Whether she had failed to see our signal, or was herself in a bad condition, or both, I am unable to say: but she moved on, and finally grew dim at the misty horizon.

Again the captain scanned the ocean on all sides; but no sail was in sight. He then, with an air of sadness and disappointment, hauled down the signal. Next, he went to Mr. Gorham, and asked him how the water was. There was no hope in that direction. He could not tell how much water was in the hold, but any one could see that the ship was slowly settling. If any one had mentioned hope to us now, we would have laughed at him—laughed with the wild laugh of despair!

A thousand thoughts of home and friends came crowding upon me; and I wondered how many months the fathomless waters would roll over me—how many months I should lie entangled, perhaps, among some slimy sea-weeds, if not immediately devoured by the monsters of the deep, before the dear ones, whom I had seen for the last time, would give me up for lost. They could never know how I perished, I mused; none would be left to tell the tale.

In an hour, perhaps the waves would be dashing a thousand fathoms above us all. Time would roll on, the BREWSTER would never be heard of, no letter from San Francisco would ever bear to my friends the welcome words, " All is well!" Years would pass away—no tidings of the wanderer—one by one, all who were dear to me would grow old and die, and sink down into the grave, thinking of the lost one who disappeared in the dim years gone by, and wondering how he died!

These thoughts were saddening indeed to one who believed that his end was nigh; but I remembered that no fretting, or repining, or yearning for loved faces, could at all help the matter; and made up my mind to die like a man!

The captain returned to the after-deck, and I went down into the cabin and stayed with Mr. Trufant, whose sufferings, as the vessel tossed about, were indeed heartrending. He was a brave fellow, though, and stood it with fortitude. He had served in the navy, and his face was disfigured from the explosion of a shell; and he told me he had been unlucky all his life. He did not know the extent of our danger —and I did not tell him—and related some of his misfortunes, as I sat there on a sofa, near his berth, clinging to it to retain my seat. He said that, only a year before, he had met with an accident on a ship, had nearly been crushed by a falling yard, that it had taken him eight or nine months to recover, during which time he had spent, in doctor-bills, and the like, all the hard-earned money he had saved up in the course of years; that now, just when he had got able to start on a voyage again, with hopes of a brighter future, this sad accident had occurred, and would lay him up for months, should we reach shore. It was hard, he said, after what he had suffered in the navy; and I thought so, too.

Well, his misfortunes and sorrows, my misfortunes and sorrows, and the misfortunes and sorrows of the whole crew would soon have ended, had the storm continued so much as an hour longer. But at six bells—vulgarly called on land, eleven o'clock—it began to abate, as though its very strength was exhausted; and by evening, had entirely subsided. The ship was again comparatively relieved from water; and there's no use in any ordinary mortal attempting to give a passable description of our joy, as we found ourselves once more basking in the full light of hope!

21

CHAPTER XLIV.

COURTESIES AT SEA.

NEXT day, (Sunday,) a fresh north-west breeze blew all day, and we made but little progress toward New York. The weather was pleasant, and the ship did not leak so much as before. The sailors were busy all day, repairing the damages, as best they could, securing the rigging and so forth ; the carpenter nailed some boards on the almost bare framework of the bulwarks, made another inspection of the hold, and got some of the leaks stopped : especially did he secure one of the stern planks, that was so loose that a man might have pulled it off with his hands.

On Monday morning, the sea was perfectly calm. Not the slightest breeze stirred, the surface of the water was glassy, and scarcely any swell was perceptible. [They have *swells* at sea, as well as on land.]

By and by, as we laid perfectly motionless, we saw a steamer coming from the southward, and the captain ran up his "ensign," as a signal that he wanted to communicate with her. It was the *Moro Castle*, from Havana for New York. As she passed astern of us, within half a cable's length, Captain Collins called out :

" This is the BREWSTER, leaking badly and returning in distress! Please report me in New York!"

" Ay, ay," replied the captain of the steamer, as she
rushed by.

On Monday evening, a stiff north-west breeze sprung
up again, as though determined to keep us away
from New York harbor; and it lasted a whole week.

On Thursday, the twenty-eighth, after we had been
tacking about for three days without gaining much
distance, a pilot-boat came dancing out to us, over
the rough waves, and a pilot left her in a yawl and
came aboard the BREWSTER.

" HAVE YOU ANY NEWSPAPERS?" was the question the captain and I asked him, in a breath, as he
came up over the bulwark.

I shall never forget the anxiety and impatience
with which we asked this question. We had been
absent from the world, as it were, about three weeks:
and so full of terror and danger had the period been
that it seemed like a moderate life-time. I almost
fancied that my country might have undergone a
revolution during my absence, and that I might find
it necessary, on going ashore, to bend my solitary
knee to a crowned monarch. However, I saw no
indications of any such state of things, in the *World*,
Herald and *Times* with which the pilot responded to
our earnest inquiries. Things seemed to be going on
about as usual in Gotham, and the remainder of the
United States : the markets appeared to be good;
whisky, cotton and iron were quoted at fair figures:
while the usual healthy number of fires, accidents and
murders were reported in the proper columns.

On Monday morning, the first day of April, having
been all this time beating about in front of the harbor,
we found ourselves becalmed again, about seventy
miles from New York.   The sky was heavily clouded,
a dull, damp, misty rain fell, and the barometer was
low.   Every thing augured ugly weather.   Soundings were taken, which indicated that we were in fifty
fathoms water.   Other sails could be seen on all
sides.

By and by, we saw a small side-wheel steamer
coming toward us, from the direction of the harbor;
whereupon the captain said to the pilot:

"Don't you think that's a steamer coming to take
us in tow?"

"It looks very like it," was the reply.

The captain then called the carpenter and instructed
him to remove from the stern of the ship the board
on which the name BREWSTER was painted.

"What is that for, Captain?" I asked.

"Don't you know?" he replied.

"No."

"How dull you are," said he.

"You would be dull, too," I retorted, "if you had
never been out of sight of land but three or four times
in your life.   But, tell me—what is it for?"

"Why, you see, we have already been reported in
distress; and if that fellow coming should recognize
us, he would ask a thousand or fifteen hundred dollars
to tow us in."

"Ah?" said I, somewhat enlightened.   "Is that
their style?"

"Yes, indeed: let them get a fellow in a tight place

once, as we are now, and they'll pile it on—no telling
how high.—Hurry, carpenter."

The steamer reached us at last, crossed our stern,
and, with a graceful curve, came round on our port
side, within hailing distance.

"Good morning," said the captain of the little
steamer—the WM. FLETCHER—who stood in the
pilot-house.

"Good morning," returned Captain Collins.

"Where are you from?" asked the steamer captain,
looking curiously at the blank place where the
BREWSTER'S name ought to have been.

"San Francisco," responded Captain Collins.

"What vessel?"

This was a stunner, and Collins, after hesitating a
moment, pretended not to have heard, and said:

"How do the Highlands bear from here?"

"About north-west," was the response. "What
ves——"

"What will you charge to tow me in?" interrupted
Captain Collins.

"Three hundred dollars," was the prompt reply.

"O, nonsense," rejoined Collins. "That's too
much. That's all they charge when the harbor is
full of ice."

"Our regular price," said the other.

"O, no, captain," said Collins; "come, be reasonable. I'll give you a hundred and fifty."

"Couldn't do it, really."

"Well," rejoined Collins, "I think we will have a
favorable wind soon, and I can get in without being
towed."

"Yes," retorted the other, ironically; "quite likely. If you have no barometer on board, I'll lend you one. The mercury has gone clean down out of sight, and we're going to have a deuce of a blow. I'll venture it will be a nor'-wester, too."

"Pooh! No danger. I'll sail in."

"All right," said the steamer captain. "Now that I come to think, I'm sorry I made so good an offer. I begin to believe you have an underwriter's job of it. You haven't been to San Francisco."

"I'll give you two hundred dollars," said Collins, without paying any attention to the other's last remark.

"No, not a cent lower than three hundred. I wouldn't do it for that, if I had not already offered to. I'll swear, I believe that is the BREWSTER! We heard of it."

"The what?" said Collins.

"The BREWSTER. Come, isn't it now? Captain Adams, of the *Moro Castle*, reported her returning in distress."

"What do I know of the *Blueskin?* I never heard of such a ship.—Come, I'll give you two hundred and fifty."

"No, three hundred; not a cent less. I'll put you alongside the pier for that."

"O, you're a hard one! Well, you can tow us in, and I'll lick you the first time I catch you in New York. Mind, now, you are to take the ship to the pier whenever I want you to. I will anchor in the harbor to-day."   .

"All right; I'll stick to that."

"Well, Mr. Gorham, give him our hawser."

"Ay, ay, sir."

The hawser is a very thick, heavy line, used for towing or making a ship fast; and one end of this rope the sailors gladly threw over to the steamer, while the other was made fast to the capstan on the forecastle deck.

We arrived in the harbor about four o'clock that afternoon, and had just cast anchor when we were visited with a rough north-west gale. But we did not care now, we were safe.

We anchored near Hart's Island, and I got on the little steamer, with Captain Collins, and went up to the city. We landed at the foot of Catharine street, and my glad heart never before bounded as it did when, after the perils of the past three weeks, I stepped upon *terra firma* once more. I felt that I wouldn't care if somebody would knock a hole in the bottom of the nasty old sea and let all the salty water run out. It isn't of any use, anyhow, only to raise sharks, and whales, and mermaids, and porpoises, and sea-horses, and sea-serpents, and such like hideous creatures, to float iron-clads and drown people; and for idiots that never saw it to write pretty verses about. I am not habitually a fighting man; on the contrary, quite a peaceably-disposed citizen of the United States; but if I ever come across the cuss that wrote,

> "A life on the ocean wave,
> A home on the rolling deep;
> Where the scattered waters rave,
> And the winds their revels keep,"

I'll lick him or he'll lick me!

CHAPTER XLV.

Ho! for California!

ABOUT the middle of April, a little more than a year after my fearful experience on board the BREWSTER, I might have been seen, (if anybody had been watching), in the vicinity of the Pacific Steamship Company's buildings, at the foot of Canal street, New York, making inquiry as to the rates of passage from New York to San Francisco. I had about recovered from my maritime scare.

"One hundred dollars, first cabin," said the clerk; "seventy-five dollars second; and forty dollars steerage. The cabin tickets, however, are all sold. We have but a few steerage tickets left."

"The deuce!" I exclaimed, forgetting my good manners, in the agony of disappointment.

It was two days prior to the sailing of the *Ocean Queen*. I did not like the idea of going in the steerage, for I had been informed that it was "rough," and that even a soldier would find it so; nor did I relish waiting eight days for the next steamer.

"Pshaw!" I ejaculated.

"You wanted a cabin ticket, I suppose?"

"Couldn't think of going in the steerage; I have distant relations who have been in Congress."

"You might," he said, with some hesitation, "be crowded into the cabin, but I have no cabin ticket to sell you. If you will take a steerage ticket, I am confident you can arrange it with the purser to get transferred to the cabin."

"Do you think so?"

"I am sure of it."

"Then I will take one."

I paid forty dollars, and the clerk filled out a steerage ticket for me—which I took with thanks, and walked away, fancying I had learned a great secret.

It *was* a great secret, for I afterward discovered that it was necessary to intrust it to a great many people in order to have it well kept.

The day the *Ocean Queen* sailed was a rainy, dismal day. The steamer was crowded, and it required the neatest bit of skill to set one's crutch down any-where on the steerage deck without injuring any one's toes. There were more than fourteen hundred pas-sengers aboard.

The steamer did not get out of the harbor before five o'clock, and the purser being busy collecting tickets, I was unable to see him in order to make that little "arrangement;" and as night closed in and we plunged out among the waves of the mighty deep, I felt myself doomed to "turn in" in the steerage.

How shall I describe that night of horror? It fairly takes away my appetite to think of it! As the shores disappeared in the darkness and distance, a strong wind blew, the waves rolled savagely, then began that pitching and tossing of the vessel so terrible to the stomachs of the unsailor-like.

No sooner had we got "outside" and some slight "motion" was perceptible, than some of the more susceptible passengers grew blue under the eyes and white as a sheet all over the face, and proceeded to manifest their regret for having dined, by violently casting up the masticated provisions, to the celebrated and popular tune of "New York!" Then, as the vessel went plunging on, growing more and more reckless in its manner of tossing itself about, others began to feel the wretched reeling of the brain and morbid heaviness of the stomach—others grew sick, while the already sick grew sicker—others turned deathly pale, groaned in agony, gasped, shrieked "New York!" and let their recently-procured nourishment rush out with a gush, and gush out with a rush; while a wild, agonizing chorus of "O, deary!" "O, Lordy!" "Oo-oo-oo-Godbemerciful," and the like, resounded and reverberated through the ship, penetrated dark recesses and corners, mingled with the dash of the surging waves without, and the dull splash of repudiated nutrition on the main deck within.

As for myself—I wasn't exactly sick; I'll never acknowledge that I was, as long as I live. That I felt slightly indisposed—just enough so not to feel in the humor for receiving visitors—I will not deny; but it was not sea-sickness. It was only a kind of nausea and dizziness, accompanied by violent spasms just beneath the lungs and a rapid ejectment from the stomach of some trifling article of food that didn't agree with me—under the circumstances. I am subject to these spells—usually on the water. On such occasions, the natural depression of spirits makes me rather morose, and I am not apt to talk much. On the occasion in question, all I said was "New York," when a man asked another where he was from, and I thought he was talking to me. I should have said "Philadelphia," instead of "New York," but I didn't care much, just then, where I was from. Realizing that I had articulated when I was not spoken to, I was about to excuse myself when the vessel plunged violently, and I simply said, "O, Lordy! Ugh!"

Such was all the conversation I indulged in that night.

I went to the purser next day—late in the day, for I felt better in the afternoon than in the morning—told him the circumstances, and requested him to make that little "arrangement;" stating that I was willing to pay the difference. He said the cabin was crowded, but that, in consideration of about thirty-five dollars, he could probably find me a place. This I paid him; and, to make the matter short, I paid thirty-five more in gold on the other side—that is, from Panama to San Francisco—making in all about one hundred and twenty-five dollars for the luxury of a voyage to San Francisco.

In a day or two, I was able to stagger about the vessel in a very successful manner, considering my means of perambulating, and on the first Sunday out —three days from New York—the weather being fine, I wended my way forward to give a drink of wine to a sick steerage-passenger, and it was on that occasion that I witnessed a very amusing scene which I shall endeaver to describe.

My sick friend was lying on the hurricane deck, shaded by an awning, and very near him were four unchristian-like passengers engaged in the absorbing game of "seven-up." About that time, a Methodist minister came over from the cabin to conduct a "divine service" or two, and enlighten the benighted steerage-passengers as to the great probability of their losing their immortal souls.

He took his position a little way from our "seven-up" party, gave out a text from memory, and proceeded to preach the gospel—during which the game went on—my attention being divided between it and the sermon.

"My Christian friends," began the minister, "I would have you know, in the beginning, that ——"

["You're bound to trump or follow *suit*, if you have it," interrupted one of the card-players.]

"—— There are two ——"

["Trumps! by jingo!"]

"—— Spheres of existence for all mankind. First ——"

["Whose deal is it?"]

"—— We are placed on earth to ——"

["Play for a quarter a game."]

"—— Live such a life of honesty, integrity, piety, and godliness, ——"

["Confound such a game!"]

"—— That when we come to ——"

["Deal a little faster."]

"—— Leave the scenes of our earthly labors, and trials, and woes, and miseries, we may be ——"

["Skunked, by thunder!"]

"——Prepared to enter upon ——"

["A new game."]

"——A new and holy existence among ——"

["Clubs or spades."]

"—— The angels."

["There! he's turned a jack!"]

"But what, my thoughtless friends, what will become of the wicked and ungodly man who ——"

["Deals all the time! That's three times that I know of!"]

"—— Persists in his evil ways till ——"

["The trump is turned."]

"—— The day of judgment? What will be the fate of those who refuse ——"

["Trump three times!"]

"—— The offers of mercy, and reject the offered salvation till it is forever too late? When the awful ——"

["Trump!"]

"—— Trumpet shall sound and they are summoned from their graves to answer for ——"

["Fifty cents: let's play another."]

"——The deeds done in the body, they shall be dumb with the consciousness of their guilt, and shall have ——"

["High, low, jack, and the game! Run 'em."]

"——Their part in the lake that burneth with ——"

["Spades."]

"—— Fire and brimstone, which is the ——"

["Third game."]

" —— Second death!"

["The deuce.   I thought it was the trey."]

"Now, my friends, you are ——"

["High, low, to our jack, game."]

" —— Aware of the uncertainty of life, at all times, but especially at ——"

["Seven-up."]

" —— Sea, where ships may ——"

["Play trump."]

" —— Go down at any moment, and where those on board may ——"

["Follow suit."]

" —— Be hurled upon the merciless waters ——"

["Without a single trump."]

" —— Without a straw between them and ——"

["The end of the game."]

" —— The awful judgment seat!   What would be your cry then?"

["There now! play the square game, or I won't play any more!"]

"What could you, who are unprepared to die, say in your defense?"

["Twenty-nine for game."]

"Nothing—simply nothing.   You could only turn away in shame and wretchedness, and cry ——"

["We're out!   Fork over the stamps!   Don't let's play any more; it's about dinner time."]

" —— Unto the rocks, 'Fall on us!' and unto the hills, 'Cover us!'"

["That makes it right.   I'm just a dollar ahead."]

The game now broke up, the sermon, for lack of

variety, began to lose its interest, and I returned to the cabin much edified by the preaching and that scientifically played game of "seven-up."

I will not attempt to give a full account of the incidents of the voyage from New York to Aspinwall —a distance of nineteen hundred and eighty-three nautical miles—but will conclude this chapter by mentioning the death of a middle-aged lady, who died the day before our arrival in port. She had been ill of pneumonia for some days, and early on the morning in question she breathed her last, leaving a sorrow-stricken husband and eight children to continue the voyage and life's cheerless journey, without the light of a wife's and mother's smile.

The children were all small—the oldest not more than ten years old—and were not able to realize their loss and their desolate condition; but that heart-broken man, whose haggard face and dark sunken eyes I can never forget, mourned enough for all. Every innocent prattle of the motherless ones was a thrust into his stricken heart, and if they did not weep he wept for them.

I have seen many horrible sights, such as the mangling of men in battle; but I never saw any thing so calculated to make the heart weep as the sorrow of that lone-hearted father of motherless children. Never can I forget how I saw him, just after a dull splash aft of the leeward wheel announced that the corpse had been committed to the deep, come languidly out of his stateroom, surrounded by his wondering little ones, sit down on the deck under the shadow of a companion-way, bury his face in his hands, and weep like a lone and friendless child!

It is sad to see a woman weep; but when a strong man sheds tears they must be wrung out by an anguish of soul too poignant for the simple name of grief!

CHAPTER XLVI.

ON THE ISTHMUS.

EARLY on the morning of the ninth day from New York we landed at Aspinwall, New Granada, United States of Columbia. The eastern shores of this country, which is a portion of Central America, are washed by the Caribbean Sea. Aspinwall is composed of a score of substantial buildings, such as we see in our own country, and a few hundred thatched huts.

A few Americans and Europeans are engaged in business there; but it might be suggested that the *natives* are the chief feature in the population.

These natives are a remarkable people—a true type of a mongrel race. We see among them every shade of complexion, from the hue of midnight in a coal-pit to that of wood ashes mixed with lime. Having stated that they are a mongrel people, it is but proper to say what races they are composed of, as nearly as I can guess, and I will do so in a tabular manner, thus:

Caucasian	$1\frac{1}{2}$	per cent.
American	$19\frac{1}{2}$	"
Mongolian	0	"
Australian	1	"
Arctic	0	"
Malay	0	"
European	1	"
Ethiopian	77	"
Amounting to	100	

22

They speak the Spanish tongue: how well I am
unable to judge, as I am unfamiliar with that language; but, considering the general character of the
benighted creatures, it is fair to presume that they
cold-bloodedly murder it.

They seldom address each other by name, but style
each other Hombre (pronounced almost *Umbra*, with
a frightful quiver on the " r "): which is equivalent
to "Fellow."

As I before remarked, they have all shades of
color; and I will add, that while some have straight,
black, glossy hair, like that of the aborigines, others
"sport" the fearfully-"kinked" article, like that of
the pure African.

They are a mean, cowardly, pusillanimous set. They
cheat, lie, swear, get drunk, steal, murder, *etc.*, with
great *nonchalance*: and for the last-named crime their
law condemns the criminal to imprisonment—*for one
year.*

There is a railroad, belonging to an American company, running from Aspinwall to Panama, a distance
of forty-seven miles. Panama, it will be remembered,
is on the Pacific side of the Isthmus. In this connection, I will remark, that persons sometimes find it
difficult to remember which of the two cities, Aspin-
wall and Panama, is on the Atlantic side, and which
on the Pacific. A rule that will always enable one
to remember it is, that the initial letter of each city
is the same as that of the ocean on whose shore it
stands. Aspinwall, beginning with the letter A, is on
the Atlantic side; Panama, with P, on the Pacific.
No one will forget this.

During our ride in the cars from Aspinwall to Panama, we saw hundreds of natives—all wearing about the same appearance as those in Aspinwall. One remarkable feature was, that their children were running about in a state of nudity that was quite shocking to modest persons. Children under twelve years wear no raiment from the neck down, and usually go bare-headed. Even the adult males wear nothing but hat and breeches, and are therefore always in trim for a pugilistic encounter. Some of the ladies wear only a petticoat and a cigar. It is fashionable for the ladies there to "use the weed."

Panama is a much larger and more important place than Aspinwall. Its population is probably ten thousand. There are many more houses of respectable appearance there, among which are several hotels. There are also two antiquated Catholic churches, one of which is said to be nearly two hundred years old.

A dilapidated old wall surrounds the city, but it would prove a feeble protection against a civilized navy.

The weather is extremely hot all the year, the temperature never falling much below ninety degrees Fahrenheit. The heat is not so extreme, however, during the "rainy season," which comprises our fall, and a portion of our summer and winter months. All kinds of tropical fruits grow there in abundance. I saw oranges, lemons, limes, bananas, pineapples, cocoanuts, and other fruits, on the trees.

The natives obtain these fruits by merely gathering them, and do a good business by selling them to travelers, at prices which, though lower than New York prices, are there considered enormous.

In justice to these natives, I will say that travelers who conduct themselves with propriety, are always civilly treated by them. But it is not safe to injure or abuse them, where they are in such a decided majority; for, like most cowards, they are brutal and vicious, and, if irritated, do not hesitate to murder foreigners.

Many, no doubt, remember the terrible riot that occurred in Panama, a dozen years ago, between foreigners and natives. It was occasioned by one rascally drunken passenger, who managed to raise a dispute with a fruit-vender, and concluded to settle the matter by knocking over the fruit-stand and shooting at the owner. Thus it originated: the natives making an assault on the offender, and his fellow-passengers attempting to defend him. The riot soon became general; and the military of the New Granadian Government being called out to quell the disturbance, did so by wantonly shooting down every white man that came in their way. The slaughter was fearful. It should be a warning to all coarse and reckless fools, like the originator of this difficulty, who do not know how to conduct themselves with common decency in a foreign country.

CHAPTER XLVII.

THE "GOLDEN CITY."

WE embarked at Panama on the steamer "Golden Age," the same day we landed at Aspinwall, and made the passage to San Francisco in fourteen days—touching at the ports of Acapulco and Manzanillo, Mexico—coaling at the former place. The distance from Panama to San Francisco is three thousand two hundred and sixty-seven nautical miles, according to the record of our run. Manzanillo is about midway between the two places, while Acapulco is about three hundred miles nearer Panama.

I will not trouble the reader with the details of this voyage, but, simply stating that we arrived in the grand harbor of San Francisco early in May, and landed early one pleasant Sunday morning, I will proceed to tell what kind of place it is, and relate what befell the redoubtable John Smith there.

First, I will briefly mention the peculiarities of San Francisco, commencing with—

THE CLIMATE.—In San Francisco, as well as along the whole coast of California and Oregon, the temperature of the air does not vary much during the year. There are no extremes of heat or cold. The trade-winds prevail during the summer, and there is no rain except in the winter months—the period of the "rainy season." It seldom snows or freezes—and never to any considerable extent. In the summer the thermometer seldom indicates a higher degree of temperature than eighty. This would be rather warm, but for the steady breeze that sweeps in from the broad Pacific.

THE HARBOR of San Francisco has not, probably, an equal in the world. The entrance is narrow, and tall, abrupt hills stand guard on either side. This entrance is termed the "Golden Gate." The harbor is large enough to float all the vessels in the world; it is adorned with several picturesque islands; and its shores, where not occupied with buildings, are beautiful and green, except on the south side near the entrance, where immense heaps (almost mountains) of sand are the prevailing feature.

THE POPULATION was fifty-six thousand in 1860, according to the National Census, but it is now *three times* as great. It is, of course, composed of people from all parts of the world, but chiefly from the United States. A large proportion of the population are the Chinese. These people are small in stature, yellow in color, pagan in religion, ingenious, industrious, inoffensive, cowardly, low-lived, filthy, and ugly as toads—creatures to which they bear a striking family resemblance. They work at any and every thing, many of them doing housework, washing and ironing, and the like. I remember seeing the following names of "Orientals" on their business signs: Wo Hop, Hung Gee, Cum Lum Sam, Sam Lee, Wo Lee, Wo Wing, Ah Sing, Wing Wo, Yek Wa. These distinguished gentlemen from the Orient, (or rather, to one in California, from the Occident) were all extensively engaged in the laundry business. There are but few negroes in San Francisco. I do not not think I saw a dozen while there.

THE MONEY in circulation in the "Golden City" is only silver and gold. No paper money of any kind is seen.

EARTHQUAKES are a luxury which this city indulges in occasionally. We had one gentle shock while I was there. A few years ago they were favored with one that did much damage, and scared many of the inhabitants out of a year's growth : and in October, 1868, they had one still more severe. Slight shocks are quite common.

San Francisco is one of the greatest fruit, vegetable, and grain markets in the world.

During my sojourn in San Francisco, I was employed as "Funny Man" of a well-known literary paper, the "GOLDEN CITY;" and shortly after my arrival I published an article, under a *nom de plume*, in which I touched up some of the peculiarities of the city as they presented themselves to me, in the following manner :

"CAT'S-EYE VIEW OF SAN FRANCISCO. BY O. JOB JONES.

"One morning, shortly after my arrival in San Francisco, I strolled out to take a view of the city as it was and is—the clerk of my hotel having kindly informed me that it was 'piled up all around us.'

"I first directed my steps to the post-office, where, making my way up to the 'J' window, I modestly inquired if there was any letter for O. Job Jones?

The clerk without looking, informed me that there wasn't. Wondering how he found it out, I asked if there were any newspapers? Yes, wrong as it was to annoy him with so many foolish questions, I did."

"What was his reply?

"I will tell you.

"The truth of the matter was, the steamer hadn't been in more than twenty-four hours, and the papers had not yet been distributed. This the clerk *might* have informed me, in calm, gentlemanly and compre-hensive language : but, did he? No. Such a course would have been inconsistent with his dignity. Here's the way he answered me ; he says—and that in a rude tone that startled me—says he :

"'YOU'D BETTER WAIT TILL THEY'RE DISTRIBUTED FIRST, HADN'T YOU !'

"Abashed and mortified at this exhibition of supe-rior greatness, and enjoying a full sense of my little-ness—my comparative *nothingness*—I turned away, trembling. If I had never before felt that I was but mortal, I felt it now—felt it sensibly, deeply, awfully, as I shrunk from the stern presence of this great being.

"I was patient, however. I remembered that the morning was a little damp; and, wishing to return good for evil, I informed this mighty man that there was a more genial climate located somewhere—a climate where they have warm weather the year round—and recommended his emigration thither at once. All this in the most laconic language imagi-nable.

"The Atheist claims that there is no God : but he is

clearly mistaken. Just let him go to that post-office window and inquire for a paper or letter inopportunely, and he will see before him the stern, exalted countenance of as fine a little god as any one would wish to see. Vulcan, the god of fire ; Mars, the god of war; Neptune, the god of the deep; and Jupiter, the great big god of all, are simply nowhere, compared with that pompous and pretentious clerk of the P. O. !

"Full of these thoughts, I wended my way westward, towards the more elevated regions of the city. I had not gone far till I met a singular being, whose name (I have since learned) was John Hung Kee Dung Kee Lung Kee Mung Kee Choo Bang. This person, I understood, constituted a considerable portion of the population of San Francisco. The most remarkable feature about him was, that he didn't resemble anybody else I had ever seen, in *any* feature. His color was a mixture about half-way between that of a bay colt and that of a cream-colored pony. His nose was the puggest of the pug, and the ugliest of the ugly. He wore a blue cotton petticoat on each leg, and a black shirt, which he hadn't the decency to stuff in anywhere. He had a pair of skates on, but the iron part was broken off, and he walked on the wood. He had no hat on, but his head was tied up in a piece of goods such as they make black cotton umbrellas of. He had no hair on his head at all, except just one single one that grew out at the back about as thick as a corn-cob, and hung down to his heels, where it came to a point. This, I fancied, would be very convenient to hang him. He appeared to be an adult male, not younger than fifteen, or older than forty-nine; but somewhere along about there.

"I have been informed that this individual was imported in large numbers from a little island, somewhere in the Pacific, called China. It is but a small island, inhabited by only a few hundred millions of these people; so they can never do much harm anywhere.

"As I walked up street, I was a little surprised to meet a house on its way down to the post-office.* It was traveling slowly, to be sure; but it looked smiling and happy, and even intelligent. I am informed that when a man gets dissatisfied with the location of his dwelling, he just ties a rope round the door-knob and leads it away, up or down street, to some more agreeable vicinity, like a man leading a horse to water with a halter. I have since met quite a number walking about. They seem quite tractable and docile, and will follow where led, just like a good-natured elephant.

"I like this system very much. I cannot help thinking how convenient it would be if I had a house up in that neighborhood where the "John" element prevails. I should just put a halter on and lead it away a mile or two to-morrow morning before breakfast.

---

* This is an allusion to the moving of buildings, which is carried on to a considerable extent in San Francisco. It is no unusual thing there, to move a frame building as much as a mile when the owner finds it profitable to sell the ground it stands on.

" I like several things about San Francisco. I like its "fractional currency" for one thing. The material it is printed on is better calculated for standing all sorts of weather, and the wear and tear of time, than that in the States. Moreover, it is not near so likely to be repudiated, and enjoys a better foreign reputation.

" I like the ladies here; they have but one fault. That fault is similar to that of the very small congregation that turned out one Sunday morning at the church I used to attend. There were not more than nineteen of us, and the parson scolded us for an hour because we didn't turn out better. It wasn't our fault that the rest didn't come. I'm sure I was all there. So, I suppose it is hardly just to censure the ladies here because there are not more of them; it isn't their fault.

" I am also pleased with the elevated points around;* they give a man a chance to rise in the world, without principle, capital or reputation. Besides, one of them would be such a fine start for a monument. One might be topped out on Telegraph Hill, for instance, with very little expense; and in a graphic description of it, it might be stated that the top was five hundred and twenty-three feet above tide-water. No allusion need be made to the bottom.

" Among other peculiarities of San Francisco, I perceive that the blacking of boots and shoes is done by grown-up adult men, and that they have regular

* I have already intimated that there were a few rough hil's in this vicinity. There are streets in San Francisco which it is difficult to ascend without ladders.

establishments for the accommodation of the customer.
This is a grand idea. The customer not only has a
comfortable seat to sit in while his brogans are being
rubbed down and shined up, but he also enjoys the
luxury of a shelter, which is ample protection against
he heavy summer rains and winter snows, which, I
believe, prevail very extensively here.

"Pardon me if I make any blunders in giving my
views of San Francisco.*

"I have perceived, in the course of my perambula-
tions, that they were moving Kearny street further
up the hill.† I didn't like to ask any questions concerning it, lest I should be considered green; but I
supposed that the reason was that it had slid down
at the time of the earthquake here, a few years ago.

"I have heard so much about the rough state of
society here, that I am surprised and delighted to find
that law and order are as strictly observed here as in
any city of the States. From what I have heard in
times gone by, I was led to anticipate that I should
hear a bullet whiz every time I should step from my
door, and that I should find a fresh dead man lying at
every corner. I am glad to find, however, that the
streets are entirely clear of such obstructions, and
that men are not killed here, except in cases of absolute necessity. I highly approve of this orderly
state of things. I don't deny that it is quite a
pleasant pastime to a new beginner to help kill a man

---

* As the reader may have already gathered, they have no
rain in summer or snow in winter.

† An allusion to the widening and improving of that street.

or two each week; but, as is the case with every other enjoyment, the novelty soon wears off, and one gets tired of it."

I carried a letter of introduction from a gentleman in Philadelphia to Mr. J. M. Foard, of the " Golden City," San Francisco, and was very cordially received.

"Mr. Foard," I said one day, shortly after my arrival, "I am very fond of the water——"

"Not as a beverage, I hope," he interrupted.

"Not as a regular beverage; but as a medium of navigation. I love riding on the water. I would like to go out and take a row."

"Where?" he asked.

"On the harbor," I replied.

"Don't do it."

"Why?"

"You are not familiar with our harbor. It is an unsafe one for an inexperienced boatman. Even some of the most skillful lose their lives. It may be calm and smooth as a river one moment; the next, the tide may change, the wind rise against it, and it may become so boisterous, all at once, that you might imagine it was ready to boil over. Don't venture out in a small boat. We have a list of drownings to record every week, and should be most unhappy to place your name in our next week's list. Don't go!"

"I won't," I replied, fully impressed with the dangers of the harbor.

I meant it.

But—perfidious as it was—I afterward basely disregarded the advice of my excellent friend Foard, and justly came to grief.

Five minutes after leaving the office of the " Golden City," I met two fellow-passengers, named Gilmore and Brooker—both good fellows, and fond of fun— the latter a nephew of a celebrated "ornament of the stage," then "drawing houses" in San Francisco.

"Smith," said Gilmore, " suppose we take a ride somewhere?"

" Where?" I asked.

"Any where," said he.

" Let us take a boat-ride," suggested Brooker.

" The very thing!" said Gilmore.

" I have been told," I interposed, " that the harbor here is rather dangerous, and——"

"O, never mind! We can manage a boat in any harbor. I am some oarsman, myself."

"There can't be much danger with three of us to run the craft," remarked Brooker. " Let us go!"

We went.

The face of the harbor was as smooth and gentle as that of a " sleeping beauty," and the three of us glided gracefully out from one of the piers—a pair of oars, in my skillful (?) hands, gently dipping into the unruffled waters at irregular intervals. The friendly warning of Foard was entirely forgotten.

O, Foard! Thou best of friends! Though John Smith may be wandering thousands of miles from the happy spot where thy kind face first smiled a welcome to him in a strange land, yet fresh in his memory is that noble and pleasing face, as on the day thy warning voice said: "Don't go out on the harbor, Smith!"

The air is usually quiet in the morning, at San Francisco, but as the day advances, a stiff breeze springs up, and, on meeting the ebbing tide, stirs up the waters of the harbor, as though a young son of Neptune were just beneath the surface, lashing them with his toy-whip: the waterman must then exercise his utmost strength and skill to navigate with safety.

We had not proceeded more than a mile, when the tide commenced to run out, the wind came sweeping in through the "Golden Gate," and the waters began to evince their illest humor.

The first trifling mishap that befel us was that a rough, ill-natured, foam-crested wave came slashing along, wrested an oar from my hand, and left it floating on the "briny deep." The boat became unmanageable, turned with her side to the waves, and lay in a trough of the—harbor.

In endeavoring to recover the truant oar, Gilmore pitched out into the "yeast of waves;" and, in endeavoring to recover *him*, by means of his coat-tail, *I* pitched out; and, in endeavoring to save himself from the same fate, Brooker pitched out; and there, with

"Nothing save the waves and"—us,

and the boat, (half-full of water,) we commenced a manly and awkward struggle for existence. With this boon in view, Gilmore clung to the oar, and Brooker and I to the boat.

By this time, the wind was blowing with actual fierceness, and the waves swept clear over our heads every second. There can be little doubt that we would all have found an eternal *nest* among the slimy *harbor*-weed, with only the monsters of the *shallow* to drop a (crocodile) tear upon our "moist, uncomfortable bodies," but for certain timely " succor " that appeared on the scene at this critical juncture. The said "succor" comprised two skillful oarsmen, who owned the boat, and, having seen that we managed it poorly, and fearing the loss of their property, had put out to our assistance some minutes prior to the startling accident—arriving just in time to save their boat (and us) from an aqueous tomb.

They hauled us and the lost oar aboard their own boat, like so many packages of damaged goods, (*flotsam* Blackstone would have styled us,) took the other boat in tow, and started for shore,—giving us a good round cursing for our awkwardness in so nearly sacrificing their property.

I never told Foard of this adventure till about two months had elapsed, and it had got a little "old." Then, having first exacted a promise from him that he would not scold me for what I was about to tell him, frankly confessed the whole affair, bringing out all the little extenuating points, such as, "The morning was *so* fine," " The harbor was *so* smooth," " We thought that three of us could surely manage one boat." " We had partaken of fluid refreshments," " We hadn't seen each other for several days, and felt so jolly glad," *et cetera.*

He did not break his promise : but——

"Smith," said he, "if I had not promised not to scold you, I would give you the (blank)est black-guarding any man ever got in San Francisco! To

think that, in the very face of the good, healthy advice I gave you, you should have the unparalleled audacity to—Well, never mind: I promised not to
scold : but if you ever do such a thing again—I
wonder what time it is ?   I feel dry."

I didn't, the day I pitched out of the boat.

23

CHAPTER XLVIII.

The Doctor.

DEAR reader, before bidding adieu to San Fran cisco, let your one-legged friend introduce you to a noble citizen of that cosmopolitan city, whom, for the sake of a name, shall be styled Dr. Charles Rowell of Kearny street.

Let us call this chapter an imaginary sketch of what might be, what has been, and what will be. Let us suppose your friend John Smith on a crutch to be only mortal: let us suppose him, after all, an ordinary object for—

"The slings and arrows of outrageous fortune,"

as well as subject to—

"The heart-ache and the thousand natural shocks
That flesh is heir to :"

let us suppose him a human being who eats, drinks— yes, *drinks!*—sleeps, and indulges in other like amuse- ments, and let us suppose him susceptible of suffering, when the means of these enjoyments are, by any chance, temporarily withheld. Let us even suppose that he may be "broke," sick, and "in a strange land," all at once. Let us suppose that the "Panama Fever," which is "no respecter of persons" may lay hold of him on any proper occasion, and let us suppose that poverty which is another "no-respecter-of-persons," may happen to pay him a friendly visit . about the same time. Let us suppose both visitors going hand in hand and calling on John Smith at the same time at his lodging-house in San Francisco.

In asking the reader to assume all this, I do not positively assert that such things did actually happen to John Smith himself, in this connection, but I can testify to the substantial truth of what I am about to relate, and it is no harm to make use of Mr. Smith as an actor.

I have heard a good deal said about angels: but as no one now living can prove to the satisfaction of the public that he ever saw one, the personal appearance and general traits of their characters can be but matters of conjecture.

We are inclined, however, when speaking or thinking of an angel, to fancy it a lovely creature—whether male or female, I cannot say—of fair complexion, blue eyes and light curling hair, and clothed in a long white robe, with the hue of the "driven snow"—the handsome toes just peeping out from beneath the lower folds. In addition to this, we fancy a pair of gentle wings protruding from the shoulder blades. These, however useful, when the angel happens to be in a hurry, are rather calculated to detract from the handsome outline of a fine figure, in case the fashionable clothing of the present day should be used, instead of the robe. I believe that every reader will readily comprehend me, without my going to the trouble to say that the wings alluded to, if covered with a neat dress coat, (or other fashionable garment,) would give the wearer a lamentable appearance of being hump-backed.

Such, however, are not my ideas of an angel. As we cannot know, positively, what shape we are to assume after leaving the scenes of our present exist-ence, I have selected my *beau ideal* of an angel from among the sons of men. The angel I shall describe has a handsome, manly, noble, genial, smiling face; the calm gray eyes twinkle with merriment and good nature; a heavy black beard flows from the lower half of the countenance; the brow is one of the intelligent order, the hair is dark; the figure is full and strong, and dressed—not in a flowing white robe—but in black pantaloons, vest and frock-coat, actually made by a corporeal tailor. For the latter article of clothing, while the owner lounges easily in his neat office, dur-ing hours of leisure, might be substituted a dressing-gown. At such times, too, place a common brier-wood pipe in the hand, and the figure of my angel is complete.

Such was Doctor Rowell, whose image, but poorly portrayed here, may well supersede the bright one of the winged angel in the fancy of John Smith.

John Smith being in San Francisco; without em-ployment; attacked with a return of Panama Fever contracted on the Isthmus; suffering a natural depres-sion of spirits; withal, in " reduced circumstances;" and being of too delicate a nature to apply to friends, —although he had some there who would have rushed to his assistance with a relish—came to the melancholy conclusion that the best thing he could do, sad as it was, was to enter the City Hospital for—say—an indefinite period.

With this view, he, languid, pale and emaciated, walked into the office of a physician—walked into the same office on a crutch—to ask for information as to the measures to be resorted to in order to gain admittance to the City Hospital.

This physician chanced to be the man whom we style Dr. Charlie Rowell. This was the angel, who, unlike the popular angel with robe and wings, wore a common black suit, a smile, a merry twinkle of the eye, and carried a pipe in his hand, at which he took occasional deliberate whiffs.

"Sit down," he said to the one-legged young man.

The latter seated himself on a sofa.

"You are the Doctor?"

"That's what they call me," answered the physician, cheerfully. Then he took a calm whiff of that pipe, and deliberately sat down in a rocking-chair.

Smith would have remarked that the weather was fine, but he remembered that the weather is always pleasant in San Francisco. So, he switched off on another subject—*the* subject—and said:

"Doctor, I have simply come in to ask for a little information. I am a stranger here, and I suppose you can tell me what I desire to know."

"What is that?"

"I wish information as to the means of gaining admittance to the City Hospital."

"Why do you want to go to the hospital?"

"Because, I am quite unwell, have no immediate business prospects, and am nearly broke."

" What seems to be the matter with you ?"

" Something like ague."

" Have you come through Panama lately ?"

"Yes, I only landed here a week or two ago. I have not felt quite well since my arrival, and since I fell out of a boat in the harbor the other day and got wet, I have felt worse."

After some discussing of symptoms, the Doctor said :

"You have what is called Panama Fever. But that's nothing. Where did you lose your leg ?"

" In the army."

" Well, it is not necessary for you to go to the hospital. It would be a hard place for you to go to, any how, and I cannot allow it. Do not be discouraged. It is nothing here for new-comers to find themselves pecuniarily reduced. Such things happen every day. A great many persons are arriving here now, and many of them come with but little spare means. As numbers do not get into business so soon as they hope, the result is very natural. Now, as for yourself, if you suppose that I, who can easily cure you in a short time, would sit here with my arms folded, smoking my pipe, and see you go into the hospital for want of treatment, and that, too, after you have lost a limb in the service of your country, I must say that it speaks poorly for your discernment of human character. I should——"

" But I am almost without means, and ——"

" Well, suppose you are? *I* am not. You shall not go into the hospital; you shall accept medicine from me; you shall also allow me to see that you want for nothing in the way of living till you are well and succeed in getting into business."

"But, Doctor, it would not be right for me to ——"

"Excuse me one moment," interrupted the Doctor, rising and going into another room.

When, after a brief absence, he returned, it was with several small packages of medicines in his hand with "directions" pasted on them.

"Take these with you to your lodging-house, and come in and see me to-morrow."

"But how can I, consistently ——"

"Come, now, after I have prepared the medicines for your particular case, you would not surely refuse them, and thus render them useless."

"Very well, Doctor, I will take them; but remember that I do not accept them gratuitously. That, however, does not lessen your kindness in offering them. I will accept treatment at present, but it must be with the understanding that I am to pay you as soon as I ——"

"Have more money than I have," interrupted the Doctor.

On arriving at his lodging-house, and entering his room, the owner of the packages began to examine them. One was a small vial with a brandy-colored liquid in it, and a label on instructing the patient to indulge in a certain number of drops at certain intervals. Another was a small, round paper box, which rattled in such a way as to entirely preclude the idea of its containing any thing else than pills. A label on this box suggested to the afflicted the expedience of enveloping one of them in his stomach each evening about bed-time.

A third box, however, was a puzzle. It was like the second in size, was heavier, did not rattle, and bore the following astounding directions:

"USE ACCORDING TO JUDGMENT."

What could this mean? How should the patient know what rules to observe in the use of this box of "medicine," limited as was his knowledge of the art of Esculapius? Still, it would do no harm to open the box and see what manner of medicine it contained.

This proceeding being carried out, developed the fact that it contained several hard, shiny, yellowish, metallic, button-shaped "pills," wrapped in paper, each containing the following strange inscription:

"ACIREMA FO SETATS DETINU. LOD EVIF."

CHAPTER XLIX.

A STARTLING BUNDLE.

EARLY one Monday morning in August, after a sojourn of about three months in San Francisco, in the course of which I had been, on the whole, rather prosperous than otherwise, I was sitting in the office of the "Golden City," when I suddenly, without knowing why, conceived the idea of returning to "the States." The steamer *Nevada*, of the "Opposition Line," was to leave for Panama on the ensuing Wednesday; and I walked down to the office of the company and bought a ticket—being just in time to secure the last stateroom.

The astonishment and sadness of my numerous friends—for by this time there were two full semicircles of them in San Francisco—on learning of this rash act, were a source of mingled amusement and pain to me. I half regretted what I had done, and if I had not already purchased my ticket, I should have relinquished the idea of going. But the die was cast, and, concealing from them the regret I felt, I lightly reminded them that they too well knew that "When I took a notion to go to any place," I was moderately certain to go.

Not till the steamer floated away from the pier,

amid the cheers and blessings of several thousand spectators, and I saw the waving hands, hats, and handkerchiefs, and heard the friendly farewells of a score who had come to see me off, and of hundreds who had come to bid other passengers adieu, did I fully realize that I was leaving the city I had so soon learned to love—again starting on a long journey of more than five thousand geographic miles. When I did realize it, it was with a depth of sadness I cannot describe: and had I not been a man, I think I should hardly have subdued that moisture of the eyes that is looked upon as an evidence of weakness—though it is sometimes a noble and heavenly weakness!

The voyage to Panama, in the course of which we put in at Manzanillo, Mexico, for coal, occupied four-teen days. Much space might be absorbed with a full description of it; but it would be scarcely perti-nent. Let us close our eyes on the voyage, imagine a lapse of two weeks, and we find the good steamer *Nevada* quietly anchored at early morn in the picturesque harbor of Panama, New Granada. There are no piers for the accommodation of large vessels at Panama, so that ocean steamers must anchor three miles from shore, in the deep water, and be relieved of their cargoes and passengers, or loaded therewith, by means of lighters and small steamboats.

We rose from our berths on the morning the *Nevada* anchored in the harbor of Panama, elated with the prospect of crossing the Isthmus and taking another steamer at Aspinwall for New York. It was, there-fore, somewhat to our chagrin that we learned that an accident had happened the connecting steamer,

Dakotah, that although due at Aspinwall five or six
days previously, she had barely arrived, and that we
must lie at Panama and wait till she should have
discharged her cargo. The prospective delay was
variously estimated by the officers at from "a few
days," to "some little time."

The natives learned that we were to lie in the
harbor for some days, and soon flocked about the
steamer in small boats, offering to convey to shore all
who wished to visit the rusty old city. The price
they asked was *cuarto rialos* per head—which means
half-a-dollar.

Many of us took advantage of this means of escaping from the confinement of the vessel, and in an
hour or two the greater portion of the steamer *Nevada's* "population" might have been seen intermingled
with the inhabitants of benighted Panama. Prominent among those who visited the city might have
been seen the owner of a certain crutch.

It was now the "rainy season," but the heat, between the showers that visited us daily, was intense
and oppressive. To counteract its effects, the thirsty
Caucasians resorted to certain iced drinks, containing
stimulants, which were to be had at the saloons at
twenty-five cents (coin) each. I regret to chronicle
the fact that many of them used these beverages to
an extent rather calculated to engender thirst (next
morning) than to allay it.

As the shades of evening began to fall over the
tropics, three persons, Monsieur Figaro, a Frenchman;
Mr. Hawes, an Englishman; and I, John Smith, Esq.,
an Americo-Caucasian, wended their way down 'a

street of Panama, with the intention of taking a small boat at the beach, and returning to the steamer *Nevada*.

Now, at the lower end of this street, near the archway in the city's wall, affording an outlet to the beach, there is a certain saloon with the alluring name of " OREGONIAN SHADES." The proprietor is an intelligent native, about the color of new leather who speaks both Spanish and English.

When we had come over to Panama, that morning, there was in " our crowd" a humorous and witty passenger named Briggs; but, in the course of the day, we had lost sight of him, and I just glanced in at the "Oregonian Shades," as we passed, deeming it possible that he might be there; and hoping for the pleasure of his company, together with that of my French and English friends, to the steamer. Mr. Briggs was not there; but there was within a lady passenger of the *Nevada*, who was one of the most remarkable persons I ever met. This lady, whose husband was also a passenger, was about twenty-eight years old, five feet four inches high, and weighed two hundred and ten pounds. Her width may be imagined. To add that she was inclined to *embonpoint*, would be rather mild language. She was obviously of Irish birth and parentage : but whatever I may have occasion to say, of her personal merits or demerits, must not be construed into any invidious insinuations against her nationality, for I am not pre· judiced against the Irish, but rather in their favor, claiming that, everything fairly considered, they possess as many noble traits as any other people.

This corpulent lady was not, I regret to say, in a rational mood. She had visited Panama early in the day, in the company of her husband—a big, ill-looking, muscular American—who had become intoxicated during the day and basely deserted her. His name was Philip—somebody—and he was termed "Pheel" by the lady in question, whose accent was peculiar. When I have stated that Mrs. "Pheel," however *temperate*, was not of the *total abstinence* "stripe," but rather given to the moderate use of aqueous stimulus, and that she had not departed a hair's breadth from her principles on the day in question, I think that the intelligent reader will not fail to comprehend the true state of things.

"*Hombre*," said I, addressing the proprietor of the *Oregonian Shades*, as I looked in, "have you seen the gentleman with side-whiskers who was in here with us to-day, and whom we called Briggs?"

"Not since two o'clock," replied *Hombre*.

At this moment Mrs. "Pheel" started up from her seat like one excited.

"Hov ye seen Pheel?" she eagerly asked.

"I have not, madam," I replied.

"Och, he's lift me!" she exclaimed, throwing herself back into her seat, and dropping two of five bundles of goods she had been buying.

This was too much for me. My sympathies were aroused in a moment. I knew by Philip's complexion that he was a drinking man, and here was the patient and gentle wife anxiously awaiting his return to the "Oregonian Shades." Can it be wondered at that, meantime, hot weather, corpulence, anxiety, and

general depression of spirits all taken into considera·
tion, she had not sat there all that time dying of
thirst, while the means of allaying it were before
her? Not rationally. The proprietor afterward in·
formed me that she had "drank nothing but ale:"
how much, he could not undertake to compute.

"Probably," said I, to the deserted woman, as I
stepped in and gently picked up her bundles for
her, "Philip has taken a little too much, and forgot·
ten you. You had better return to the steamer."

"Is he in there?" asked my English companion at
the door.

"Who?—Briggs?"

"Yes."

"No, *he* is not: but here is a lady whom you have
seen on the steamer, and who has lost sight of her
husband. Had she not better return with us?"

"I suppose so."

"Well, madam," said I, "we are going back to the
steamer now; will you come with us? Phil will be
all right. No doubt he is there by this time."

"Och, Mr. Smith, ye won't desart me, will ye!" she
exclaimed, letting two more bundles fall.

Mr. Smith! she actually called me by name! That
she knew my name I was not aware. How she had
learned it was a mystery to me; but it was more
marvelous still that, having learned so strange and
rare a name, she remembered it!

"No, madam," said I, "you shall go with us to the
ship. Come." And I gallantly picked up her two
bundles and restored them to her fulsome arms.

By this time Monsieur Figaro was looking over

Mr. Hawes's shoulder at the door, and I fancied I saw him smile. It may have been imagination.

"Come, madam," said I, "we are going down to hire a boat immediately. Will you go with us?"

"Och! Indade I wull!"

She now rose—being very little taller standing than when sitting—dropping all her bundles but one.

I picked up all but one.

"Come, let us go."

It was now fully dark.

Somewhat to my chagrin, this charming and confiding creature grasped my gallant arm, as a support; and we all started for the beach.

With the care of two hundred and ten unsteady pounds on my arm, and I walking on a frail crutch, I confess that I experienced a difficulty in traveling to the beach which I did not acknowledge at the time.

On the way to the boat, my voluptuous companion dropped all her bundles, one by one, and they were promptly picked up, taken care of, and carried after us, by a little native with nothing but a hat on—whose attention and fidelity I generously rewarded with a silver half-dollar on arriving at the water's edge.

I will not take it upon myself to say that Mrs. "Pheel" had drank too much, as I should not wish to do her the slightest injustice: it may have been the extreme heat of the climate; it may have been her obesity; it may have been her anxiety; it may have been that she was not blessed with a strong constitution; it may have been all or part of these combined that governed her conduct: but certain it is, that Mrs. "Pheel," acted strangely and unlike a lady at the beach. Some little delay was occasioned there, by the fact that the native who engaged to take us to the steamer, had to go and hunt up his partner ; and during the interval, Mrs. "Pheel" not only talked strangely, walked strangely, and bore herself in an unaccountable manner ; but actually became unreasonable, unmanageable, and even pugnacious. She first opened our eyes by declaring that we were going to rob her, and adding :

"Bedad, I'll make Pheel put a head on yez all !"

This was somewhat startling to me, as I had one head that suited me very well, and, with my means of perambulating, did not desire to be encumbered with another.

"Madam," I remonstrated, "I pray that you will be quiet. We are your friends, and you are welcome to go with us to the steamer. I hope——"

"Where's my fan ?" she interrupted, springing with some abruptness to a new theme of conversation.

"I do not know. Have you lost one ?"

"Bedad some one's sthole it," she vociferated.

By this time a dozen natives had collected on the beach, and were viewing the female Caucasian with mingled wonder and amusement.

Mr. Hawes was sitting on an old spar at this time, calmly fanning himself with a palm-leaf fan he had carried all day. The object, at this unfortunate moment, caught the eye of Mrs. Pheel.

"Ye *blaggard* ye !" she fairly screamed, staggering

clumsily toward the startled Englishman; "ye hov
me fan! Bad luck to ye, ye divil! Give me that!"

Without waiting for a word of remonstrance from
Mr. Hawes, she dealt him a blow on the cheek bone
that sent him backward over the spar, with his feet
elevated in the night air; and, at the same time, stag-
gered, herself, whirled round and fell prostrate on
the rough stones and sand of the beach.

She was actually crazy. She screamed, struggled
convulsively, swore a few regular brimstone oaths,
then lay a little while appare*tly insensible, and
gasping as though she were in a retort and the air
had suddenly been pumped away.

By this time, quite a concourse of curious natives
had collected around us.

After an apparent death-struggle of three-quarters
of a minute, she actually ceased to breathe, and I
feared she was dead. I took her ample wrist in my
hand and there was not the slightest perceptible pulsa-
tion. Here was a go! Here was a fix for John
Smith! Night; foreign country; a dead woman on
the beach; only two of my race present, and they
scared like the deuce; surrounded by a score or two
of the swarthy, blood-thirsty natives of a semi-bar-
barous land! O, how I wished that crutch of mine
were but clicking on the side-walk in front of Trinity
church, New York; or the State House, Philadelphia.
But no, there I was; and the gloom of night, mingled
with the black faces of vicious and cowardly ruf-
fians, frowned on me. O, Smith! Smith!

What was to be done? What *could* be done?
Fortunately, the boat was soon after ready, and I

24

thought the best thing we could do would be to have
the "body" put aboard, and take it along. My companions concurred. But how should we get it into
the boat? The quickest way was to hire the natives;
so, I spoke to them. In my extremity, I remembered
that but a small proportion of those present could
speak English, so I endeavored to address them with
a mixture of both English and Spanish. As nearly
as I can recollect, I thus spoke to any and all of
them, individually and collectively:

"*Hombre! Signor! Carryo this hero fatwomano
into boato for cuarto rialos! Do you mind!*"

It appears they comprehended me, for eight of them,
in view of half-a-dollar each, laid hold of the "form"
and proceeded to carry it into the boat. It was indeed a clumsy burden. Yet they conveyed it to the
boat on scientific principles. The following was the
programme: any anatomist will readily comprehend:

Two of the *Hombres* supported their share of the
weight by locking hands beneath the *glutæus maximi;*
two others, in like manner, supported the *clavi· les,*
coracoid process and *acromion* of *scapula*, the *humeri,*
ulna, radius, et cetera, besides the *sternum* and *latissimus
dorsi;* two others supported the *tibia, fibula, gastrocne-
mius, tibialis anticus* and *extensor communis digitorum;*
the seventh supported the base of *tibia, astragalus,
peronæus tertius, abductor minimi digiti,* and *extensor
pollicis proprius;* while the eighth took charge of the
occipito-frontalis temporalis, os frontis, parietal and *orbi-
cularis palpebrarum.*

Thus they conveyed the inanimate form to the
small boat; but they were just on the point of "dump-

ing" it in, when it returned to consciousness, opened
its eyes and mouth, breathed, and was once more
Mrs. " Pheel."

" Murther!" was the first articulate sound of the
resuscitated.

" Hush, my good woman," I implored. " You are
all right now. We are starting for the steamer."

Thereupon, she opened her mouth and uttered a
series of screams that made the night hateful, and
causes me to shudder yet, when I think of them.
The substance of them was:

" Murther ! Murther ! Murther ! Robbery!
Robbery ! Help ! Police ! Watch ! Watch !
Police ! Murther ! Murther ! Watch ! Help !
Help ! Help ! Murther ! Murther ! Murther !
Police ! Police ! Police ! Och ! ye bloody divils!
Murther ! Murther ! Murther !"

This, however, is but an abridged edition of the
original. For five minutes—every one seeming like
an age—she continued to scream in this manner,
making the old walls of Panama to resound as with
the voices of all the fiends.

Had this happened at the piers of any civilized
town or city, the *gens-d'armes* would soon have been
down upon us and arrested the whole party ; but as it
was, we were not molested, and much to our relief, at
last succeeded in getting clear of shore, and we glided
away toward the steamer in the dim darkness, with
our baleful charge.

CHAPTER L.

EXIT SMITH.

ENOUGH. I need not tell of our arrival at the steamer; of the trouble the sailors had getting the drunken woman up the gang-ladder; of our meeting Briggs there; of his suggesting, while they were tugging away at the again insensible creature, pulling her up step by step, to " send for the *baggage-master*," as the proper person to take charge of the immense bundle ; of our lying in the harbor five days; of my meeting drunken " Pheel " in Panama, the day after our adventure with his charming bigger half; of his threatening to "punch a hole through " me with a sword-cane, for "running away with " his gentle wife—the proprietor of the *Oregonian Shades* having told him, on inquiry, that " she went away with that one-legged fellow ;"—of our final crossing the Isthmus; of our embarking at last on the crippled *Dakotah ;* of our tedious voyage of fourteen days, from Aspinwall to New York ; of the various events on the passage; of the death and burial at sea of a bright little boy, who had eaten too much tropical fruit; of our suffering for cold water—there being no ice on board the miserable ship; of our poor food, and but little of it—being restricted to two meals a day ; of the

machinery giving out off the coast of Cuba, and our
danger of not being able to reach any port; of our
being towed by a bark, to whom we showed a signal
of distress; of a fire on board, which was happily extinguished; of a hard blow off Cape Hatteras; of our
final arrival in New York: *et cetera*, and all that.

It is proper, in this chapter, to make some disposition of myself, as writers usually do of their principal
characters in the concluding chapter. Therefore, pre-
pare to bid John Smith an everlasting farewell.

To wind up by stating that I got married to a beautiful heiress, after the usual stern opposition, but final
consent of her stony-hearted old " parient," and that
I settled down after my rambles, and lived to a green
old age, would be a very happy termination; but the
events narrated are of too recent occurence, and
would appear like anachronisms. So, I must abandon
that idea.

Still, I must make some disposition of myself, for
if the reader is allowed to suppose me still perambulating over the world with the inevitable CRUTCH, he
will feel that he has not yet read the conclusion of
my story, and will look forward to the publication of
a supplementary volume of adventures, similar to
these—look forwar', I heartily assure him, only to
be bitterly disappointed. Linger over this volume,
gentle reader, for when you have laid it down you
will hear of John Smith, the man of the CRUTCH, no
more. He is a dead letter.

But now for that disposition. This remarkable
character must be got rid of some how. But how?
I can think of no end for him so fitting as *death*.

So, dear reader, as I have abandoned the idea of concluding with an account of my marriage; as death is a circumstance of almost as much importance in one's history; and as I am supported in this course by eminent precedent—Moses having given a graphic account of his own death in Deuteronomy; and as, moreover, this may be read years hence, when the hand that is writing it has indeed grown cold, and the pen fallen from its weary grasp, (and when there will be a vacant crutch to let,) I will conclude by simply stating that I died.

J·o·h·n·S·m·i·t·h.

NEW AND LATE BOOKS

PUBLISHED BY

JOHN E. POTTER & CO.

MAILING NOTICE.—*Any books on the following list will be sent, post paid, to any address, on receipt of price.* *Address* **JOHN E. POTTER & CO.,** Publishers, 614 and 617 Sansom Street, **PHILADELPHIA.**

HISTORICAL AND SECRET MEMOIRS OF THE

EMPRESS JOSEPHINE. A secret and truthful history of one of the most remarkable of women, uniting all the value of absorbing facts with that of the most exciting romance. Translated from the French of M'lle Le Normand, by JACOB M. HOWARD Esq. 2 vols. in one. Cloth. Price $1 75.

MEMOIRS OF THE COURT OF MARIE ANTOI-

NETTE. An instructive work—one of the most intensely interesting ever issued from the American press—the events of which should be familiar to all. By MADAME CAMPAN. With Biographical Introduction by M. DE LAMARTINE. 4 vols. in one. Cloth. Price $1 75.

MEMOIRS OF THE LIFE OF MARY, QUEEN OF

SCOTS. Affording a complete and authentic history of the unfortunate Mary, with materials and letters not used by other authors, making up a volume of rare interest and value. By MISS BENGER. With portrait on steel. 2 vols. in one. Cloth. Price $1 75.

MEMOIRS OF THE QUEENS OF FRANCE. Writ-

ten in France, carefully compiled from researches made there, commended by
the press generally, and published from the Tenth London Edition. It is a truly
valuable work for the reader and student of history. By Mrs. FORBES BUSH.
2 vols. in one. Cloth. Price $1 75.

MEMOIRS OF THE LIFE OF ANNE BOLEYN,

QUEEN OF HENRY VIII. In the records of biography there is no character that
more forcibly exemplifies the vanity of human ambition, or more thoroughly
enlists the attention of the reader than this—the Seventh American, and from
the Third London Edition. By Miss BENGER. With portrait on steel. Cloth. $1 75.

HEROIC WOMEN OF HISTORY. Containing the

most extraordinary examples of female courage of ancient and modern times,
and set before the wives, sisters, and daughters of the country, in the hope that
it may make them even more renowned for resolution, fortitude, and self-sacrifice
than the Spartan females of old. By HENRY C. WATSON. With Illustrations.
Cloth. $1 75.

PUBLIC AND PRIVATE HISTORY OF LOUIS NA-

POLEON, EMPEROR OF THE FRENCH. An impartial view of the public and private
career of this extraordinary man, giving full information in regard to his most
distinguished ministers, generals, relatives and favorites. By SAMUEL M.
SCHMUCKER, LL. D. With portraits on Steel. Cloth. $1 75.

LIFE AND REIGN OF NICHOLAS I., EMPEROR

OF RUSSIA. The only complete history of this great personage that has appeared
in the English language, and furnishes interesting facts in connection with Rus-
sian society and government of great practical value to the attentive reader. By
SAMUEL M. SCHMUCKER, LL. D. With Illustrations. Cloth. $1 75.

LIFE AND TIMES OF GEORGE WASHINGTON.

A concise and condensed narrative of Washington's career, especially adapted to
the popular reader, and presented as the best matter upon this immortal theme—
one especially worthy the attention and admiration of every American. By
SAMUEL M. SCHMUCKER, LL. D. With Portrait on steel. Cloth. $1 75.

LIFE AND TIMES OF ALEXANDER HAMILTON.

Incidents of a career that will never lose its singular power to attract and instruct, while giving impressive lessons of the brightest elements of character, surrounded and assailed by the basest. By SAMUEL M. SCHMUCKER, LL. D. With Portrait on steel. Cloth. $1 75.

LIFE AND TIMES OF THOMAS JEFFERSON. In

which the author has presented both the merits and defects of this great representative hero in their true light, and has studiously avoided indiscriminate praise or wholesale censure. By SAMUEL M. SCHMUCKER, LL. D. With Portrait. Cloth. $1 75.

LIFE OF BENJAMIN FRANKLIN. Furnishing a

superior and comprehensive record of this celebrated Statesman and Philosopher—rich beyond parallel in lessons of wisdom for every age, calling and condition in life, public and private. By O. L. HOLLEY. With Portrait on steel and Illustrations on wood. Cloth. $1 75.

PUBLIC AND PRIVATE LIFE OF DANIEL WEB-

STER. The most copious and attractive collection of personal memorials concerning the great Statesman that has hitherto been published, and by one whose intimate and confidential relations with him afford a guarantee for their authenticity. By Gen. S. P. LYMAN. With Illustrations. Cloth. $1 75.

LIFE AND TIMES OF HENRY CLAY. An impar-

tial biography, presenting, by bold and simple strokes of the historic pencil, a portraiture of the illustrious theme which no one should fail to read, and no library be without. By SAMUEL M. SCHMUCKER, LL. D. With Portrait on steel. Cloth. $1 75.

LIFE AND PUBLIC SERVICES OF STEPHEN A.

DOUGLAS. A true and faithful exposition of the leading incidents of his brilliant career arranged so as to instruct the reader and produce the careful study which the life of so great a man deserves. By H. M. FLINT. With Portrait on steel. Cloth. $1 75.

LIFE AND PUBLIC SERVICES OF ABRAHAM LIN-

COLN. (In both the English and German languages) As a record of this great man it is a most desirable work, admirably arranged for reference, with an index over each page, from which the reader can familiarize himself with the contents by glancing through it. By FRANK CROSBY, of the Philadelphia Bar. With Portrait on steel. Cloth. $1 75.

LIFE OF DANIEL BOONE, THE GREAT WESTERN

HUNTER AND PIONEER. Comprising graphic and authentic accounts of his daring, thrilling adventures, wonderful skill, coolness and sagacity under the most hazardous circumstances, with an autobiography dictated by himself By CECIL B. HARTLEY. With Illustrations. Cloth. $1 75.

LIFE OF COLONEL DAVID CROCKET, THE ORI-

GINAL HUMORIST AND IRREPRESSIBLE BACKWOODSMAN. Showing his strong will and indomitable spirit, his bear hunting, his military services, his career in Congress, and his triumphal tour through the States—written by himself; to which is added the account of his glorious death at the Alamo. With Illustrations. Cloth. $1 75.

LIFE OF KIT CARSON, THE GREAT WESTERN

HUNTER AND GUIDE. An exciting volume of wild and romantic exploits, thrilling adventures, hair-breadth escapes, daring coolness, moral and physical courage, and invaluable services—such as rarely transpire in the history of the world. By CHARLES BURDETT. With Illustrations. Cloth. $1 75.

LIFE OF CAPTAIN JOHN SMITH, THE FOUNDER

OF VIRGINIA. The adventures contained herein serve to denote the more noble and daring events of a period distinguished by its spirit, its courage, and its passion, and challenges the attention of the American people. By W. GILMORE SIMMS. With Illustrations. Price $1 75.

LIFE OF GENERAL FRANCIS MARION, THE

CELEBRATED P   .ISAN HERO OF THE REVOLUTION. This was one of the most distinguished   n who _ ....: grand theatre of war during the times that "tried men's so .!," and his br.......... .... has scarcely a parallel in history. By CECIL B. HARTLEY. With Illustrations. Cloth. $1 75.

Life of General Andrew Jackson, the

CELEBRATED PATRIOT AND STATESMAN. The character here shown as firm in will, clear in judgment, rapid in decision and decidedly pronounced, sprung from comparative obscurity to the highest gift within the power of the American people, and is prolific in interest. By ALEXANDER WALKER. $1 75.

Life and Times of General Sam Houston,

THE HUNTER, PATRIOT, AND STATESMAN. It reminds one of the story of Romulus—who was nurtured by the beasts of the forest till he planted the foundations of a mighty empire—and stands alone as an authentic memoir. With Maps, Portrait, and Illustrations. Cloth. $1 75.

Lives of the Three Mrs. Judsons, the

CELEBRATED FEMALE MISSIONARIES. The domestic lives and individual labors of these three bright stars in the galaxy of American heroines, who in ministering to the souls of heathens, experienced much of persecution. By CECIL B. HARTLEY. With steel Portraits. Cloth. $1 75.

Life of Elisha Kent Kane, and of Other

DISTINGUISHED AMERICAN EXPLORERS. A narrative of the discoverers who possess the strongest hold upon public interest and attention, and one of the few deeply interesting volumes of distinguished Americans of this class. By SAMUEL M. SCHMUCKER, LL. D. With Portrait on steel. Cloth. $1 75.

The Life and Adventures of Pauline

CUSHMAN, THE CELEBRATED UNION SPY AND SCOUT. Stirring details from the lips of the subject herself, whose courage, heroism, and devotion to the old flag, endeared her to the Army of the Southwest. By F. L. SARMIENTO, Esq., Member of the Philadelphia Bar. With Portrait on steel and Illustrations on wood. Cloth. $1 75.

Jefferson Davis and Stonewall Jackson:

THE LIFE AND PUBLIC SERVICES OF EACH. Truths from the lives of these men, both of whom served their country before the war, and afterwards threw themselves into the cause of the South with unbounded zeal—affording valuable historic facts for all, North and South. With Illustrations. Cloth. $1 75.

CORSICA, AND THE EARLY LIFE OF NAPOLEON.

Delicately drawn idyllic descriptions of the Island, yielding new light to political history, exciting much attention in Germany and England, and altogether making a book of rare character and value. Translated by Hon. E. JOY MORRIS. With Portrait on steel. Cloth. $1 75.

THE HORSE AND HIS DISEASES: EMBRACING

HIS HISTORY AND VARIETIES, BREEDING AND MANAGEMENT, AND VICES. A splendid, complete, and reliable book—the work of more than fifteen years' careful study—pointing out diseases accurately, and recommending remedies that have stood the test of actual trial. To which is added "RAREY's METHOD OF TRAINING HORSES." By ROBERT JENNINGS, V. S. With nearly one hundred Illustrations. Cloth. $1 75.

SHEEP, SWINE, AND POULTRY. Enumerating

their varieties and histories; the best modes of breeding, feeding, and managing; the diseases to which they are subject; the best remedies—and offering the best practical treatise of its kind now published. By ROBERT JENNINGS, V. S. With numerous Illustrations. Cloth. $1 75.

CATTLE AND THEIR DISEASES. Giving their

history and breeds, crossing and breeding, feeding and management; with the diseases to which they are subject, and the remedies best adapted to their cure; to which is added a list of remedies used in treating cattle. By ROBERT JENNINGS, V. S. With numerous Illustrations. Cloth. $1 75.

HORSE TRAINING MADE EASY. A new and

practical system of Teaching and Educating the Horse, including whip training and thorough instructions in regard to shoeing—full of information of a useful and well-tested character. By ROBERT JENNINGS, V. S. With numerous Illustrations. Cloth. $1 25.

600 RECEIPTS WORTH THEIR WEIGHT IN GOLD.

An unequalled variety in kind, the collection and testing of which have extended through a period of thirty years—a number of them having never before appeared in print, while all are simple, plain, and highly meritorious. By JOHN MARQUART, of Lebanon, Pa. Cloth. $1 75.

500 Employments Adapted to Women.

Throwing open to womankind productive fields of labor everywhere, and affording full opportunity to select employments best adapted to their tastes—all the result of over three years' constant care and investigation. By Miss VIRGINIA PENNY. Cloth. $1 75.

Everybody's Lawyer and Book of Forms.

The simplicity of its instructions, the comprehensiveness of its subject, and the accuracy of its details, together with its perfect arrangement, conciseness, attractiveness and cheapness make it the most desirable of all legal hand-books. By FRANK CROSBY, Esq. Thoroughly revised to date by S. J. VANDERSLOOT, Esq. 606 pp. Law Style. $2 00.

The Family Doctor. Intended to guard

against diseases in the family; to furnish the proper treatment for the sick; to impart knowledge in regard to medicines, herbs, and plants; to show how to preserve a sound body and mind, and written in plain language, free from medical terms. By Prof. HENRY TAYLOR, M. D. Profusely Illustrated. Cloth. $1 75.

The American Practical Cookery Book.

A faithful and highly useful guide, whose directions all can safely follow, making housekeeping easy, pleasant, and economical in all its departments, and based upon the personal test, throughout, of an intelligent practical housekeeper. Illustrated with Fifty Engravings. Cloth. $1 75.

Modern Cookery in all its Branches. De-

signed to interest and benefit housekeepers everywhere by its plain and simple instructions in regard to the judicious preparation of food, and altogether a work of superior merit. By Miss ELIZA ACTON. Carefully revised by Mrs. SARAH J. HALE. With many Illustrations and a copious Index. Cloth. $1 75.

Thirty Years in the Arctic Regions. The

graphic narrative of Sir John Franklin, the most celebrated of Arctic Travellers, in which Sir John tells his own story—unsurpassed for intense and all-absorbing interest—sketching his three expeditions, and that part of the fourth not shrouded in mystery to the world. Cloth. $1 75.

EXPLORATIONS AND DISCOVERIES DURING

FOUR YEARS' WANDERINGS IN THE WILDS OF SOUTHWESTERN AFRICA. Important and exciting experiences, full of wild adventure and instructive facts, wh.c, seem to possess a mysterious charm for every mind, and in which the spiri o intelligent and adventurous curiosity is everywhere prominent. By CHARLES JOHN ANDERSON. With Illustrations. Cloth. $1 75.

LIVINGSTONE'S TRAVELS AND RESEARCHES IN

SOUTH AFRICA. Given in the pleasing language of Dr. Livingstone, and rich in his personal adventures and hair-breadth escapes of that most indefatigable discoverer and interesting Christian gentleman—making a work of special value. By DAVID LIVINGSTONE, LL. D., D. C. S. Profusely Illustrated. Cloth. $1 75.

TRAVELS AND DISCOVERIES IN NORTH AND

CENTRAL AFRICA. Recounting an expedition undertaken under the auspices o. H. B M.'s Government, exhibiting the most remarkable courage, perseverance, presence of mind, and contempt of danger and death, and immensely important as a work of information. By HENRY BARTH, Ph. D., D. C. L., etc. With Illustrations. Cloth. $1 75.

ELLIS' THREE VISITS TO MADAGASCAR. Writ-

ten in Madagascar, while on a visit to the queen and people, in which is carefully described the singularly beautiful country and the manners and customs of .ts people, and from which an unusual amount of information is obtainable. By Rev. WILLIAM ELLIS, F. H. S. Profusely Illustrated. Cloth. $1 75.

ORIENTAL AND WESTERN SIBERIA. A Stir-

ring narrative of seven years' explorations in Siberia, Mongolia, the Kirghes Steppes, Chinese Tartary, and part of Central Asia, revealing extraordinary facts, showing much of hunger, thirst, and perilous adventure, and forming a work o. rare attractiveness for every reader. By THOMAS WILLIAM ATKINSON. With numerous Illustrations. Cloth. $1 75.

HUNTING SCENES IN THE WILDS OF AFRICA.

Thrilling adventures of daring hunters—Cummings, Harris. and others—among the Lions, Elephants, Giraffes, Buffaloes, and other animals—than which few, if any works, are more exciting. With numerous Illustrations. Cloth. $1 75.

Hunting Adventures in the Northern

WILDS. A tramp in the Chateaugay Woods, over hills, lakes and forest streams, at a time when millions of acres lay in a perfect wilderness, affording incidents, descriptions, and adventures of extraordinary interest. By S. H. HAMMOND. With Illustrations. Cloth. $1 75.

Wild Northern Scenes; or, Sporting Ad-

VENTURES WITH THE RIFLE AND THE ROD. Affording remarkably interesting experiences in a section where the howl of the Wolf, the scream of the Panther, and the hoarse bellow of the Moose could be heard—presenting a racy book. By S. H. HAMMOND. With Illustrations. Cloth. $1 75.

Perils and Pleasures of a Hunter's Life;

OR, THE ROMANCE OF HUNTING. Replete with thrilling incidents and hair-breadth escapes, and fascinating in the extreme, while depicting the romance of hunting. By PEREGRINE HERNE. With Illustrations. Cloth. $1 75.

Hunting Sports in the West. An amount

of novelty and variety, of bold enterprise and noble hardihood, of heroic daring and fierce encounters, which seem to be much more entertaining by the quiet fireside than they would be to the one going through them in the forest or field. By CECIL B. HARTLEY. With numerous Illustrations. Cloth. $1 75.

Fanny Hunter's Western Adventures.

Vividly portraying the stirring scenes enacted in Kansas and Missouri during a sojourn of several years on the Western Border, and fully representing social and domestic affairs in frontier life—containing curious pictures of character. With Illustrations. Cloth. $1 75.

Wonderful Adventures, by Land and Sea,

OF THE SEVEN QUEER TRAVELLERS WHO MET AT AN INN. Revelations of a singular and unusually entertaining character, in which the most terrible circumstances and mysterious occurrences are faithfully and forcibly placed before the reader By JOSIAH BARNES. Cloth. $1 75.

Nicaragua; Past, Present, and Future.

Setting forth its history, the manners and customs of its inhabitants, its mines, its minerals, and other productions, and throwing light upon a subject of very great importance to the masses of our people. By Peter F. Stout, Esq., late U. S. Vice-Consul. Cloth. $1 75.

Female Life Among the Mormons; or,

Maria Ward's Disclosures. Romantic incidents, bordering or the marvelous, which show the evils, horrors, and abominations of the Mormon system—the degradation of its females, and the consequent vices of its society. By Maria Ward, the Wife of a Mormon Elder. With Illustrations. 40,000 copies sold. Cloth. $1 75.

Male Life Among the Mormons. Detailing

sights and scenes among the Mormons, with important remarks on their moral and social economy; being a true transcript of events, viewing Mormonism from a man's standpoint, and forming a companion to the preceding volume. By Austin N. Ward. Edited by Maria Ward. With Illustrations. Cloth. $1 75.

Pioneer Life in the West. Describing the

adventures of Boone, Kenton, Brady, Clark, the Whetzels, the Johnsons, and others, in their fierce encounters with the Indians, and making up a work of the most entertaining and instructive character for those who delight in history and adventure. With numerous Illustrations. Cloth. $1 75.

Thrilling Stories of the Great Rebel-

lion. Fearful adventures of soldiers, scouts, spies, and refugees; daring exploits of smugglers, guerillas, desperadoes, and others; tales of loyal and disloyal women; stories of the negro, and incidents of fun and merriment in camp and field. By Lieut. Charles S. Greene, late of the U. S. Army. With Illustrations in Oil. Cloth. $1 75.

History of the War in India. Furnishing

the complete history of British India, together with interesting and thrilling details which have scarcely a parallel in the world's history, to which is added a memoir of General Sir Henry Havelock. By Henry Frederick Malcolm. Illustrated with numerous Engravings. Cloth. $1 75.

www.ingramcontent.com/pod-product-compliance
Lightning Source LLC
Chambersburg PA
CBHW032341280326
41935CB00008B/406